PRAISE FOR *INSPIRING* CONSUMER CHOICE

"Marketers are increasingly recognizing the value of viewing consumer behavior through the lenses of neuroscience and behavioral economics. This ground-breaking new book extends the application of such insights to the problem of encouraging sustainable consumption. In it the author outlines pathways to accelerate the transition to a greener marketplace. A must-read!"
Carla Nagel, Executive Director, Neuromarketing Science and Business Association

"This much-needed book lays the ground for public and private organizations to take action that promote sustainable behaviors in consumers and citizens. Dr. Michael Smith leverages his expertise in consumer neuroscience and the behavioral sciences to develop a practical guide that could help mitigate the impact of the traditional consumer economy on the planet through changes in consumer behavior."
Manuel Garcia-Garcia, PhD Global Lead of Neuroscience, Ipsos

"The gap between consumers' good green intentions and their actual behavior is a key leverage point in the urgent fight for a greener economy. This book will help anyone in the business of marketing and selling understand the reasons for this gap, so they can develop ways to overcome it. It's rare that a book on consumer behavior has historic importance but I believe this one truly does. The message is clear: to save the planet we must understand the human mind."
Darren Bridger, Chief Research Officer at CloudArmy and author of *Neuro Design*

"In this terrific new book, Michael E. Smith applies his deep knowledge of both brain science and consumer behavior to answer one of the most challenging questions of our time: how can we change the mental models that guide consumer behavior to encourage more sustainable and environmentally-friendly choices in the marketplace? The answer is often surprising and counterintuitive. If you care about practical solutions for the planet and the future of humanity, you need to read this book, closely and without delay."
Stephen Genco, author of *Intuitive Marketing* and *Neuromarketing for Dummies*

Inspiring Green Consumer Choices

Leverage Neuroscience to Reshape Marketplace Behavior

Michael E. Smith

First published in Great Britain and the United States in 2021 by Kogan Page Limited

2nd Floor, 45 Gee Street	122 W 27th St, 10th Floor	4737/23 Ansari Road
London EC1V 3RS	New York, NY 10001	Daryaganj
United Kingdom	USA	New Delhi 110002
		India
		www.koganpage.com

www.koganpage.com

Kogan Page books are printed on paper from sustainable forests.

© Michael E. Smith 2021

The right of Michael E. Smith to be identified as the author of this work has been asserted by him in accordance with the Copyright, Designs and Patents Act 1988.

ISBNs

Hardback   9781398601024
Paperback 9781398601000
Ebook   9781398601017

British Library Cataloguing-in-Publication Data

A CIP record for this book is available from the British Library.

Library of Congress Control Number

2021029201

Typeset by Integra
Printed and bound by CPI Group (UK) Ltd, Croydon CR0 4YY

For Huxley, Jennifer and Linda

CONTENTS

ACKNOWLEDGEMENTS

I would like to thank my editors Kathe Sweeney and Heather Wood, as well as the production and marketing staff at Kogan Page, for their help in bringing this book to life. For their early influences on my subsequent path towards becoming a cognitive psychologist, I would also like to thank Professors Richard Nisbett and the late Stephen Kaplan from the University of Michigan, who helped me to better understand how people think about people and about their relationship to the environment they inhabit. And I am indebted to the friends and colleagues I've worked with in the market research industry over the years, who through discussion and debate (often late at night and in far-flung corners of the world), have provided me with invaluable insights into the underlying drivers of consumer behavior. They are too numerous to fully acknowledge here, but I would especially like to thank David Brandt, Steve Genco, Thom Noble, Horst Stipp, Deepak Varma and Joe Willke for their tutelage and support.

Introduction

This book explores the ways in which the traditional consumer economy has impacted the ecosystem we inhabit, and the prospect that an improved understanding of consumer behavior might contribute to efforts to mitigate that impact. I started it one night in the spring of 2020, when in the moonless dark with Venus rising to the west above where I stood on the coast of Southern California, the crests of the ocean waves lit up in a phosphorescent blue glow. So did the wake-patterns trailing the boards of the otherwise invisible surfers riding the curls. And as amazed spectators walked along the waterline, for a moment they too left trails of glowing blue footprints behind them. The light show was one of the more charming, and less awful, examples of a growing "global weirding," the oft-cited term used in reference to the emergence of a variety of extreme events accompanying the planet's warming and the associated degradation of the biosphere.

In that case the weirdness was the result of an unprecedented bloom of a type of nitrogen-dependent and warm-water-loving bioluminescent single-cell dinoflagellate named *Lingulodinium polyedra*. Under the right circumstances this photosynthetic microorganism emits brilliant flickers of light when it is jostled *en masse* by breaking surf or a passing boat. While lovely to watch, this event occurred as a result of an unnatural influx of pollution from runoff of agricultural chemicals, which in turn was the result of a highly abnormal seasonal variation in typical rainfall patterns. Fortunately this algal bloom turned out to be both entertaining and relatively harmless—other "red tide" events that we have experienced in recent years were from microorganisms that were more toxic and caused die-offs of local fish, birds, seals, and sea lions. Both the brilliant and the bad blooms are becoming more frequent as the local waters grow warmer.

This odd aquatic phenomenon was made more special by the fact that the beach had only recently reopened for careful visitation. The audience for the lightshow was tentative and a little disoriented, having just been liberated from sheltering in their homes for weeks in response to the COVID-19 pandemic that spread quickly around the globe as a result of our deeply interwoven consumer economy. Weeks during which, for the first time in their lives, the audience also experienced the fragility of that interconnectivity as supply chains for common consumer products ranging from toilet paper to dried pasta were disrupted worldwide.

While the quality of life for most of these people had until very recently been pretty comfortable, they now suddenly faced widening political strife, a shocking economic recession, increasingly obvious amounts of plastic detritus on the beach, and growing concern about the implications of accelerating coastal erosion from sea-level rise. There was also an expectation that the coming summer would only grow hotter, and a budding realization that the future was more uncertain than ever and that business-as-usual was not working anymore.

This book will explore the role of consumer behavior in creating that uncertainty and the potential for changing it to enable a more sustainable and less threatening future. In it we will take a deep dive into the brain of the consumer and the consequences of the way that organ works for choices in the marketplace. And we will investigate strategies that marketers and policymakers can adopt to move those choices in a more promising direction.

The coming chapters outline an overview of the modern view of consumer decision-making that is being informed by advances in neuroscience, experimental psychology, behavioral economics, and other disciplines. They will also identify some potential barriers to the transition to more sustainable patterns of consumption implied by this developing view of the consumer's brain/mind. In them we will consider examples, policies, and best practices from the applied behavioral science literature that illustrate how to best reduce those barriers and minimize cognitive friction along the road to a circular economy.

We'll start by asking the question, "How did we get here?" Chapter 1 charts the rise of consumer activity in the modern economy, its growing excess and planetary impacts, and emerging views of ways to shift consumer behavior in more sustainable directions. Chapter 2 examines the gap between the reported "green" intentions of consumers and their actual behavior, and begins to consider the cognitive resource limitations and associated mental shortcuts that may contribute to that difference. Chapter 3 takes a deep dive into the brain mechanisms underlying purchase decisions, how those mechanisms bias consumption towards short-term goals rather than longer-term considerations, and how they can be hijacked by marketing efforts to drive unsustainable consumption.

Chapters 4 and 5 review the neuropsychology of human learning and memory and the role of habit formation in consumer behavior. In them we will see how consumption habits imply both opportunities for, and barriers to, shifting consumers towards the adoption of "greener" products and services.

Chapters 6–8 explore a variety of aspects of the social brain. They include a deep dive into the ways in which social norms influence behavior and the power of invoking such norms, even those that are nascent and emerging, for encouraging pro-environmental behaviors. They also consider some implications of the brain's social and affective information processing characteristics and biases for the likelihood of consumer engagement with the circular economy. Throughout there will be an emphasis on the negative impacts that the industry's history of greenwashing has had on attitudes and environmentally friendly market choices, and the challenges inherent in addressing related concerns.

Finally, Chapter 9 focuses on the widely recognized need for companies and policymakers to reduce barriers to green consumption. In that section we'll consider the potential impacts of policies that reduce environmental impacts by incorporating incentives and disincentives to reduce negative externalities while beneficially shaping consumer choice. We will also consider technological and marketing approaches that might facilitate consumer engagement with the green economy.

01

Growing Cracks in the Consumer Economy

Recent years have seen an unprecedented expansion of the global "middle class." According to research from the Brookings Institute, "the next decade could see a faster expansion of the middle class than at any other time in history. Within a few years, based on current forecasts, a majority of the world's population could have middle-class or rich lifestyles for the first time ever" (Kharas, 2017). Much of this will come from growth in Asian economies and other parts of the developing world as consumers strive to attain lifestyles in line with developed nations. What will that mean for the world? By way of setting some broader context, let's first consider a few facts about the typical middle-class American consumer lifestyle in the early 21st century.

Overflowing With Stuff

The average household in the US currently has about 2.6 people in it (Fry, 2019). That number is a notable reduction relative to the average of about 4.5 people per household that was the norm a century earlier. Over that same period of time, the average size of the homes those households inhabit has increased by about 75 percent (Muresan, 2016). As a result, the average individual living in a relatively modern home in the US now has over 200 percent more personal space in which to stretch out, consume media, and store their own personal collections of "stuff" in comparison with their forebears who lived a few generations back.

On first impression one might suppose that expansion would have provided the occupants a comfortable increase in roominess, one a little less crowded and confining. But, in a typical year Americans also spend over $1.2 trillion on nonessential goods and services (Whitehouse, 2011). And by some counts the average household now contains 300,000 material things of one sort or another (Becker, 2015). A number presumably many times that which was owned by the typical household a hundred years ago. As a result, modern householders must invest some quality time figuring out where to put those things.

Accompanying many of these modern-day living units are additional two-car garages intended for the automobiles of their occupants. Yet a quarter of those garages are also filled with too much extraneous stuff to park any cars in them. An additional third of the households with two-car garages have room for only one car in them, at least in a best-case scenario when other things that have been dead-ended in the garage are fastidiously arranged. And it's not like those occupants don't need the parking space. On average there are also about two cars owned by the members of each average US household. Those frequently upgraded vehicles are obviously taking up yet more space by being parked somewhere, unused around 95 percent of each day, rusting as their resale value rapidly degrades. That is the baseline reality of the situation.

And even that extra garage storage does not suffice—apparently almost one in every 11 Americans pays for yet more space outside of their home to house an ever-growing inventory of extraneous material possessions. The almost $40 billion annual revenue self-storage industry has become one of the most profitable arenas of the real estate market, accruing growth of almost 50 percent over the last decade (Gardner, 2019; Sisson, 2018). That growth was already enough a decade ago to spawn the American reality television series *STORAGE WAR$*, which focused entirely on the efforts of modern-day treasure hunters to acquire at auction the contents of such storage spaces that end up abandoned by their owners. With the occupancy rate of self-storage facilities hovering around 90 percent in many areas, the square-footage dedicated to these warehousing operations will likely continue to rapidly grow. Seemingly, the much-hyped current social media trends of #minimalism, #tinyhouses and even, born out of choice or necessity, #vanlife, do not seem to be doing much to reverse this overall trajectory.

Classic Views on the Psychological Drivers of Consumption

This strangely obsessive acquisitiveness and hoarding behavior that is driving the growth of the self-storage industry is a relatively new phenomenon.

However, the consumer characteristics that underlie those behaviors have been recognized and thoughtfully discussed for as long as critical thinkers have been considering the drivers of human social and economic activity. As a relatively recent example, long before writing his better-known 1776 classic *The Wealth of Nations*, the Scottish philosopher and economist Adam Smith in 1759 published *The Theory of Moral Sentiments*. As we will see, the ideas explored in that treatise were not so different than many of those considered in the modern social and affective neuroscience literature. In particular, without the benefit of neuroimaging technology to evaluate his intuitions, Smith posited that the capacity to intuit and empathize with the thoughts and feelings being experienced by another person—that is, in current parlance, to have a "theory of mind" about them—is a key factor in understanding both individual morality and the dynamics of interpersonal relations. I imagine that if he had known of the present-day notion of "mirror neurons" and their hypothesized role in things like empathy (Iacoboni, 2008) he almost certainly would have subscribed to it.

In any case he further developed one part of that overarching viewpoint in terms of its importance for understanding consumer behavior. His view of the psychology of the consumer was that of an individual driven to seek the imagined veneration of others, and he saw this motivation as a key driver of the acquisition of material possessions (rather than the intrinsic utility provided by the objects themselves). Foreshadowing the growth of the self-storage industry, Smith observed of his contemporaries: "All their pockets are stuffed with little conveniences. They contrive new pockets, unknown in the clothes of other people, in order to carry a greater number" (Smith, 1759).

Smith correctly saw that people were consuming increasing amounts of material possessions, and that they did so in part as a way to look good in the eyes of others. He also presciently viewed the perceived social approval (or envy) itself as something of a key reward that reinforced the cycle of buying over and above any concrete benefit provided by the new possession.

In Smith's view, the seeking of social approval through the accumulation of possessions wasn't such a bad thing; rather he saw it as a key driver of human endeavor. Smith believed that the economic development that resulted from productive labor and the acquisition of more material goods ultimately justified those efforts by improving the human condition. Western societies have largely accepted and promoted this notion, at least as evidenced by the fact that among countries that are members of the Organization for Economic Co-operation and Development (OECD), consumer expenditures account on average for well over 60 percent of national GDPs.

Smith's observations about the psychological drivers of buying behavior in some ways foreshadowed the concepts of "conspicuous consumption" and "conspicuous leisure" subsequently described by the American social economist (and noted critic of capitalism) Thorstein Veblen, as outlined in his 1899 book *The Theory of the Leisure Class*. Like Smith, Veblen emphasized the social and psychological aspects of consumer behavior, in particular noting that consumption often served a symbolic and emotional purpose related to social status signaling rather than reflecting choices made through a process of cold, logical decision-making by rational economic actors.

Unlike Smith, though, rather than portraying superfluous consumption as an engine of economic progress, Veblen characterized it more as a vain waste of time and resources—and akin to an addiction. He described it as a means of social stratification that keeps laborers stuck on an aspirational treadmill from which they can never truly advance their position. One has to wonder how Veblen would react to his ideas about conspicuous consumption and conspicuous leisure in the ways that they are now being co-opted by brand advertisers through the digitized, institutionalized, and monetized rise of legions of social media "influencers" who help package products and experiences for sale.

Consumption and Perceived Wellbeing

Regardless of whether one views the consumer economy as a means to improve the human condition or as a mechanism of social control, it is clear that our current grand market experiment of accelerating consumerism is not improving subjective wellbeing. According to the 2020 edition of the *World Happiness Report* (Helliwell et al, 2020), a summary of research published annually by the United Nations Sustainable Development Solutions Network, between-country differences in GDP can explain only a portion of the differences between countries in the subjective sense of wellbeing that their citizens have. And despite a significant increase in global GDP over the years that the study has been conducted, across countries people were found to be more worried, sad, and angry than they were in past measurement periods despite general increases in access to goods and services.

Of course, people who have adequate financial resources with which to acquire all the things they need for themselves and their families to survive are generally happier than people who struggle to meet basic requirements for food, shelter, and security. But once those basic needs are met the difference is not so stark. The *Gallup World Poll*, a recurring representative sample of 1.7 million respondents worldwide, provides some of the key data underlying the *World Happiness Report*. Among other things it includes questions about household income as well as queries that ask respondents to rate their quality of life and emotional wellbeing from the best to the worst possible. In past years those data have been mined for deeper insights into the complex relationship between income and subjective wellbeing.

In one such heavily reported study a group of researchers examined the relationship between subjective wellbeing and incomes in different regions around the world (Jebb et al, 2018). For each region they were able to identify a "satiation point" beyond which higher income did not result in much of an increase in sense of wellbeing. Of course, that dollar-value satiation point varied for different countries around the world, but in general an income that would provide for a reasonably comfortable and slightly above-average lifestyle in each region was also enough to reach that region's sense of wellbeing satiation point. "Stuff" appears to have a decreasing marginal utility as you accumulate more of it, yet people tend to get stuck on something of a hamster wheel in an endless effort to find rewards from it (Diener et al, 2006).

It also appears to be a path that people may want an exit from. For example, in 1990 when US citizens were asked by the Gallup organization whether environmental protection or GDP growth was more important, 71 percent ranked environmental protection as more important versus just 19 percent preferring GDP growth. The magnitude of that preference gradually eroded over the years, and by 2009 in the aftermath of the "great recession" the preference actually flipped for a short period (Figure 1.1). Despite that momentary flip, over the last decade the preference has shifted back such that as of this writing almost twice as many respondents were again prioritizing environmental protection over GDP growth (Saad, 2020).

Undesired Byproducts of Consumption

Maybe there is more going on to subtract from happiness than just the mere fact that at some point more stuff stops being rewarding? Let's go back to our average household and their growing storage needs. Of course, that growth in storage space mainly just reflects the expansion of extraneous stuff that people choose to keep for a while before discarding. But there are bigger problems afoot and some related facts should also be considered. For example, much of the material that comes into their homes is not actually

FIGURE 1.1   Preference for Environmental Protection over GDP Growth

Relative Importance of Environment vs Economy

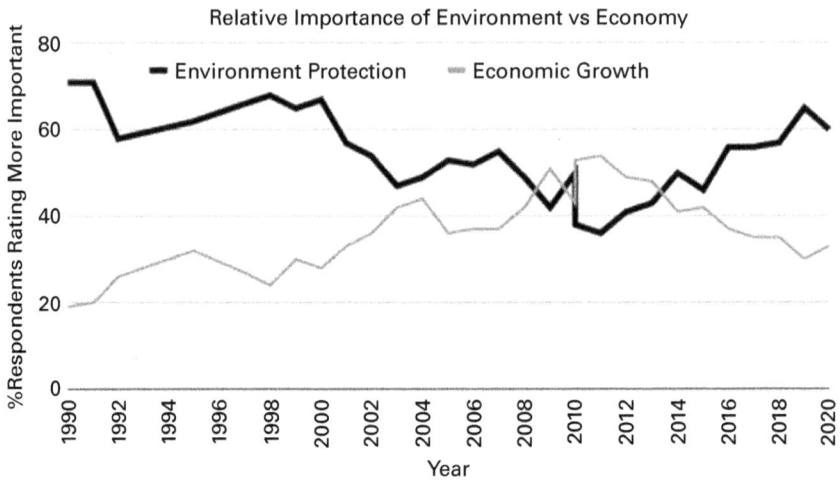

FIGURE 1.2   2018 Daily Per Capita Municipal Solid Waste Generation (in kg)

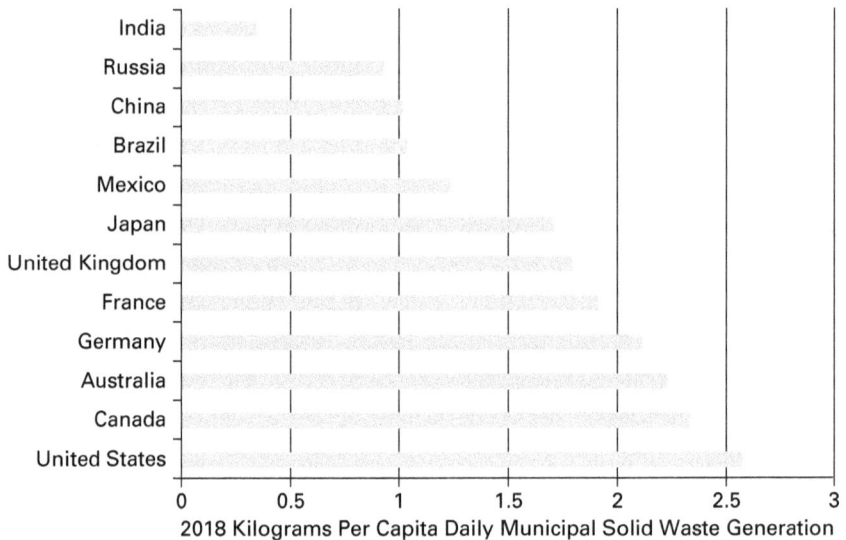

stored but instead just serves as throughput—material byproducts of consumption that very quickly become some form of household waste.

In terms of municipal solid waste, in 2018 the average US consumer discarded on average about 2.5kg of such materials per day, over seven times the amount discarded by the average consumer in India (Figure 1.2; Statista, 2018). In other words, collectively each average modern household of 2.6 people in the US was responsible for discarding over two tons of solid waste per year.

More intimately, in that same year each member of an average household was also responsible on a daily basis for discharging from their home around 100 US gallons of "waste water" (and all that it might have contained). That is, around 100,000 US gallons each year in total by the average household, which also has to go… somewhere. More invisibly, the typical American in 2017 was also responsible for approximately 85 daily pounds of carbon dioxide emissions. That is, collectively, roughly 40 tons each year for that average household. Which also have to go… well, we know where it goes, it gets trapped in the atmosphere and absorbed by the sea, in both cases with somewhat nasty long-term consequences.

These household discharges, and their analogues in industry, once accomplished, have traditionally followed the adage of "out of sight, out of mind" by the folks who discharged them. They were just a routine component of everyday life that busy householders or industrialists didn't concern themselves with much. Waste was a temporary nuisance, not worth expending mental effort to think about. Not something of importance to everyday lives or business models. But such convenient ignorance is becoming much more difficult to maintain, at least for many people and businesses. And the potential long-term negative consequences of that profligacy are starting to become more immediately and less abstractly felt. Even the wasteful behavior itself is starting to become unpopular. No wonder folks are feeling moody despite having plenty of stuff and, for many, otherwise comfortable lives.

Limits to a Linear Consumer Economy

Well, how did we get here? Let's dig a little deeper and consider yet more facts that may be driving the (hopefully) incipient change of heart. Since the dawn of the Industrial Revolution, sometimes argued as coincident with James Watt's introduction of a new and much improved steam engine in 1764 and in the zeitgeist between when Adam Smith published his *Theory of Moral Sentiments* and subsequently *The Wealth of Nations*, Western society has relied on a linear model of consumption: (1) extract resources, (2) create stuff, (3) use stuff, and (4) bury the bodies (aka the "take-make-waste" approach).

Environmental Impacts of Consumption

In order to be profitable, this take-make-waste approach for satisfying consumer wants and needs, while demonstrably being both energy- and resource-intensive, also depends on externalizing and failing to price the costs of environmental contamination and resource depletion. In part to better understand the historical trajectory and physical implications of the current consumption approach, in 1987 the International Council of Scientific Unions—a global coordinating body of national science organizations— established the International Geosphere-Biosphere Programme (the IGBP). The IGBP was a multinational, multiyear research project designed to foster collaborative efforts to look at changes in Earth systems over time and any impact that human actions might be having on those systems.

One of the major activities of the IGBP was the compilation and synthesis of key annual data from 1750 to 2010 that included a variety of indicators of both socioeconomic activity and Earth system health over that time. Socioeconomic indicators available from 1750 onwards included such things as global population, the urbanization of that population, energy use, and real GDP. From about 1900 onwards data were available for additional indicators such as fertilizer consumption, large dam construction, and overall water use. And proxy indicator data from about 1960 onwards were available for the extent of paper production, telecommunications, and transportation. Earth system health indicators from 1750 onward included estimates of atmospheric carbon dioxide concentration and those of other greenhouse gases (GHGs), loss of ozone in the stratosphere, planet surface temperature, ocean acidification, marine fish capture, coastal nitrogen concentration from agricultural runoff, amount of land domesticated and corresponding tropical forest loss, and biosphere degradation.

The trend lines for how such indicators have changed between 1750 and 2010 dramatically illustrate a few key things (Steffen et al, 2015). From a global perspective, the socioeconomic indicators reveal a fairly gradual increase until accelerating into explosive growth after 1950 or so. Pretty much across the board. Among other things, while the world population grew by over 250 percent between 1950 and 2010, global GDP increased by over 900 percent! Notably given the relatively slow growth before then, that jump represents a tremendous increase. Since consumer activity reflects over 60 percent of global GDP, we can assume that this rapid growth primarily reflected the overall effect of individual consumers buying more material possessions.

The second finding to note is, on the downside, the Earth system indicators over that period also displayed dramatic evidence of growing environmental stress. For example, greenhouse gas (GHG) emissions increased gradually from 1750 onward, and then much more rapidly after about 1950. Similar trajectories were observed for the other indicators. The planet's surface temperature increased more rapidly, the oceans acidified from absorbing carbon dioxide while also becoming more polluted from coastal fertilizer runoff, the amount of domesticated land grew and tropical rainforests shrank, and the biosphere degraded. And as early as 1962, when Rachel Carson published her classic alarm bell *Silent Spring* about the growing threat of pesticide pollution on the biosphere, a growing subset of the population was beginning to become aware of the rising threats from such impacts.

While it wasn't included as either a socioeconomic or Earth system indicator in the IGBP studies, it's also worth noting that plastic production rose from about 2 million tons in 1950 to over 380 million tons in 2015 (Figure 1.3; note that the figure depicts change in log scale), an eye-popping increase of over 25,000 percent in that time frame (Geyer et al, 2017). Over 90 percent of that plastic is still lurking around somewhere, un-recycled, and either buried, strewn about the land, or floating in the ocean. On a per capita basis the US and the UK lead the world in plastic waste creation, with consumers in both countries responsible for generating around 100kg of it on average each year (Lau et al, 2020).

FIGURE 1.3   Inflation-Adjusted Global GDP Growth Versus Growth in Plastics Production, 1950–2015

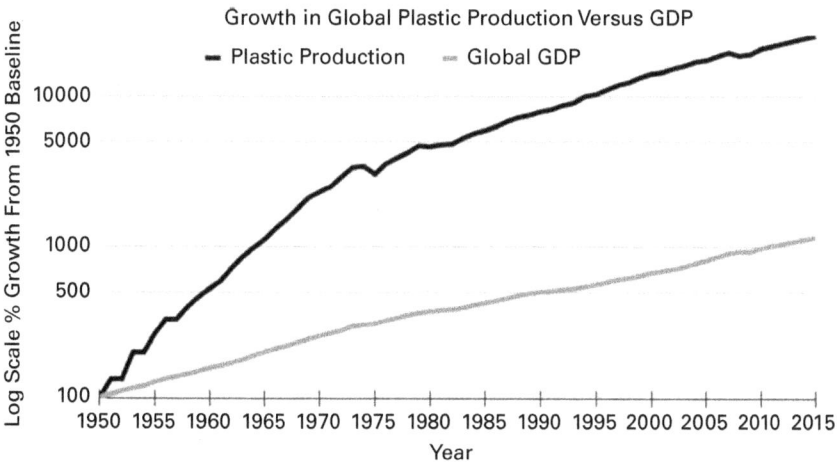

Apparently the rapid growth in GDP over this period also came with some important costs. On a net basis, it's not really clear how much progress towards increasing long-term wellbeing we've made during this economic great leap forward. During the last 12,000 years or so, the relatively stable and comfortable interglacial epoch that geophysical scientists refer to as the *Holocene*, agriculture was developed, the shift from roaming "hunting and gathering" societies to more sedentary communities grew, people became global circumnavigators, and sociologically, technologically, and economically sophisticated communities had a chance to develop. But the kind of changes in Earth system indicators described above, concurrent with the accelerating rise in socioeconomic indicators of the factors that stress that system, provides evidence of a growing threat of severe destabilization of the human forms of cooperation that enabled such development.

This destabilization threatens the integrity of the biosphere itself. IGBP vice-chair Paul Crutzen and his colleagues have helped to popularize the notion that the planet has entered a new geological epoch, the *Anthropocene* (Crutzen, 2002). As of this writing geophysical scientists continue to debate whether formally calling an end to the Holocene and naming such a new epoch defined by modern human consumer behavior is yet warranted (and if so when to demarcate its starting point), but the winds of change are blowing in that direction.

One last, very relevant, thing to consider from the findings of the IGBP work is that while world human population and the extent of environmental degradation have both risen sharply in recent decades, population growth itself does not seem to be the root cause of the Earth system problems. A third key finding from the IGBP studies is that, whatever benefits which may have accrued from global GDP growth, those benefits were mainly enjoyed by a relatively small portion of the global population. In particular, while the overwhelming majority of population growth from 1950–2010 occurred in the non-OECD countries, the overwhelmingly consumption-driven GDP growth in that period took place in the OECD. Another way to phrase it is that the 18 percent of global population represented by the busy OECD shoppers in 2010 walked away with the vast majority of the stuff created by the take-make-waste economy. And, wittingly or not, they shared the ensuing environmental degradation from their shopping with everyone else on the planet.

Consumption and Its Impacts Are Exceeding Planetary Boundaries

The research of an NGO, the Global Footprint Network, focuses on developing a comprehensive sustainability metric, called an Ecological Footprint, which quantifies the impact that the behavior (i.e., the economic activity) of people in different regions has on the environment, and on developing additional metrics of the carrying capacity of the planet in terms of the ecological resources that can be used and the waste that can be absorbed in a year without reducing the planet's capacity to provide resources and absorb waste in the future. Clearly one can imagine that this is a complicated if not intractable problem, and that any such calculations could be called into question on a variety of grounds. Yet valiantly, nevertheless, they persist.

In recent decades they have been calculating an "Earth Overshoot Day," which projects the day in the calendar year on which human activity has used as much in the way of ecological resources as the Earth's biosphere can regenerate in a year. In the year 2000, that date was September 23, and it has since regularly continued to shift towards earlier dates in the year such that by 2019 the overshoot date was July 29. In 2020 this steady trend reversed course by a few weeks to land on August 22, but that anomaly reflected the dramatic slowdown in economic activity across the globe that was associated with the pandemic—and so it can't rightly be viewed as a hopeful harbinger of virtuous change (Global Footprint Network, 2020).

They also make projections for what the date would theoretically be if every country in the world had the same Ecological Footprint as that of any given country in their dataset. For the collection of the average US households that we considered above that date would be March 23, just barely past the vernal equinox and the fifth earliest time point for all countries in the world. It would probably be a good idea if we don't continue to strive to meet that benchmark in the developing world as a whole.

That is, we are now in the midst of the "Great Acceleration" of our environmental impacts and we are rapidly reaching a point where the side effects of human behavior on the Earth's climate and biosphere may change them in profound and highly unpleasant ways (Steffen et al, 2018). The traditional linear economy is becoming more than the biosphere can bear. And since consumer behavior has been at the core of this growing problem, consumer behavior will also need to change in profound ways in order to address it. Part of that change will need to come in the systems that enable the consumer economy, and another part of that will need to come in the form of changes in the way consumers think about themselves and their role in the world. In coming chapters we'll take a deep dive into the brain and behavior of the consumer in order to glean insights that might help inform efforts to reduce barriers to making such changes.

From Linear to Circular Views of the Consumer Economy

The Scottish philosopher and psychologist Kenneth Craik introduced the notion of a "mental model" into the vernacular of cognitive science. Writing in a small but highly influential book published shortly before an untimely accidental death in his early thirties, he observed that:

> If the organism carries a "small-scale model" of external reality and of its own possible actions within its head, it is able to try out various alternatives, conclude which is the best of them, react to future situations before they arise, utilize the knowledge of past events in dealing with the present and future, and in every way to react in a much fuller, safer, and more competent manner to the emergencies which face it (Craik, 1943).

This notion has become commonplace in many fields, and researchers often try to understand the parameters of such models that people might possess and the implications of those models for successful system design. In essence the notion is that the brain builds a representation of some aspect of the world and the contingencies that it implies, bases behavioral acts on that understanding, and then uses the outcomes from those behaviors as either reinforcement for the model or to update it as needed (Figure 1.4). In the commercial world people employ such mental models to understand and predict both their potential range of market actions and their relationship to the broader environment they inhabit.

FIGURE 1.4   Mental Models of the World Guide Behavior

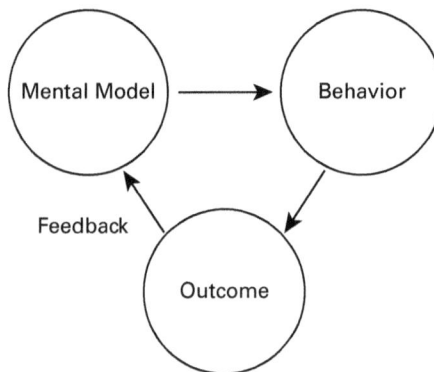

Evolving Mental Models of the Consumer–Environment Relationship

Long before the IGBP undertook their epoch-defining work, some thoughtful scholars and commentators already had a good sense of where things were unsustainably headed and the ways in which people would need to adapt their mental models to confront pressing environmental issues. Prominent among those deep thinkers was a UK-born but very American Quaker, peace activist, economist, early social and general systems theorist, and, in the deepest meaning of the word, polymath. Kenneth E Boulding was nominated at different times for both the Nobel Peace Prize and the Nobel Prize in Economics, but at present might be seen as a seldom-referenced and relatively obscure (and definitely underappreciated) iconoclastic historical figure.

Among his many other interests, he was somewhat of a cognitive scientist. Or at the very least, one might call him a philosopher of cognitive function. A recurring theme in Boulding's writing focused on the role of learned cognitive structures, or organizing frameworks, or mental models, in the human brain, as they are manifested at a societal level. His work especially focused on their role in interpersonal and economic behavior.

His ideas in that regard were most clearly outlined in his classic text *The Image: Knowledge in life and society* (Boulding, 1956). In that treatise Boulding hypothesized that people have subjective worldviews, or in his words, that they possessed an "Image" that was grounded in their sense of place and embedded in a network of associations that include both implicit emotional responses and more general and sometimes naïve structural knowledge about the environment they live in. Some of those associations clearly include beliefs about the nature of, and the rules governing, interpersonal relations, as well as beliefs about that subset of such rules related to economic transactions. The *Image* Boulding described can effectively be seen as our understanding of the collective, normative context or social "operating system" that our individual mental models are embedded in.

Boulding saw individual decision-making and behavior as shaped by such an underlying collective context. A decade later he expanded on those thoughts in an essay entitled "The Economics of the Coming Spaceship Earth" that he first presented at the Sixth Resources for the Future Forum on Environmental Quality in a Growing Economy held in Washington, DC (Boulding, 1966). In that talk he described what he saw as a dominant shared understanding of the world that guided the economy in the past, one of a metaphorical open world characterized by a vista of a limitless frontier and filled with unending resources to be exploited. He contrasted that with a growing need for adoption of a newer model, one of a more self-contained world with finite resources that can be used for economic development—resources that were limited except for the energy of the sun:

> For the sake of picturesqueness, I am tempted to call the open economy the "cowboy economy," the cowboy being symbolic of the illimitable plains and also associated with reckless, exploitative, romantic, and violent behavior, which is characteristic of open societies. The closed economy of the future might similarly be called the "spaceman" economy, in which the earth has become a single spaceship, without unlimited reservoirs of anything, either for extraction or for pollution, and in which, therefore, man must find his place in a cyclical ecological system which is capable of continuous reproduction of material form even though it cannot escape having inputs of energy.

Boulding noted a key difference between these worldviews was in the attitudes they implied concerning resource exploitation and consumption. "In the cowboy economy, consumption is regarded as a good thing and production likewise; and the success of the economy is measured by the amount of the throughput." In contrast, he notes that in the spaceman economy "throughput is by no means a desideratum, and is indeed to be regarded as something to be minimized rather than maximized" (Boulding, 1966).

The colorful and easily understood metaphors he described are often credited with helping to facilitate the emergence of a strain of more environmentally aware economic thought in the late 1960s. And with some—but not small—amount of prescience on his part, the metaphorical image of a Spaceship Earth soon manifested itself even more clearly and much more widely in *Earthrise*, a stunning pictorial image that has become the most famous picture ever taken from space. The iconic Earthrise image depicts the distant, relatively smallish, and clearly self-contained Earth as viewed above the lunar surface, and as photographed from lunar orbit by astronauts on the 1968 Apollo 8 moon mission. The beauty and fragility and immediacy of that image in turn has often been credited as playing an important role in the emergence of a populist environmental movement during that same period (Dent, 2018). Two years later, in April 1970, the first Earth Day was celebrated, a tradition that has persisted for the past 50 years. That same year the US Congress authorized the creation of a new federal agency designed to focus on related issues—the Environmental Protection Agency (EPA).

Despite this promising beginning, a half century thereafter Boulding's Spaceship Earth economy is still struggling to be more fully imagined and implemented. There are, though, a lot of growing signs that his influence, even if unrecognized, is still being felt—and that the type of societal and economic transformations that he foretold as both necessary and inevitable are slowly starting to emerge. There is in fact growing general awareness, both by individuals and organizations, that the throughput of the unidirectional take-make-waste economic system is greatly exceeding the planet's carrying capacity while taking a disastrous toll on the biosphere. There is also a growing recognition of the business imperative to begin transitioning to a more sustainable, "circular" economic model.

The Accelerating Shift to More Sustainable Business Models

The emerging economic model largely resembles Boulding's systems thinking approach. It is a model in which products and services are designed in such a way as to keep materials and other resources within a closed loop. The global management consultancy Bain & Company (Davis-Peccoud et al, 2020) has recently compared the rapidly developing business and political imperative to focus more strategically on sustainability in operational and product marketing issues with that of the digital revolution, noting that this trend "is disrupting industries in ways that could not have been imagined even a few short years ago, poised to do what Amazon did to bookstores, Airbnb did to hotels and Uber did to taxis." And in the consumer packaged goods (CPG) industry, over the past five years sustainably marketed products appeared to drive more than half of all growth for brands in the category (Crawford, 2020).

Much of the discussion around the topic of circular economics has been informed primarily by the emerging discipline of *industrial ecology*, which focuses on the flow of energy and materials through industrial systems. It conceives of manufacturing as a human-built ecosystem analogous to natural ecosystems, where in an ideal scenario the wastes or byproducts that are generated by industrial activities become feedstock for other processes rather than simply as something to be disposed of (Chertow, 2007). Writers and business practitioners seeking to advance a circular economy have most often focused on things like reimagining supply chains and business models.

In the conceptualization of circularity described by the influential Ellen MacArthur Foundation (2013), a circular economy is one that is self-contained and restorative by design, and is based on three key principles: (1)

designing out waste and pollution, (2) keeping products and materials in use, and (3) regenerating natural systems. That view is often conveyed in more detail by an oft-cited "butterfly diagram" that traces material flows through separate technical and biological systems depicted as the "wings" in the figure. In both wings consumers and their actions are depicted as a key and central component of material flows.

Circular Business Models Need Consumers With Updated Mental Models

To date relatively little serious consideration has been given to the intrinsic implications that the existing mental models of the marketplace that consumers have built in their brains might have for the operation of this systems thinking circular economy. Or, for that matter, any consideration of the implications of those models and human nature more generally that might help marketers to more effectively engage in that transition. This is despite the fact that achieving a successful transition to a circular economy will require not only dramatic changes in the way products are designed and produced, but also dramatic changes in consumer behavior and the ways in which marketers think about the relationship between manufacturers and their customers. This book will highlight ways in which a modern understanding of consumer behavior and decision-making may ultimately be critical in the shift towards sustainable consumption.

The mental models that people have for interacting with the commercial world have been built on the reinforcements provided by the traditional linear consumer economy. Thoughtful consumers increasingly say they understand that their current marketplace practices are unsustainable, and growing numbers of them profess a desire to engage in behaviors that are more environmentally friendly. But there remains a big gap between such intentions and actual consumer choice.

Fortunately, the study of consumer behavior is getting better at explaining why this gap exists. In particular, over the last several decades there has emerged a view of the mind that is at stark odds with the naïve classical view of *homo economicus*, which presumed that people are rational decision-makers that attempt to maximize personal utility as a consumer and to maximize profit as a producer. Instead, when viewing consumer behavior through the lens of advances in the brain and behavioral sciences, a very different view emerges.

As we will see in coming chapters, consumers are increasingly recognized as having limited aptitude or desire for engaging in conscious rational deliberation with respect to most day-to-day routine purchase decisions. After all, there are a lot of more pressing things to think about in our lives. Instead, people act more as model-driven creatures of habit, creatures for which automatic behaviors are triggered by situational cues and colored by implicit emotional responses. Consumers use heuristics and take mental shortcuts that predictably bias the choices they will make. Those same consumers are risk-averse and hyper-alert to threats in the short term, yet they severely discount the potential for rewards in the longer term. They are also quick to conform to prevailing social norms; most commonly, they are followers of influencers rather than influencers themselves. And they often seek information not to illuminate and improve their understanding of a situation, but rather to confirm their existing beliefs—tending to dismiss inconvenient truths as "fake news."

Moreover, these traits aren't easily mutable, and so they need to be acknowledged, understood, and designed for in advance—in products, marketing campaigns, and policy proposals. As somewhat darkly noted by the author and social commentator Jonathan Franzen, "call me a pessimist or call me a humanist, but I don't see human nature fundamentally changing anytime soon" (Franzen, 2019). And that same human nature stands as a potential challenge to the circular economy agenda, as any attempts to shift consumers to more sustainable ways of thinking and behaving will need to overcome significant mental barriers.

In the user interface/system design world the term *cognitive friction* is often used to describe the heightened mental effort, confusion, and errors users experience when their mental model of the world has been upended because of a system change or upgrade. It is the opposite of something being intuitive and effortless. That is, cognitive friction is experienced when existing beliefs are violated, existing habits are made ineffectual, and expected rewards are denied. Rather than expend the extra effort needed to learn the offered rewards of an upgrade and overcome such violations, a potential user might instead just walk away from a new system—to instead cling to a familiar and comfortable, if fundamentally flawed, older alternative. This book will identify sources of cognitive friction, and ways to reduce it, in the transition to a green economy.

In what follows I will describe science-based insights and general principles aimed at bridging the gap between the preferences that many consumers state that they have for sustainable options, and their frequent failure to act on those preferences in the marketplace. Implicitly I'll assume that sustainable consumption refers to choices that address the individual's basic needs and improves their quality of life without undermining the similar needs we can expect future generations will have. And when referring to a hypothetical "green" consumer I will intend one that recognizes and values the need to move towards more sustainable models of consumption and one who might generally value the natural environment they are part of.

References

Becker, J (2015) Twenty-one surprising statistics that reveal how much stuff we actually own, *Becoming Minimalist*, www.becomingminimalist.com/clutter-stats/ (archived at https://perma.cc/BNS8-VLT4)

Boulding, K E (1956) *The Image: Knowledge in life and society*, University of Michigan Press, Ann Arbor, MI

Boulding, K E (1966) The economics of the coming Spaceship Earth, in H Jarrett (ed.) *Environmental Quality in a Growing Economy*, Resources for the Future/ Johns Hopkins University Press, Baltimore, MD

Carson, R (1962) *Silent Spring*, Houghton Mifflin, Boston, MA

Chertow, M R (2007) "Uncovering" industrial symbiosis, *Journal of Industrial Ecology*, 11(1), 11–30

Craik, K J W (1943) *The Nature of Explanation*, Cambridge University Press, Cambridge

Crawford, E (2020). Sustainably-marketed products drove more than half of all growth across CPGs in past five years, *Food Navigator*, 23 July, www.foodnavigator-usa.com/Article/2020/07/23/Sustainably-marketed-products-drove-more-than-half-of-all-growth-across-CPGs-in-past-five-years (archived at https://perma.cc/VT3G-W42U)

Crutzen, P J (2002) Geology of mankind—The Anthropocene, *Nature*, 415, 23

Davis-Peccoud, J, van den Branden, J-C, Brahm, C and Mattios, G (2020) Sustainability is the next digital, *Bain & Company*, 8 September, www.bain.com/insights/sustainability-is-the-next-digital/ (archived at https://perma.cc/MR4D-QW8T)

Dent, S (2018) 50 years ago, Earthrise inspired the environmental movement, *Engadget*, 24 December, www.engadget.com/2018-12-24-earthrise-50-years-the-big-picture.html (archived at https://perma.cc/C4KV-LM3M)

Diener, E, Lucas, R E and Scollon, C N (2006) Beyond the hedonic treadmill: Revising the adaptation theory of wellbeing, *American Psychologist*, 61, 305–314

Ellen MacArthur Foundation (2013) *Towards the Circular Economy*, www.ellenmacarthurfoundation.org/assets/downloads/publications/Ellen-MacArthur-Foundation-Towards-the-Circular-Economy-vol.1.pdf (archived at https://perma.cc/P9YR-YTMF)

Franzen, J (2019) What if we stopped pretending? The climate apocalypse is coming. To prepare for it we have to admit that we can't prevent it, *The New Yorker*, 8 September

Friedman, T L (2010) Global weirding is here, *New York Times*, 17 February, www.nytimes.com/2010/02/17/opinion/17friedman.html (archived at https://perma.cc/R7DV-7X7Z)

Fry, R (2019) The number of people in the average U.S. household is going up for the first time in over 160 years, *Pew Research*, 1 October, www.pewresearch.org/fact-tank/2019/10/01/the-number-of-people-in-the-average-u-s-household-is-going-up-for-the-first-time-in-over-160-years/ (archived at https://perma.cc/6H8Z-3PKR)

Gardner, C (2019) Self storage industry statistics 2020, *Neighbor*, 18 December, www.neighbor.com/storage-blog/self-storage-industry-statistics/ (archived at https://perma.cc/QH66-QEN6)

Geyer, R, Jambeck, J R and Law, K R (2017) Production, use, and fate of all plastics ever made, *Sciences Advances*, 3, e1700782

Global Footprint Network (2020) About Earth Overshoot Day, www.overshootday.org/about-earth-overshoot-day/ (archived at https://perma.cc/KAK5-A48C)

Helliwell, J F, Layard, R, Sachs, J D, and De Neve, J-E (2020) World Happiness Report 2020, 20 March, worldhappiness.report/ (archived at https://perma.cc/YJ2J-U7G7)

Iacoboni, M (2008) *Mirroring People: The new science of how we connect with others*, Macmillan, New York

Jebb, A T, Yau, L, Diener, E and Oishi, S. (2018) Happiness, income satiation and turning points around the world, *Nature Human Behaviour*, 2, 33–38

Kharas, H (2017) The unprecedented expansion of the global middle class, February, www.brookings.edu/wp-content/uploads/2017/02/global_20170228_global-middle-class.pdf (archived at https://perma.cc/KDS4-3N3S)

Lau, W W Y, Shiran, Y, et al (2020) Evaluating scenarios toward zero plastic pollution, *Science*, 269(6510), 1455–1461

Muresan, A (2016) Who lives largest? The growth of urban American homes over the last 100 years, *Property Shark*, 8 September, www.propertyshark.com/Real-Estate-Reports/2016/09/08/the-growth-of-urban-american-homes-in-the-last-100-years/ (archived at https://perma.cc/7X5X-65WF)

Saad, L (2020) Environmental ratings, global warming concern, flat in 2020, *Gallup*, 20 April, news.gallup.com/poll/308876/environmental-ratings-global-warming-concern-flat-2020.aspx (archived at https://perma.cc/8RRZ-7EAG)

Sisson, P (2018) Self-storage: How warehouses for personal junk became a $38 billion industry, *Curbed*, 27 March, archive.curbed.com/2018/3/27/17168088/cheap-storage-warehouse-self-storage-real-estate (archived at https://perma.cc/8UXH-VXRB)

Smith, A (1759) *The Theory of Moral Sentiments*, A. Millar, London

Smith, A (1776) *The Wealth of Nations*, W Strahan and T Cadell, London

Statista (2018) Daily municipal solid waste generation per capita worldwide in 2018, by select country, www.statista.com/statistics/689809/per-capital-msw-generation-by-country-worldwide/ (archived at https://perma.cc/6G2V-64JF)

Steffen, W, Broadgate, W, Deutsch, L, Gaffney, O, Ludwig, C (2015) The trajectory of the Anthropocene: The great acceleration, *Anthropocene Review*, 2, 81–98

Steffan, W, Rockstrom, J, Richardson, K, et al (2018) Trajectories of the Earth System in the Anthropocene, *Proceedings of the National Academy of Sciences*, 115(33), 8252–8259

Veblen, T (1899) *The Theory of the Leisure Class: An economic study of institutions*, Macmillan, New York

Whitehouse, M (2011) Number of the week: Americans buy more stuff they don't need [blog] *Wall Street Journal*, 23 April, blogs.wsj.com/economics/2011/04/23/number-of-the-week-americans-buy-more-stuff-they-dont-need/ (archived at https://perma.cc/X5FN-MV2D)

02

The Not-So-Conscious Consumer

Let me start by sharing a personal shopping vignette not so different from the kind of customer journey that many consumers who are striving-to-be-more-environmentally-friendly experience. One day recently a drain in my home was clogged and I walked over to a neighborhood store to consider my options. I found the shelf display of drain-opening products, and quickly recognized a couple of comfortably familiar, leading brands. The packages portrayed compelling imagery of free-flowing drains, and the product descriptions promised powerful unclogging action. Both were competitively and fairly inexpensively priced. Since they lacked obvious distinctive brand attributes to help me decide between them, I struggled for a moment trying to identify a unique selling proposition that would convince me to pick one, while also scanning the shelf to try to figure out which of the various sub-brand versions being displayed would best suit my particular needs.

In the process of considering my options I noticed another, less familiar, alternative that was inconveniently displayed on a shelf off to the lower right-hand side. This shelf position is sometimes referred to as the "corner of death" by eye tracking researchers who study consumer behavior because it is the last place people look in a display, and then only if they haven't already found what they need. The package lacked compelling imagery, but it told a kinder, gentler story of natural enzymatic action that would use friendly microbes to clean my pipes without harsh chemicals. It unfortunately was priced at about twice that of other alternatives. While I harbored some concern that it might not actually work, I found this option appealing and I could afford it. So, I walked back home with this bottle of mystery liquid. And then dumped twice the recommended dose down my drain—just to make sure. And waited. And waited some more. And then gave up and walked back to the store and bought a container of one of the brand-category leaders. And went back home and dumped that in my drain. And waited and waited as has often been my past experience with those same brand-category leaders. And then I called a plumber. As in the famous words of Kermit the frog, "It's not easy bein' green." Hold on to this example as foreshadowing. We'll come back to it.

The Intention–Action Gap

In the Introduction I alluded to the notion that there is a gap between what consumers say about the importance of sustainability considerations in their purchase decisions and the actual choices and post-purchase pro-environmental behaviors that they engage in. Let's examine this issue a little more closely. What are people actually saying and doing? And what is the disconnect between those two things that marketers need to better understand if we are to try to bridge that gap? Well, to start, many more people are expressing concerns about environmental degradation than in the past.

PUBLIC AWARENESS AND CONCERN ABOUT ENVIRONMENTAL IMPACTS OF CONSUMPTION

- In the US most people believe global warming is occurring, realize it is from human activity, and are concerned about it. Many are very concerned and believe people are already being harmed by it (Leiserowitz et al, 2020).

- Most people believe the government isn't doing enough to protect the environment, and a majority claim to be trying to change their lifestyles to lessen their impacts by driving less, wasting less, and using fewer single-use plastic items (Pew Research Center, 2019; Shelton Group, 2019).

- Similar sentiments are shared by the majority in the EU, where climate change, air and water pollution, and the growing amount of consumer waste, are top-of-mind issues, and where most also acknowledge that this degradation is a direct result of consumer habits (Eurobarometer, 2020).

- Globally, four out of five consumers feel strongly that companies have a responsibility to help protect and improve the environment, and a majority claim they are willing to pay more for sustainably produced products (Nielsen, 2015, 2018).

Given this growing awareness and concern about environmental issues, why do people who support sustainable consumption often fail to align their actions with their intentions? In 2017, a team of public opinion and market research organizations conducted a study (European Commission, 2018) of consumer engagement with the notion of an emerging "circular economy" as described in the Introduction. In particular they sought to better understand how consumers decide whether to purchase a more-or-less durable product, whether to have a product repaired instead of replacing it, whether they would consider switching to "shared" product use through a renting/ leasing arrangement, and how they felt about buying used or refurbished products.

They found that while most respondents espoused a willingness to engage in these types of more sustainable consumer behaviors, many have little experience with sharing businesses or with buying products secondhand, perhaps in part because such options don't convey the same social cachet or elicit the same sense of intrinsic personal rewards associated with acquiring new alternatives. Consumers also fail to repair many products and instead will replace them when that is the easiest thing to do. The evidence suggested more generally that if consumers lacked sufficient information about product durability and reparability, if sharing was too inconvenient, and if the whole thing required too much mental effort, they wouldn't bother. That is, there appeared to be a large gap between respondents' stated willingness to participate in the circular economy and how much work they would do to actually engage with it.

Similarly, in the spring of 2019 GlobeScan and partner organizations representing major consumer brands (including such heavyweights as Ikea, Pepsico, Procter & Gamble, and Visa) conducted a survey across 25 countries that was intended to help companies and other organizations to better understand the barriers to, and ways to enable, more sustainable consumer behavior. Across the countries studied, over 60 percent of respondents rated as "very serious" issues such as environmental degradation, pollution, climate change, and plastic waste.

But the researchers in this case again found a significant gap between the respondents' personal attitudes and their actions with respect to sustainability. Over 50 percent of respondents rated living in a sustainable way as a priority, but only about a third said they were actually doing so. Some barriers cited by the respondents as preventing them from achieving a more sustainable lifestyle were personal and motivational in nature—inconvenience,

FIGURE 2.1   Drivers of the Sustainable Consumption Intention–Action Gap

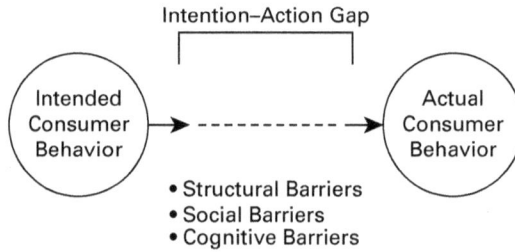

Intention–Action Gap

Intended
Consumer
Behavior

Actual
Consumer
Behavior

- Structural Barriers
- Social Barriers
- Cognitive Barriers

a lack of time, a lack of trust in brands, a lack of social support, or a sense of futility. But the barriers that were the most commonly cited were more systemic and structural—unaffordable green product choices and a lack of adequate support from governments, companies, and NGOs for engaging in pro-environmental behaviors.

Structural, social, and psychological factors all appear to contribute to the gap between consumer intentions to attain a more sustainable lifestyle and their actual behaviors in that regard (Figure 2.1). Regardless of who one might assign responsibility for bridging this intention–action gap, there are reasons to assume it may actually be a wider divide than research indicates. First is the fact that there isn't yet much evidence that consumer attitude change is leading to proportional changes in pro-environmental behaviors. Waste continues to pile up, vehicle miles traveled steadily increase, biodiversity continues to decline, and emissions continue to rise.

Second, there is clear evidence that consumers routinely overstate the degree to which they personally engage in environmentally friendly activities relative to their peers. Take the problem of food waste. In much of the world over 30 percent of post-harvest food is wasted rather than eaten, and that waste has multiple adverse environmental impacts. In 2014 a nationally representative survey was fielded in the US to examine the knowledge and attitudes of consumers about this issue (Neff et al, 2015). The survey indicated widespread self-reported awareness of the problem, self-reported knowledge of ways to address it, and personal efforts to do so. Somewhat improbably, it also found that three-quarters of respondents said they waste less food than the average person!

Subsequent research conducted across the US, Europe, and Asia has established that most people generally also believe that they personally are more environmentally virtuous in their behaviors than others across a variety of activities (Bergquist, 2020). Of course, part of this "better-than-average" effect in reported behavior might just reflect the type of social-desirability response bias that impacts many forms of consumer research. But as we will see, there may be more fundamental factors at play than respondents just wanting to be viewed positively in the eyes of researchers.

Third, and perhaps as importantly, while consumers might increasingly express growing knowledge and concern about the environmental impacts of their everyday lives, they might also lack accurate insight into their own behavior and the factors that influence it. For example, at least one study has shown that the actual ecological footprints of consumers who indicated that they were concerned about their environmental impacts and sought to reduce them did not differ on average from those of less concerned individuals in the same income bracket (Csutora, 2012).

Automaticity in Everyday Behavior

Why do presumably well-meaning people severely misjudge the nature of their choices and the extent of their actions with respect to sustainability issues? Part of the explanation for this gap is that people in general do not appear to have much direct conscious access to the causes of their choices or other aspects of their behavior.

What People Say About Why They Do Things Is Often Wrong

In a landmark paper entitled "Telling More Than We Can Know: Verbal reports on mental processes," the social psychologists Richard Nisbett and Timothy Wilson (1977) described a wide variety of findings indicating that people, both in the laboratory and in everyday life, appear to be extremely limited in their ability to predict their own personal behavior and to accurately report on their own mental processes and the factors that influence their actions. This notion has become conventional wisdom and is widely influential among researchers and practitioners in psychology and behavioral economics. Commenting about such research, Nisbett (2006) later noted that:

> The most important thing that social psychologists have discovered over the last
> 50 years is that people are very unreliable informants about why they behaved
> as they did, made the judgment they did, or liked or disliked something. In

short, we don't know nearly as much about what goes on in our heads as we think. In fact, for a shocking range of things, we don't know the answer to "Why did I?" any better than an observer.

A year after Nisbett and Wilson's seminal paper, another social psychologist named Ellen Langer published a paper entitled "The Mindlessness of Ostensibly Thoughtful Action" (Langer et al, 1978). That team reported results from experiments that suggested that people walk through many of their everyday activities in a sort of autopilot mode, oblivious to the contents of common interpersonal interactions, and to contextual cues and other influences that demonstrably shape their activities. That is, they found that there are many situations in which people are assumed to behave with conscious intent, but in reality those situations receive little consideration or rational thought. Such situations could certainly extend to that of a busy shopper working their way down a list of everyday items while their conscious thoughts are more concerned with other aspects of their lives.

So, what might one conclude from such studies? For one, that people don't, and perhaps can't, consciously think accurately about their cognitive processes. Additionally, that they have little direct insight into the factors that drive their own routine, everyday acts. Both might seem to be "inconvenient truths" during a time when the need to change thoughts and acts is becoming ever more paramount. So why should these limitations exist? And what minimally do we need to understand about them?

Experimental psychologists have long observed that people appear to have two very different, yet concurrent, ways of interacting with the world. According to one such "dual mode" or "dual process" model (Schneider and Shiffrin, 1977; Shiffrin and Schneider, 1977), one mode operates more or less automatically, below the level of conscious thought or deliberate intention. It predominates in situations that are routine, where stimuli can be readily classified, and where suitable responses are habitual. It relies on the rapid activation of overlearned semantic, motoric, and emotional associations, and enables efficient, if nonetheless stereotyped, action. The other mode is more cautious and deliberate, requires mental control and conscious effort, and predominates under circumstances that are less familiar and that may require greater behavioral and cognitive flexibility to contend with. This type of dual process view of the nature of thought has become widely popularized in recent years, including in the marketing community, through publications such as the Nobel Laureate Daniel Kahneman's best-selling 2011 book *Thinking, Fast and Slow*.

Relying on Habits and Mental Models Is an Efficient Mode of Thought

We'll come back to some of the implications that this dichotomous view of human nature has for shedding light on the "aspiring to-be-green consumer's" intention–action gap, but let's first delve into why these two modes of thought might exist. In broad strokes, it can be advantageous and adaptive to operate quickly, efficiently, and instinctively wherever possible. But it is undeniably also adaptive and useful to possess a sophisticated capacity to be thoughtful and creatively flexible when novel circumstances demand it. A key thing to understand is that there are trade-offs involved when invoking that behavioral and cognitive flexibility.

The human brain contains over 80 billion neurons and on average constitutes about 2–3 percent of an adult's overall bodyweight. Yet it is responsible for around 20 percent of the body's energy use—an order-of-magnitude increase in caloric requirements relative to the average body part (Raichle and Gusnard, 2002). Most of this caloric expenditure is devoted to maintaining ongoing activity associated with just keeping the brain and the body it inhabits alive. Thinking hard thoughts might increase energy use in some areas of the brain, but this change amounts at best to only a few percentage points difference overall—as that is all that can be afforded. And it is usually localized in extent across cortical regions—those areas more necessary for a task transiently increase their metabolism. In order for the brain to maintain itself within a range of optimal functioning, transient perturbations of demanding thoughts are necessarily and normally rapidly resolved by reducing the activity of brain regions not involved in the task (Bruckmaier et al, 2020), and by shifting to energetically cheaper ways to guide behavior.

Cognitive neuroscientists study these dynamics in the laboratory in order to explore their implications for improving our understanding of how thinking unfolds and how the brain adapts to new challenges in the environment. Some of those researchers use tools that measure changes in the electrical activity of the brain during some experimental context, either measuring such changes at the microscale by indexing the charging and discharging of individual brain cells as they chatter among themselves, or by measuring changes in the rhythmic oscillations in electrical activity observed at the macroscale from large populations of neurons acting in synchrony. Other tools can be used to study regional increases or decreases in the brain's metabolic demands for oxygen and glucose that occur as a consequence of changes in its electrical activity.

At the most general level, one thing has been made very clear from such measurements. When a person is confronted with some type of new stimulus event or is required to engage in some type of outward-facing activity, the brain dynamically shifts from its more spontaneous ongoing variable mode of electrical activity into a different and more focused and effortful one. The magnitude of that shift is somewhat proportional to the complexity of the task the brain is confronted with, especially if it is one that requires active conscious attention. Within seconds, the cells involved in that shift signal that they need more fuel.

To maintain biological homeostasis while keeping on top of the never-ending perception–action cycle we have to live with, brains have come to be Bayesian prediction machines. That is, they have evolved the capacity to detect and encode regularities in the environment, to learn expected sequences of events as well as appropriate responses to them, so that what might come next can be anticipated. The brain builds mental models of the contingencies and expected rewards of any task environment it is operating in. This enables any new information to be rapidly organized and assimilated into its network so that the neural resources necessary to confront the dynamic world it operates in can be successfully deployed quickly and in a metabolically efficient way. Feedback from any discrepancies between the internal predictive models that the brain builds of itself and of the environment, and the course of the actual real-world events that occur, can trigger more thoughtful responses. These in turn help to initiate error-corrective learning in response to the anomalies, helping to enable the organism to survive the present and to make better predictions in the future.

The unfolding of such activities can be observed in real time to some degree. Imagine you are compelled to play a new, and not especially fun, video game. The game is designed to challenge your ability to process information and make quick decisions about it. At first, you'll make lots of errors, but with practice you'll gradually get better and won't expend as much mental effort while playing it. Those changes that your brain is undergoing are observable in the laboratory using the types of tools outlined above.

In my own research and that of others, a distinct pattern of functional changes can be seen in such circumstances. When first confronted with such a situation, the electrical activity of the learner's brain displays a pattern that is consistent with a more effortful mode of thinking, activating broad areas of the cortex, especially in more difficult levels of a game (Smith et al, 2001). The brain demands increased oxygen and glucose to feed it (Haier, 1992).

And the learner's scoring reflects lots of errors. Players subjectively report that keeping up with things requires a lot of effortful, and stressful, mental work. However, with practice the typical learner objectively scores better and feels less stressed by the situation over time (Gevins et al, 1997; Smith et al, 1999). The learner's brain activity, in turn, reflects less widespread activation and lower mental effort, with reduced metabolic demands (Chein and Schneider, 2005).

While people can build new mental models on the fly, the thing is, people also think that the state of heightened mental effort required at first to do so is somewhat aversive and would prefer to avoid it. And, unless that effort was otherwise expended on something they might find intrinsically rewarding, they feel their extra effort should at least be financially rewarded. Herein lies a potential problem for the sustainable product marketing agenda. That is, any extra effort expended towards achieving some goal can be perceived as a cost. This is not exactly a new idea—Adam Smith noted as much in *The Wealth of Nations*, where he wrote: "The real price of everything, what everything really costs to the man who wants to acquire it, is the toil and trouble of acquiring it."

Simply put, when given a choice, both humans and other animals tend to seek least-effort solutions when trying to accomplish some goal. In his classic 1943 text *Principles of Behavior*, the experimental psychologist and learning theorist Clark Hull in a manner elaborated upon Smith's observation when he described his "law of less work." In particular he proposed that:

> If two or more behavioral sequences, each involving a different amount of energy consumption of work, have been equally well reinforced an equal number of times, the organism will gradually learn to choose the less laborious behavior sequence leading to the reinforcing state of affairs.

A wide variety of evidence suggests that this proposition generally holds true. When given task options that lead to equivalent rewards, people and rats both display a bias towards choosing whichever route is easier. No surprise there. And while Hull was mainly focused on physical effort, more recent psychometric research indicates that the proposition generally holds true also for the mental effort associated with complex tasks. All other things (such as short-term incentives) being equal, people tend to choose tasks that require less mental effort (Kool et al, 2010). And this is not just a result of some coldly calculated cost–benefit analysis. Modern neuroimaging research indicates that tasks requiring high degrees of mental effort tend to activate regions of the brain (such as the anterior insula and the anterior cingulate cortex) that are also activated by such aversive conditions as physical pain and social rejection (Otto et al, 2014; Lu et al, 2016). The added costs of unnecessary effort appear to be experienced at a visceral level!

The key take-away from these considerations is that if you ask people to expend extra mental effort in making a purchase decision and then additionally ask them to actually pay more for a product that offers uncertain and temporally distant benefits over alternative choices, those people are unlikely to choose the more demanding and costly product over competitors. Consider the drain opener anecdote that I shared at the opening of this chapter. I ended up expending more mental effort, more physical effort, and much more money, by choosing the questionably more-sustainable option, with ultimately little received benefit or reinforcement except for a fleeting moment of feeling that I was doing the right thing on some abstract level and for benefits that might accrue to someone else in the distant future. It shouldn't be surprising that there exists a big sustainable consumption intention–action gap.

Mental Heuristics: Judgment Under Uncertainty

We need to consider a few more key issues before moving on—one of which is the related view of Herbert Simon, another polymath who variously contributed in large ways to the fields of economics, cognitive science, and political science, who received the Nobel Prize in Economics for his development of the idea of "bounded rationality." According to Simon, the rationality of any striving *homo economicus* must necessarily be limited by the facts that: (1) the brain is limited in its computational capability, (2) the decision problems that the owners of those brains must confront can be very complex, (3) the information they have available to work with is often woefully incomplete, and (4) the time available in which to make a decision is often quite limited.

"Satisficing"—Finding Good-Enough Solutions When Information Is Limited

Simon introduced the notion of "*satisficing*" in order to explain human decision-making behavior under these conditions. With this notion he was referring to a good-enough decision, one that makes the best of a situation given that with which a human choice-taker has to work. As he noted in his Nobel acceptance speech, "decision-makers can satisfice either by finding optimum solutions for a simplified world, or by finding satisfactory solutions for a more realistic world. Neither approach, in general, dominates the other, and both have continued to co-exist in the world."

Herb Simon's views on the realities of choice behavior acknowledge the limits of how much mental effort we can comfortably expend. We are biologically bandwidth-limited. While we can act quite cleverly, our thoughts and behaviors have had to be streamlined and compromised in the evolutionary process. Our decision-making ability within the limits Simon noted is a growing issue now that the brains that enable our efficient over-achieving are no longer operating in the world they were programmed to exploit. Our brains are much better suited to Kenneth Boulding's (1966) metaphor of an archaic and anarchic "cowboy" frontier rather than a planet of increasingly constrained resources.

One well-documented aspect of our problematic streamlining is the fact that, instead of thinking in a slow and effortful fashion when encountering every situation, the satisficing that people do instead can involve reliance on convenient shortcuts or mental heuristics that enable good-enough judgments much of the time. These (often strategic) "rules of thumb" help people to make decisions about problems in a fast and efficient manner, often without having to spend a lot of time pondering the most optimal course of action. Because such shortcuts sometimes yield judgments that differ from more reasoned correct results (as adjudicated by formal logic or probability theory), they are often popularly referred to as "cognitive biases." Regardless, they persist as handy tools of thought. Heuristic-based judgments and decisions can often be good enough to satisfy an immediate need, but they can be blind to the future.

Ease-of-Processing and Fluency-Based Modes of Satisficing

Several types of frequently discussed mental heuristics depend on the notion of "processing fluency," which is the subjective experience of the relative ease versus difficulty one has when making sense of the world. Processing fluency can take different forms. For example, the term "perceptual fluency" refers to a feeling that an external stimulus is perceptually salient and easy to distinguish and encode, rather than something that is difficult to discern from its background or something hard to categorize. In contrast, the notion of "retrieval fluency" refers to the relative ease by which information can be retrieved from memory. For mental heuristics that rely on processing fluency, the mere fact that something is easy to comprehend or recall gives it a special status.

People who have an experience of perceptual fluency for an item can judge it as more familiar, or more likable, than something that is more difficult to process. This is regardless of whether there is any objective basis for doing so. Similarly, the ease by which a general idea or personal experience can be retrieved from memory can also be used as a basis from which to infer the likelihood that it is objectively factual, that it reflects something that is representative of a category, and that things like it have a higher probability of occurrence in the world.

Because every personal confrontation with the world subjectively falls somewhere along a continuum from effortless to overwhelming, subjective fluency can serve as a useful metacognitive cue in reasoning and social judgment. Given its importance, the general implications for marketing practitioners of mental heuristics based on processing fluency or related factors have already been discussed at length elsewhere (Bridger, 2017; Genco, 2019).

There is another type of fluency-based mental shortcut, the "availability heuristic." First described by Daniel Kahneman and his collaborator Amos Tversky (Tversky and Kahneman, 1973), the availability heuristic depends on retrieval fluency. In particular, the availability heuristic is an automatic inference that if something comes to an individual's mind relatively easily when considering a specific problem or topic, that is, if it is more or less conceptually salient, it must then be relatively important or representative of the facts of the real world.

The availability heuristic played a central role in Byron Sharp's 2010 classic review of the buying behavior and marketing performance literature, entitled *How Brands Grow: What marketers don't know*. In his book, he argued that brand growth comes primarily from gaining new users rather than increasing brand loyalty. Moreover, to achieve such growth a brand has to be both easily available on a physical basis, and it must readily come to mind as a solution to a need that a potential buyer has. In other words, it must have "mental availability."

The role of advertising and marketing in his view then is to initially build, and continue to refresh, the memory structures necessary to implicitly activate the distinct features of a brand. Such structures serve to bring the brand to mind in a salient fashion when associated attributes are cued in a market context. For example, in-store displays in a retail environment might serve to activate a brand representation right when a consumer is making their purchase decision. In this view, for brands to grow in market share, marketers need to minimize both the physical difficulty and mental effort that potential customers have to overcome in order to access brand characteristics from memory when they think they need something from the product category, and thereby make it more effortless for those potential customers to choose those brands over the other options that may be competing in the marketplace.

Let's consider this in the context of my drain opener anecdote. In Sharp's view the advantage of brand leaders is that they easily come to mind (and physically often can demand an advantaged shelf position as well), such that a potential shopper is unlikely to even think about or consider a niche competitor, especially in the absence of any prominently displayed price promotions that might interfere with the mindless script the consumer is following. This would certainly characterize my experience. I undertook my shopping journey with the brand leaders top of mind, and that mental salience and their privileged shelf positions both helped me to physically find them. But the top two product-space brand competitors were not that distinctive in their features—otherwise I probably would have just grabbed the more distinctive one, and not have noticed or considered the more explicitly claimed sustainable, but niche, competitor. I also had to expend the extra mental effort necessary to justify a higher price and less certain benefits in order to add it to my shopping basket and there was no subsequent reward—either immediately or psychologically in the abstract long term—signaling that the extra effort and expense were worth it. That is, the "green" challenger was unfamiliar and not top of mind, nor obvious on the shelf. It espoused claims I had no way to easily evaluate, and it cost significantly more.

Implicit Networks of Association Guide Product Choice

The availability heuristic might also have some potential explanatory power for helping to illuminate at least one factor that might be contributing to the intention–action gap in sustainable consumption behavior we reviewed at the beginning of this chapter. In their initial study of mental availability, Tversky and Kahneman (1973) found that examples that are mentally salient and easily brought to mind are also judged to be more representative of a category and more likely to occur in the real world than they in fact do. Given this, one might expect that when a survey respondent is asked about their own sustainable behaviors, it seems reasonable to suppose that such a respondent might more easily bring to mind some salient examples of their own sustainable behaviors when asked to judge their personal virtues relative to that of some abstract other—whereas few or no vivid examples of the sustainable behaviors of that generic other person may be available to retrieve even with effort. That is, a reliance on the availability heuristic might also at least in part explain the robust better-than-average effect observed when respondents are asked to make such comparative judgments.

Automatic Behavior Depends on Implicit Activation of Associative Memory

The more effortless, intuitive mode of thinking we have been considering is driven by habits and the automatic activation of associated memories, thoughts, and feelings defined by learning from past experiences. Those associations are then sparked by some proximal event or environmental cue. Associative networks are models of the structure of human memory that represent key features of how we organize and understand the world. Their essence has been discussed for millennia and explored empirically for over a century. When two things co-occur in the world or in the mind, through learning processes they may become linked in a memory structure and organized as connected nodes in a network. Experimental psychologists have long used reaction time-based methods to study the organizational structure and the relative strengths of those connections. One basic finding that has emerged from such research is that associative networks in the human brain have a degree of hierarchical and categorical structure (Collins and Quillian, 1969). For example, things that can be described by nouns subsume things that are the descriptive attributes of those nouns. For example, fruits are generally things that contain seeds.

Similarly, nouns that are exemplars of categories have some associative relationship to the superordinate nouns that may describe the general category. So bananas and apples are both fruits (Figure 2.2). And all of these associations will vary in strength depending on the particulars of one's experience with the world—both those direct personal experiences we have had and more indirect, manufactured experiences delivered via media

FIGURE 2.2 Associative Organization of Semantic Memory

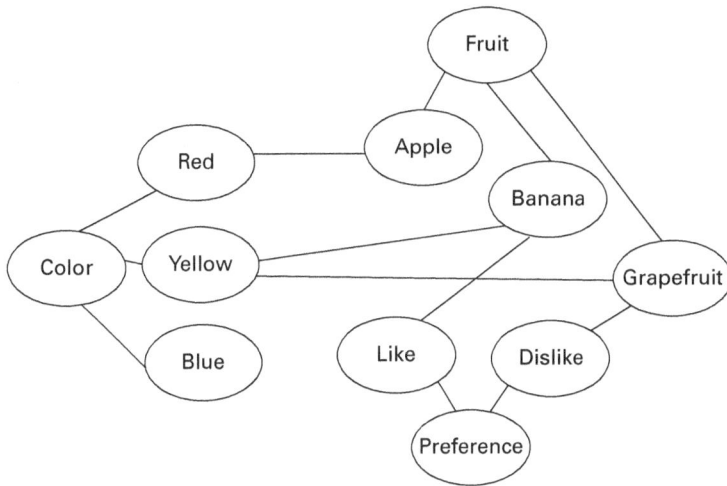

impressions. And given my personal experiences with the world if I was asked whether a banana is a yellow fruit, I would be relatively fast to say yes, and relatively slow when asked whether a mango is a yellow fruit. It is important to also note that a key finding from past research is that such networks are not just semantic in nature; they also incorporate associations to the attitudes and emotional responses evoked by those past experiences (Fazio et al, 1986). For example, while a banana and a lemon both fall under the category of "fruits," and share the property of being yellow, I might like to eat the former but not the latter.

As noted by the marketing theorist David Aaker (1995) in his classic work *Building Strong Brands*, individual brands and product categories can also be represented as associative networks with a hierarchical organization. In fact, the success of brand marketing may depend heavily on the degree to which a branded exemplar of a product category is immediately available to the mind when thinking about the category, and how distinctive the particular attributes associated with that brand exemplar are. Given such an organization, at the more general level of the product category itself, might there also be some generic concept of what the attributes of a "sustainable" or "green" product might be? And if so, what generic attributes might be associated with it and activated by situational cues that relate to those concepts?

Implicit Associations Can Guide "Green" Purchasing Decisions

Some researchers using reaction time methods to study the organization of associative networks have begun to apply those tools to the problem of exploring how such networks impact the sustainability of the choices consumers make. One finding from such research is that the implicit associations and attitudes of consumers can be better predictors of whether consumers will choose "green" products than the explicit verbal reports made by those same consumers, especially when they are operating under time pressure.

In one such study researchers explicitly asked participants to rate the degree to which they preferred "low-carbon" products, that is, those that were associated with lower GHG emissions, from low to high on a Likert scale (Beattie and Sale, 2011). They then had the same participants engage in a reaction-time-based study to examine implicit associations between pictorial exemplars of "low-carbon" versus "high-carbon" products and the positive versus negative attitudes activated by those pictorial depictions.

After the study they provided the participants with the opportunity to choose a gift bag containing either low-carbon (a locally grown apple with an LED light bulb and an ink pen made of recycled materials) versus high-carbon products (an imported, tropically grown banana with an incandescent light bulb and a regular ink pen). They found that across subjects there was little correlation between their explicitly stated attitudes towards low-carbon products and their implicit associations as revealed from the reaction-time measures. They further found that the implicit measure of associational strength was a significantly better predictor of the type of gift bag they would select than the explicitly stated preference measure was, suggesting that implicit association strength contributes to product choice

Of additional relevance to the current discussion is a relatively granular finding from research of this nature—one identifying a potential liability for sustainable products in some circumstances (Luchs et al, 2010). The researchers involved found that even if consumers care about environmental issues, the degree to which claims of sustainability might influence product preference may be category-specific. They measured implicit associations to products with and without sustainability claims and found that "sustainable" products were more strongly associated with gentleness-related attributes, whereas products without such claims were more closely associated with strength-related attributes. Further, in product categories for which gentleness was a perceived benefit (e.g., baby shampoo), sustainability claims were associated with increased product preference judgments. But, for product categories for which strength was a perceived benefit (e.g., car wash detergent), sustainability claims actually reduced or eliminated that effect, and sometimes even resulted in a higher preference for less sustainable alternatives.

In light of such a finding, let's return one last time to my drain opener anecdote. Drain opening is clearly a product category where strength-related attributes could be better predictors of product preference than gentleness-related attributes. In addition to the other shortcomings we have covered, my existing belief and need state likely activated an almost instinctual implicit association that strength was a more important attribute for product choice in the drain opener category than gentleness was. Clearly, at least in this example, the overall situation was not a great position from which to get the green brand to grow. Indeed, if our desired vantage point is by necessity consistent with Boulding's (1966) proposed spaceman image of the future, then to quote a line from Apollo 13, "Houston... we have a problem."

1   Routine behaviors tend to be governed by existing mental models and automatic habits that override more mindful decision-making, especially when choices are made under stress and in the face of distractions.

2   Overcoming automaticity requires exerting limited reserves of cognitive effort and control, which itself imposes a perceived cost, and when combined with the financial costs of some green choices it may become hard to balance the trade-offs.

3   To minimize the need for effortful thinking about complex problems, the brain tends to employ mental heuristics and shortcuts to enable decision-making under pressure. Such heuristics may supersede pro-environmental decisions.

4   Existing networks of associations in the brain may implicitly color the way some product choices are factually and emotionally perceived, which may in turn unconsciously color and bias consumer preferences towards either more traditional or green alternatives.

References

Aaker, D A (1995) *Building Strong Brands*, Jossey Bass, San Francisco, CA

Beattie, G and Sale, L (2011) Shopping to save the planet? Implicit rather than explicit attitudes predict low carbon footprint consumer choice, *International Journal of Environmental, Cultural, Economic and Social Sustainability*, 7(4), 211–232

Bergquist, M (2020) Most people think they are more pro-environmental than others: A demonstration of the better-than-average effect in perceived pro-environmental behavioral engagement, *Basic and Applied Social Psychology*, 42(1), 1–12

Boulding, K E (1966) The economics of the coming Spaceship Earth, in H Jarrett (ed.) *Environmental Quality in a Growing Economy*, Resources for the Future/ Johns Hopkins University Press, Baltimore, MD

Bridger, D (2017) *Neuro Design: Neuromarketing insights to boost engagement and profitability*, Kogan Page, London

Bruckmaier, M, Tachtsidis, I, Phan, P, and Lavie, N (2020) Attention and capacity limits in perception: A cellular metabolism account, *Journal of Neuroscience*, 40(35), 6801–6811

Chein, J M and Schneider, W (2005) Neuroimaging studies of practice-related change: fMRI and meta-analytic evidence of a domain-general control network for learning, *Cognitive Brain Research*, 25(3): 607–623

Collins, A M and Quillian, M R (1969) Retrieval time from semantic memory, *Journal of Verbal Learning & Verbal Behavior*, 8(2), 240–247

Csutora, M (2012) One more awareness gap? The behaviour-impact gap problem, *Journal of Consumer Policy*, 35, 145–163

Eurobarometer (2020) Attitudes of European citizens about the environment, ec. europa.eu/commfrontoffice/publicopinion/index.cfm/survey/getSurveydetail/ instruments/special/surveyky/2257 (archived at https://perma.cc/SKF2-EZ89)

European Commission (2018) Behavioural study on consumers' engagement in the circular economy ec.europa.eu/info/sites/info/files/ec_circular_economy_final_ report_0.pdf (archived at https://perma.cc/G6Y5-2TZ9)

Fazio, R H, Sanbonmatsu, D M, Powell, M and Kardes, F R (1986) On the automatic activation of attitudes, *Journal of Personality and Social Psychology*, 50(2), 229–238

Genco, S J (2019) *Intuitive Marketing: What marketers can learn from brain science*, Intuitive Consumer Insights, LLC

Gevins, A, Smith, M E, McEvoy, L, and Yu, D. (1997) High resolution EEG mapping of cortical activation related to working memory: Effects of task difficulty, type of processing, and practice, *Cerebral Cortex*, 7, 374–385

GlobeScan. (2019) Healthy and sustainable living: A global consumer insights study, globescan.com/wpcontent/uploads/2019/09/Healthy_Sustainable_Living_2019_GlobeScan_Highlights.pdf (archived at https://perma.cc/ZHR4-PU8A)

Haier, R J, Siegal, B V, MacLachlan, A, Soderling, E, Lottenberg, S and Bushsbaum, M S (1992) Regional glucose metabolic changes after learning a complex visuospatial/motor task: a positron emission tomographic study, *Brain Research*, 570, 132–143

Hull, C L (1943) *Principles of Behavior: An introduction to behavior theory*, Appleton-Century-Crofts, New York

Kahneman, D (2011) *Thinking, Fast and Slow*, Farrar, Straus, and Giroux, New York

Kool, W, McGuire, J T, Rosen, Z, and Botvinick, M M (2010) Decision-making and the avoidance of cognitive demand, *Journal of Experimental Psychology: General*, 139(4), 665–682

Langer, E, Blank, A and Chanowitz, B (1978) The mindlessness of ostensibly thoughtful action: The role of "placebic" information in interpersonal interaction, *Journal of Personality and Social Psychology*, 36(6), 633–642

Leiserowitz, A, Maibach, E Rosenthal, S, Kotcher, J, Bergquist, P, Ballew, M, Goldberg, M, Gustafson, A and Wang, X (2020) Climate change in the American mind, 19 May, climatecommunication.yale.edu/publications/climate-change-in-the-american-mind-april-2020/ (archived at https://perma.cc/VK62-VAFN)

Lu C, Yang T, Zhao H, et al (2016) Insular cortex is critical for the perception, modulation, and chronification of pain, *Neuroscience Bulletin*, 32(2), 191–201

Luchs, M G, Walker-Naylor, R, Irwin, J R and Raghunathan, R (2010) The sustainability liability: Potential negative effects of ethicality on product preference, *Journal of Marketing*, 74(September), 18–31

Neff, R A, Spiker, M L, and Truant, P L (2015) Wasted food: U.S. consumers' reported awareness, attitudes, and behaviors, *PLoS ONE*, 10(6), 1–16

Nielsen (2015) The sustainability imperative: New insights on consumer expectations, nielseniq.com/global/en/insights/analysis/2015/the-sustainability-imperative-2/ (archived at https://perma.cc/T5LD-XZGN)

Nielsen (2018) The evolution of the sustainability mindset, www.nielsen.com/us/en/insights/report/2018/the-education-of-the-sustainable-mindset/ (archived at https://perma.cc/BM7X-VNG8)

Nisbett, R (2006) Telling more than we can know, *Edge*, www.edge.org/response-detail/10581 (archived at https://perma.cc/9YDA-FU8Y)

Nisbett, R and Wilson, T (1977) Telling more than we can know: Verbal reports on mental processes, *Psychological Review*, 84(3), 231–259

Otto, T, Zjistra, F R H and Goebel, R (2014) Neural correlates of mental effort evaluation: Involvement of structures related to self-awareness, *Social, Cognitive, and Affective Neuroscience*, 9, 307–315

Pew Research Center (2019) U.S. Public Views on Climate and Energy Report, www.pewresearch.org/science/2019/11/25/u-s-public-views-on-climate-and-energy/ (archived at https://perma.cc/WXV6-FFLM)

Raichle, M E and Gusnard, D A (2002) Appraising the brain's energy budget, *Proceedings of the National Academy of Sciences USA*, 99(16), 10237–10239

Schneider W and Shiffrin, R M (1977) Controlled and automatic human information processing: I. Detection, search, and attention, *Psychological Review*, 84(1), 1–66

Sharp, B (2010) *How Brands Grow: What marketers don't know*, Oxford University Press, Oxford

Shelton Group (2019) Waking the sleeping giant: What middle America knows about plastic pollution and how they're taking action, sheltongrp.com/work/circularity-2019-special-report-waking-the-sleeping-giant (archived at https://perma.cc/PWY4-3YSK)

Shiffrin R M and Schneider, W (1977) Controlled and automatic information processing: II. Perceptual learning, automatic attending, and a general theory, *Psychological Review*, 84(2), 127–190

Smith, A (1776) *The Wealth of Nations*, W Strahan and T Cadell, London

Smith, M E, Gevins, A, Brown, H, Karnik, A and Du, R (2001) Monitoring task load with multivariate EEG measures during complex forms of human computer interaction, *Human Factors*, 43, 366–380

Smith, M E, McEvoy, L and Gevins, A (1999) Neurophysiological indices of strategy development and skill acquisition, *Cognitive Brain Research*, 7, 389–404

Tversky, A and Kahneman, D (1973) Availability: A heuristic for judging frequency and probability, *Cognitive Psychology*, 5(2), 207–232

03

Decoding Consumer Wanting and Liking

New insights into the preferences that people express and the decisions they make in the marketplace are being provided by modern brain and behavioral research. Those insights are helping to better inform retail marketing and advertising strategies and they have implications for understanding the neural underpinnings of brand loyalty. They also suggest that brands aiming to introduce new, sustainable, product options may face an uphill battle, especially if those options are positioned at a high price point and if the predicated benefits of the products may be remote in time and impersonal in nature.

What's happening in your brain when you experience a sense of desire for, well, whatever you desire, even if that thing is something relatively mundane, or crass, or instead beautiful? Or if that something is purportedly "green"? If our aim is to help people make more sustainable choices in the consumer sphere, we need to better understand what's happening when they make product choices more generally. So let's take a look!

The Shopping Brain

We're going to step into a magnetic resonance imaging suite to make some measurements of your brain's functional activity (fMRI). First you're going to have to remove any metal objects you may have on you or in your clothes and then you will undergo something like an airport magnetometer screening to make sure nothing ferromagnetic remains. The scanner itself incorporates a superconducting magnet that creates an intense magnetic field that is always turned on. Loose ferromagnetic objects in such a room (like your car keys) have an unfortunate tendency to sometimes fly across the room into the scanner.

After entering the imaging suite, you lay down on a narrow, movable table. The table projects out from a machine that looks like a giant donut with a tubular hole through its middle. The hole is snug enough for your body, but not much more. You are given a pair of special sound-attenuating headphones to protect your ears from the sharp hammering sounds that accompany the scanning process. A cage-like structure that is a type of antenna that detects and transmits radio waves is clamped somewhat snugly over your head. Some of the radio waves that will be detected by the antenna will come from inside your head, as the atoms in your brain try to adjust to sudden fluxes of strong magnetic fields. Then the table you are lying on is drawn deep into the donut-like hole in the scanner. The nice MRI technician who helped you into this situation will leave you in the darkened room to shelter in a safe control center outside.

Try not to be anxious or deterred by claustrophobia—very seldom do serious problems occur. Oh, and try to keep your head very still in its cage and to not gasp for breath. Those things would interfere with the measurements to be made. And don't worry... these types of procedures are conducted for clinical reasons on thousands of people around the world every day.

Looking up through an opening in the head cage, just above your eyes, you see a small video screen. Over the headphones you hear the voice of an experimenter out in the control room. The voice reminds you that you will receive a reasonable hourly rate for participating and that, for fun, you're going shopping! You are awarded a "virtual wallet" you can spend on your virtual purchases during your shopper journey—at least one of which you will actually receive in the real world if you purchase things. If you don't buy anything, you get to keep all the money in your virtual wallet. All of the products you will be considering for purchase have been selected because they are considered to be non-objectionable—such as tasty high-end chocolate. As the consumer, the only things you need to consider are your preferences for the products and their price.

And so the fun begins. You first see a picture of a product on offer. Initially you just view the object and a label for it during a four-second presentation. Then a price pops up on the screen under the product so that you know what it will cost you. You see the product plus price illustration for another four seconds. Finally, a yes/no question appears and you have four seconds to press one or another button to indicate your purchase decision. After a brief pause, another product/price/buy-or-not sequence occurs.

Brain Activity That Predicts Product Choices

What I just described approximates the experience of participants in a study conducted by Brian Knutson and colleagues at Stanford University some years ago (Knutson et al, 2007). Overall those researchers found that several brain regions turned on in advance of the participants' decisions about whether or not to purchase a product and the pattern of those activations was predictive of the choices participants subsequently made. The earliest such discrimination observed was a significant increase in activation in an area of the brain called the ventral striatum, which is the underside of the striatum (Figure 3.1). The ventral striatum is one of the major structures in the basal ganglia—a group of subcortical cell clusters or nuclei in the brain that lie at the base of the forebrain and above the midbrain.

A large part of the ventral striatum is occupied by the nucleus accumbens (NAcc). The NAcc is located deep within each of the brain's cerebral

FIGURE 3.1 Brain Regions Activated During Virtual Purchase Decisions

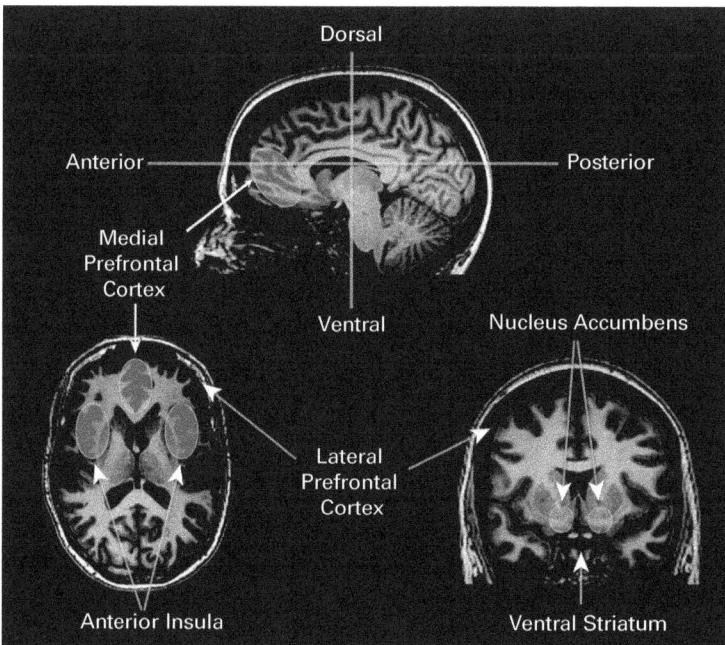

hemispheres and is a key part of the brain's reward circuitry—it is reliably activated during a wide range of experiences that promise reinforcement. Through its connections with other brain regions, it plays a role in motivating behavior towards things that might be beneficial—and away from things that might be harmful. It is also thought to play an important role in the process of associative learning, which in turn allows an organism to better anticipate potential upcoming rewards in response to future environmental cues.

In the shopping task described above, activity in the NAcc increased for displayed items that were subsequently purchased. This differential activation started soon after the picture of a product appeared, even before pricing information was available, and long before a behavioral choice was made. This type of early NAcc response is sometimes referred to as a sign of "reward anticipation." And in this case it was also positively correlated with participants' subjective ratings of product preference.

The next region to display differential activation between subsequently purchased and subsequently rejected offerings was the medial (towards the midline) prefrontal cortex (MPFC), and particularly its ventral (v) or bottom aspect. The vMPFC area is involved in many important cognitive functions, two of which are closely related and are of special importance here: assessing the potential value of, and judging the self-relevance of, an object or event. That is, it seems instrumental in helping you evaluate what something is worth to *you* specifically rather than its worth on a more absolute and abstract level. The NAcc and the vMPFC share tight anatomical and functional connectivity. In this study activation in the vMPFC was also significantly greater for items that were subsequently purchased... but not until after pricing information was displayed. And it was relatively deactivated for items that participants subjectively judged to be overpriced. So at a basic neural level, having unusually high prices drives down neural correlates of purchase intent for things you might otherwise want.

The third region of activation that was significantly related to subsequent choice, the anterior portion of the insula, displayed a very different pattern. The insula is a region of cortex tucked behind the temporal lobes in the lateral sulcus of each cerebral hemisphere, and the anterior portion is the extent of it that is closer to the front of the head. The anterior insula is differentially activated under many sorts of conditions; consequently, it's not entirely clear what it does. Results from many studies though suggest that it integrates and modulates some bodily states with respect to whatever is going on in your thinking brain.

In any case, during the virtual shopping exercise, activity in this region peaked in activation after the other areas, and participants were less likely to choose to purchase items when activity in this region was high. At least on the right side of the brain, activation in the anterior insula was especially enhanced for items that participants also subjectively judged to be overpriced.

The anterior insula is often described as a key node in a putative "salience network" that detects unexpected or otherwise important stimuli and then engages other relevant functional networks to prioritize their processing (Menon and Uddin, 2010). It also seems to have some degree of hemispheric asymmetry in its organization; the anterior insula in the right hemisphere appears to be particularly involved in aversive states such as anxiety, fear, and anticipatory pain (Craig, 2009; Critchley et al, 2004; Gu et al, 2013). The right anterior insula also appears to play an important role in modulating peripheral nervous system activity—moments after it is activated changes in such things as blood pressure, heart rate, skin conductance, and pupil dilation can be observed (Kucyi and Parvizi, 2020).

A related putative role for the right anterior insula is in the resolution of approach–avoidance conflicts (Aupperle et al, 2015), in part through increasing arousal and promoting recruitment of a functional network involved in inhibiting or stopping an ongoing response (Cai et al, 2014). For example, in the shopping context we have been considering, if your level of reward anticipation in response to a product was high enough to prime a purchase choice, but new information (such as a high price) conflicted with that initial predilection, signaling from the right insula might help activate inhibitory processes involved with keeping that item out of your virtual shopping cart.

In sum, this experimental exercise indicated that neural processes involved in registering preference, in calculating the potential personal value of a purchase opportunity, and in stopping you from overpaying, all seem to play a role in purchase choices about everyday items. In a review of research on both purchase decisions and hypothetical investment choices that involved monetary rewards and losses, the authors suggested that: "NAcc activation promotes approach towards uncertain outcomes, while anterior insula activation promotes avoidance of uncertain outcomes" (Knutson and Greer, 2008). Presumably relative activation in subjective valuation-related regions such as the vMPFC helps to modulate the ultimate direction of such influences. Collectively these brain regions thus seem to be intimately involved with approach versus avoidance behavioral responses.

Interestingly, many neuropsychiatric problems are associated with disordered processing in this system. This includes such diverse things as obsessive-compulsive disorders, eating disorders, and physical addictions such as substance abuse disorders (Dichter et al, 2012). In many of these cases an environmental cue of one sort or another hyper-activates the NAcc and associated structures involved in reward anticipation and approach behaviors. For example, on average people who struggle with obesity or binge eating often display greater NAcc activation in response to pictures of tasty food than do comparison control groups (Reichelt et al, 2015). A similar hyper-activation in this system is seen in response to alcohol, nicotine, and cocaine cues in addicts to those substances relative to control groups.

A growing literature also implicates this system in behavioral disorders such as pathological gambling. And more speculative, but intriguing and germane to the present discussion, is the notion that compulsive shopping also represents a disruption of this same reward processing and motivational system (Hartson, 2012).

Neuroelectric Measures of Approach Motivation

There are additional brain-based markers of approach versus avoidance motivation that can be obtained outside of an MRI scanner. For example, some changes in the electroencephalogram or EEG are functionally similar to those observed in the NAcc and right anterior insula during equivalent task conditions. At a macroscale, if you affix EEG electrodes to the left and right sides of the lateral frontal regions of a head, in particular about midway and an inch or so above a line drawn between the lateral corners of the eyes and the ears, one can measure the relative degree of activation of the left and right sides of your frontal lobes as changes in the oscillatory activity of the EEG.

As it happens, if brain activation in response to a cue is relatively higher in the left frontal region than in the right, in general people tend to be experiencing some sort of "approach motivation." And conversely, if instead activation is greater over the right frontal region than the left, in general people appear to be experiencing more of a withdrawal or "avoidance" motivation (Davidson et al, 1990). This dynamic has been explored in the same type of virtual shopping task as that employed by Knutson and colleagues as described above. And the investigators in that case found that a relative pre-purchase approach motivation as derived from EEG metrics was also associated with pro-purchase decisions, and a relative pro-avoidance motivation was associated with product-price rejections (Ravaja et al, 2013).

Other similar research has demonstrated that frontal EEG asymmetries can also be associated with increased "willingness-to-pay" in virtual shopping tasks (Ramsøy et al, 2018). More generally this type of EEG-based approach–avoidance metric reacts similarly to the types of experimental conditions that elicit reward anticipation signals across a wide range of conditions. But the exact anatomical and physiological mechanism that mediates this functional similarity is poorly understood at present.

Mental Effort and Temporal Delay Reduce the Value of a Reward

Harking back to the last chapter, the same regions of the brain we have been considering in the context of purchase decisions also seem to be involved in judgments of how much mental effort it is worth allocating to a task. In particular, and all things being equal, tasks with higher potential monetary payoffs elicit greater activation in the NAcc and other regions associated with reward anticipation. And, again all other things being equal, the costs associated with tasks requiring greater mental effort elicit more activity in the anterior insula (Prevost et al, 2010). When given a choice between a high-reward, high-effort task and a lower-reward, low-effort task, a subjective valuation network that includes the vMPFC appears to be involved with weighing the benefits of increased reward versus the costs of increased mental effort (Croxson et al, 2009; Westbrook et al, 2019). In terms of subjective valuation, potential rewards in a situation are discounted by the expected degree of mental effort that would be required to obtain them. Given that it may take extra mental effort to gauge the unsubstantiated validity of any claimed environmental benefits for "green" products, such results suggest that consumers may be relatively disinclined to expend that effort.

Much like the way in which the dollar cost or the mental effort needed to acquire a reward tends to discount the value of the reward, so does any delay in receiving it. While behavioral research has shown that people prefer bigger or better rewards to smaller or worse rewards, it has also shown that the way in which a reward is valued is heavily discounted such that lesser rewards received sooner are preferred over greater rewards received later.

While in absolute terms areas like the NAcc and the vMPFC increase their activity more for a future large reward than a future small reward, their activity is more closely correlated with choices for immediate rewards; other regions of the brain involved in executive control must be more critically engaged in order to override this preference for immediacy and to enable long-term goal attainment when rewards are more distant (Ballard and Knutson, 2009; Kable and Glimcher, 2007; McClure et al, 2004). Given that most product promises of environmental benefits reflect abstract rewards that are both vague and distant in time, this is not a great dynamic for the in-the-moment purchase intent elicited by those products.

From Laboratory to Marketplace

While the results described above are interesting, do we really need to worry about such toy-like laboratory-based shopping exercises? Do such results have any real-world implications? As it turns out, one of the most interesting trends in the consumer neuroscience field over the last decade has been research aimed at extrapolating results from small laboratory-based studies to predict population-level marketplace behavior. In one early such example, researchers at Emory University (Berns and Moore, 2012) published results from a study where they had previously measured the fMRI response of a small group of participants who were scanned while they listened to 15-second clips of popular music from relatively unknown artists, and then rated each clip in terms of its subjective likability. Several years later they compared those data with the subsequent cultural appeal and marketplace success of those same songs as measured by Nielsen Soundscan, a syndicated service that tracks music sales. No relationship was observed between the listener's subjective liking ratings and marketplace success. Nonetheless, a significant positive correlation was found between the songs eliciting the highest activation in the reward systems of the listener's brains (in particular the NAcc) and the subsequent population-level popularity and sales success of those same songs.

A similar result was obtained in another study that examined neural predictors of crowd-funding success (Genevsky et al, 2017). In that study researchers used fMRI to scan the brains of a small sample of 30 people who were asked to read descriptions of proposed projects on an internet crowd-funding website. And for each project they read they then were asked to decide whether or not to contribute to it. At an individual participant level, increased activity in both the vMPFC and the NAcc was found to be predictive of their yes/no funding decisions. And at a group level, relative activation of the NAcc was positively predictive of the ultimate real-world financial outcomes for each crowd-funding request as indexed weeks later when the projects completed their funding requests. This is despite the fact that no such significant prediction was observed when looking solely at the aggregate behavioral choices the participants made.

A third example of successful prediction outcome of real-world population-level behavior is one where a "neural focus group" of participants (smokers) watched anti-smoking public service advertisements (PSAs) while their brains were scanned (Falk et al, 2012). Three alternative PSAs of this nature were presented to the participants, and after viewing each the participants were asked to subjectively rate them as to their relative messaging effectiveness. All of the advertisements included a toll-free telephone number where viewers could call to get more information on how to quit smoking. The volume of calls to those numbers in response to each PSA might be seen as an objective real-world measurement of each PSA's actual messaging effectiveness. While the experimental participant's subjective ratings of the PSA's impacts were not significantly related to relative call center volume response, the investigators reported that the relative level of activation of the group's vMPFC while watching each of the advertisements did in fact correlate with the call center data.

At least two other studies have addressed the broader issue of the impact of advertising on consumer product choice at scale. Both examined the relationship between advertising effectiveness for major consumer brands as measured in the laboratory at the neural level, and the results of marketing mix modeling (MMM) of the effectiveness of the same advertisements for impacting sales at the population level. MMM is an econometric technique that utilizes multivariate regression methods applied to time series of sales and marketing data to estimate the degree to which different marketing methods (such as advertising or price promotions) influenced past sales, and for estimating the potential impact of proposed marketing plans on future sales.

In one such study organized by the Advertising Research Foundation, a group of researchers at the Center for Neural Decision-making at Temple University in Philadelphia used fMRI and other methods to scan the brains of a sample of participants as they viewed a collection of advertisements provided by major brand advertisers (Venkatraman et al, 2015). Each of those television commercials were for well-known consumer products portrayed in campaigns for which the brand advertisers had previously conducted MMM analyses and had reliable estimates of the degree to which those commercials impacted sales within the marketing campaigns they were part of. The investigators reported that out of all the variables they studied, advertisements with content that resulted in greater NAcc activation were also associated with greater marketplace impact.

A conceptually similar study reported by the market research firm Nielsen (2016; Smith and Marci, 2016) also found a significant relationship between neural measures of advertising engagement and MMM estimates of advertising marketplace effectiveness. At the time of the study Nielsen was a market leader in providing MMM services to the consumer packaged goods (CPG) industry and in providing brands with EEG-based measures of video advertising engagement. Using the type of laboratory-based, EEG-derived metrics of approach motivation as described above as well as complementary EEG measures of memory activation, it was possible to compare the neurological engagement elicited by a set of television commercials to the MMM measures of advertising effectiveness from the same campaigns those advertisements were part of. And a significant correlation between the two was reported. In particular, other things being equal, commercials that elicited greater approach motivation were associated with above-average marketplace sales lift. Commercials that were most successful at engaging consumers for a given brand were responsible for around 25 percent greater sales lift for that brand, whereas advertisements that scored below average for a brand on the EEG measures were instead associated with below-average sales lift.

Brain Activity and the Green Intention–Action Gap

So where does all this leave us? We know that in the laboratory, in the moment of purchasing, brain measurements of "reward anticipation" or "approach motivation" are predictive of purchase choices. Additionally it seems that those measures can be predictive of population-scale, real-world behavior. And it appears that advertisements that successfully activate such brain signals of desire facilitate better sales performance for the products they promote. All interesting and important things for brand advertisers to understand, but the focus of this book is on identifying ways to reduce barriers to making green choices and to encourage more sustainable consumption decisions. Is there related research that speaks more directly to that goal?

At least one study has employed brain-imaging methods to try to directly elucidate the neural underpinnings of the sustainability intention–action gap (Vezich et al, 2017). In it the authors started from the position that most consumers say on self-report measures that they prefer "green" products more than conventional products that don't emphasize environmental benefits in their market positioning. Yet actual marketplace performance of such green products had historically lagged that of the conventional alternatives. In the study the researchers exposed participants to a series of product advertisements while simultaneously scanning their brains. Half of the advertisements included marketing claims related to environmental sustainability. The other half were matched control advertisements that depicted equivalent products but which lacked any such green claims. After viewing each advertisement participants rated it on both subjective likability and the degree to which they felt it was a sustainable product. Not surprisingly, on average they rated the green advertisements as both more likable and more sustainable than the control advertisements.

But when comparing such subjective ratings to the brain imaging data, a less intuitive pattern of results emerged. Despite subjectively "liking" the green advertisements more than the controls, activity in brain regions associated with reward anticipation, self-relevance, and subjective valuation (the NAcc and the vMPFC) was not greater for the green advertisements relative to the control condition—there was actually a trend in the opposite direction, with the control advertisements leading to marginally greater activation in these regions. Moreover, for the control advertisements, activity in the vMPFC was significantly positively correlated with self-reported liking, while activity in the NAcc also displayed a trend in that direction. Yet no such positive association was found between subjective liking ratings and brain activation in these regions for the "green" ads. That is, despite stating an overall subjective preference for the green advertisements, regions of the participants' brains that have otherwise been identified as being predictive of choice behavior and advertising effectiveness were relatively unresponsive to sustainability messaging.

What are we to make of this? The authors speculate that the subjective ratings of preference for the green advertisements may be prone to social desirability bias. Or that latent expectations about such things as potentially higher cost and lower effectiveness of such products might undermine their ability to engage the viewer or result in lowered estimates of subjective value. Or that participants lack confidence that choosing such products makes much difference in the bigger picture.

Participants might have instead lacked trust in the claims being made and mentally counterargued them. In fact, other research has shown that vague or deceptive claims made in communicating the benefits of "green" products can yield more cognitive processing of those claims and, especially with more knowledgeable consumers, can adversely affect attitudes towards brands and products (Schmuck et al, 2018). We'll further consider the issue of "greenwashing" in later chapters.

And lastly, of course, perhaps the sort of mental effort and/or time-related discounting of anticipated reward and subjective valuation discussed above might have also contributed to undermining any positive response to the green advertisements. Most likely, several of these factors may have been at play. Marketers of sustainable products will need to confront such issues if their efforts are to be successful.

Preferences and the Default Heuristic

Let's go back a little further in time in the purchase cycle from that described above, where we saw that presentation of an image quickly elicited brain signals of approach motivation that, providing that product pricing was not too egregiously high, were predictive of subsequent virtual shopping choices in the form of purchase decisions and rated preferences. How do some images trigger such a response in the first place? I won't leave you hanging: The answer is that they are often comfortingly familiar, and speak to one's primary motivations, and it's easy to continue to do the same thing one always has done, especially if staying put is also financially cost-effective, whereas change can be risky, anxiety-producing, and can require more mental effort. And sometimes change requires greater financial costs, at least in the short term. No one likes that.

Existing Product Preferences Are Local Minima in the Choice Landscape

Herb Simon's notion of "satisficing" described a strategy or cognitive heuristic that involves examining alternatives until an acceptable one is found, regardless of whether that alternative is normatively "optimal." Similarly, in physics there is a view that systems tend toward a state of lowest possible potential energy, and there is a related notion of an "energy well," or a state of stable equilibrium that is not the lowest possible state of potential energy, but a state that a system can get stuck in without external inputs.

Imagine being at a chairlift at the bottom of a run in a ski village and tired after hours of hitting the slopes. You are on a mountain, so in principle there is a lot of potential energy to be expended to get to a lower altitude, but you're not going to walk out of the village to traverse that un-groomed slope below it, especially as there might be some minor uphill bumps in the landscape before the downhill part. To get back to the top of the ski run you need to expend additional energy either in the form of a painful climb or that required for standing in a long line for a ski lift that will pull you out of the place you've settled in. You are stuck in an energy well, but not one that is completely uncomfortable. So instead of taking another run you go have a beer or a hot chocolate or a snack at the nearby ski chalet. Similar ideas about being stuck in local minima exist both in statistical theory and in the process of how neural networks learn. Sometimes where one is comfortable at is the most feel-good place to be at the moment, especially compared with any of the proximal alternatives (Figure 3.2)—at least it is in the absence of notable countervailing pressure to change your position. As the 18th-century English writer Samuel Johnson noted: "to do nothing is in every man's power" (Johnson, 1751).

Getting back to shopping preferences, *a priori* associations we might have to a stimulus object influence how the brain processes that object, often in dramatic ways. Having a habitual product preference or brand loyalty when shopping is a bit like being stuck in a metaphorical energy well—a stable equilibrium solution that can satisfice even when it isn't necessarily an optimum solution to some unmet need.

Value-Based Prioritization for Capturing Attention

The slippery slope towards choice starts with early perceptual processes. For example, a wide variety of research indicates that a stimulus that has emotional associations or connotations is easier to find in an array of items

FIGURE 3.2 Existing Preferences Are a Local Minima in the Choice Landscape

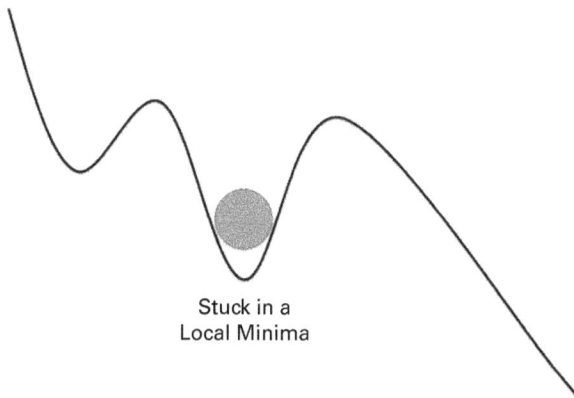

Stuck in a
Local Minima

than are similar stimuli that are emotionally neutral. Accordingly, eye-tracking studies indicate that emotional stimuli are more likely to attract overt fixations and to be looked at longer than neutral stimuli, even if they are not directly relevant to a task being performed (Calvo and Lang, 2004; Alpers, 2008). And stimuli with emotional valence are more likely to be subsequently remembered than neutral stimuli. Even when an emotional stimulus is not consciously seen it can influence consumption behavior, particularly when the person doing the consumption is in a motivational need state (Winkielman et al, 2005).

Similar phenomena occur with stimuli that may have initially been neutral but past experience has shown to be particularly valuable. That is, when experimental participants have been pre-trained to associate a stimulus with a subsequent reward, the features of such a stimulus will automatically capture attention even if it is irrelevant to the task at hand (Anderson and Yantis, 2012). If a product associated with distinctive brand assets, a learned emotional response, and expected value has insinuated itself into a consumer's mind, it visually almost leaps off the shelf from the perspective of the consumer, at least relative to less distinct members of its competitive set. We'll return to this issue in the next chapter.

Other factors are at play that further advantage products privileged enough to have one's existing brand loyalties. In the prior chapter I introduced the notion of processing fluency and the types of mental shortcuts or heuristics that emerge from experiences of relatively fluent perception or memory retrieval. The experience of processing fluency can be associated with greater "liking" and preference, and the attention-capture advantages that positively valenced, value-associated stimuli enjoy also bestows them with a comforting fluency advantage when it comes time to choose between them or an alternative. Moreover, even in the absence of associations of valence or value *per se*, simply having prior experience with an object can endow it with increased processing fluency—leading to increased liking and preference.

Often dubbed the "mere exposure effect" and most commonly associated with the work of the late social psychologist Robert Zajonc, experimentation on this phenomenon grew from the notion that unfamiliar objects with no indication of whether they represent a threat or a potential reward can instinctively elicit an initial withdrawal reaction from organisms that encounter them. But with repeated exposure they can be habituated to or even preferred. In a famous if somewhat controversial paper that Zajonc published in 1980, entitled "Feeling and Thinking: Preferences need no inferences," he proposed that instead of affective reactions being the result of a cold cognitive dissection of what a stimulus means to the organism, reactions such as liking occurred automatically and before much rational thought. And that such reactions color the way in which subsequently cognitive assessments proceed.

Zajonc tested this hypothesis by pre-exposing research participants with meaningless objects or symbols, either incidentally or at exposure durations too short to lead to conscious recognition. When participants were subsequently asked to rate the likability of those pre-exposed stimuli relative to other items that did not benefit from such pre-exposure, he and his colleagues found a reliable tendency for the pre-exposed items to be scored as more subjectively likable and preferred in choice experiments. Subsequent studies by both academic psychologists and applied market researchers have provided convergent evidence for the reliability of the mere exposure effect. So not only do market-leading brands enjoy a superior ability to attract attention because of their ability to activate emotions and attitudes about product value, in general they are more liked simply because they are better at eliciting a comforting familiarity.

The Default Bias and Being Stuck in the Status Quo

Behavioral economists have also identified a mental heuristic called the "default" or "status quo" bias (Samuelson and Zeckhauser, 1988). You intuitively will know it well as I'm sure most of you are personally guilty of it. That is, the average person will more often than not persist in a behavior of some form that they have performed in the past even though the situation that reinforced it in the first place and which drives their choices has demonstrably changed in important ways. People hate to change their habits (we'll also explore consumer habits in more detail in the next chapter). In general, they avoid adaptive change mainly because such change requires mental effort and willpower, and because it is somewhat aversive for people to draw on either.

Experimental psychologists examining the determinants of this bias have identified a number of factors that contribute to it (Anderson, 2003). Sometimes people will just put off a choice between an existing default and an alternative. Sometimes they don't bother and go with the status quo. Sometimes they don't want to expend the mental effort necessary to include an unfamiliar alternative in their consideration set. When they do consider alternatives, they are inclined to worry that they are not worth the effort, anxious that they will regret a decision to change, and/or just find it hard to judge the relative costs and benefits of other things compared with those they are familiar with.

Kahneman and colleagues (1991) suggested that the status quo bias is closely related to the phenomenon of "loss aversion" wherein the potential losses associated with a risky alternative are weighted more heavily in decision-making than any potential gains that it might provide. And even though default choices may sometimes also be suboptimal, prior research has shown that when asked to choose between typical and atypical scenarios in order to obtain rewards or losses, even when losses are equated between them people tend to regret losses obtained in atypical scenarios more than the same losses accrued in more typical scenarios (Kahneman and Miller, 1986). People are loath to change, and in the real world brand or product loyalty most likely reflects some high degree of default bias on the part of consumers.

Given the earlier discussion of the brain dynamics of purchase decisions, it is noteworthy that the default or status quo bias has also been a topic of recent brain imaging investigations. And results from such work appear to align in interesting ways with the prior research on purchase decisions. For example, Yu and colleagues (2010) used fMRI to study brain activation during a simple gambling task. For each decision-making trial in that study, participants in a scanner were first presented with two possible outcomes—a monetary win versus a loss. They were then presented with a choice of a "default" option that they could accept, or an alternative to it they could switch to. After making that decision they were then shown the outcome of that choice—what they had won or lost. After the outcome of each decision was revealed, participants rated their relative frustration versus satisfaction with the choice they had just made.

Unbeknownst to the gamblers in this study the probability and magnitude of wins and losses across trials were exactly the same for either choice. That is, there was no inherent advantage or disadvantage to staying with the default or switching to the alternative. Nonetheless, both the subjective emotional experience and the objective brain activity of participants differed between when they chose to stay with the default versus switch to the alternative. First, consistent with prior expectations given the default bias effect, participants were on average more likely to choose the default than to switch to the alternative. Second, participants expressed more frustration with a loss outcome when they had chosen to switch to the alternative rather than remain with the default. Third, when considering the choice phase of the test trials, activity in the reward-related NAcc area discussed earlier was higher for trials in which the default was chosen versus the alternative, suggesting that just staying with a default is rewarding in itself versus making a choice. And activity in the right anterior insula, which as noted above can be associated with outcome anxiety and loss aversion (see also Paulus et al, 2003), was higher on the trials when participants chose to override their default bias and brave a switch.

The pattern of activity during the outcome phase was more complicated. On average, win trials elicited more NAcc activity than loss trials. And trials in which a loss occurred elicited more activity in the right anterior insula. The magnitude of this latter effect was enhanced when a loss occurred in trials for which participants chose to switch from the default and was correlated with the degree to which they subjectively felt more frustrated in that condition. That is, it hurts more to lose when taking a chance on something new rather than when sticking with the status quo.

1   Purchase decisions involve a network of neural activity that includes nodes involved in anticipating upcoming rewards, evaluating the subjective value of alternatives, and interrupting choice for a valued option if the price seems too high.

2   Under normal circumstances activation of the reward and subjective valuation nodes of this network while consumers process marketing communications is predictive of subsequent buying behavior for advertised products, but some evidence suggests that this relationship may not hold for communications making "green" marketing claims.

3   Factors such as the mental effort required to obtain a reward and a more distant temporal proximity between a reward and the choice in question appear to negatively modulate the perceived value of an option, which suggests that marketing claims that are hard to analyze and that promise rewards in some vague, impersonal future will be ineffective.

4   Familiar options tend to be liked more than unfamiliar options simply because of their familiarity, and people tend to default to their past decision-making when choosing between options. Traditional options have an advantage because people are hesitant to explore new options both because they have an aversion to losses and take comfort in the status quo.

References

Alpers, G (2008) Eye-catching: Right hemisphere attentional bias for emotional pictures, *Laterality: Asymmetries of Body, Brain & Cognition*, 13(2), 158–178

Anderson, B A and Yantis, S (2012) Value-driven attentional and oculomotor capture during goal-directed, unconstrained viewing, *Attention, Perception, and Psychophysics*, 74, 1644–1653

Anderson, C J (2003) The psychology of doing nothing: Forms of decision avoidance result from reason and emotion, *Psychological Bulletin*, 129(1), 139–167

Aupperle, R L, Melrose, A J, Francisco, A, Paulus, M P and Stein, M B (2015) Neural substrates of approach-avoidance conflict decision-making, *Human Brain Mapping*, 36, 449–462

Ballard, K and Knutson, B (2009) Dissociable neural representations of future reward magnitude and delay during temporal discounting, *NeuroImage*, 45(1), 143–150

Berns, G and Moore, S E (2012) A neural predictor of cultural popularity, *Journal of Consumer Psychology*, 22, 154–160

Cai, W, Ryali, S, Chen, T, Li, C S and Menon, V (2014) Dissociable roles of right inferior frontal cortex and anterior insula in inhibitory control: Evidence from intrinsic and task-related functional parcellation, connectivity, and response profile analyses across multiple datasets, *Journal of Neuroscience*, 34, 14652–14667

Calvo, M G and Lang, P J (2004) Gaze patterns when looking at emotional pictures: Motivationally biased attention, *Motivation and Emotion*, 28(3), 221–243

Craig, A D (2009) How do you feel—now? The anterior insula and human awareness, *Nature Reviews Neuroscience*, 10 (1), 59–70

Critchley, H D, Wiens, S, Rotshtein, P, Ohman, A and Dolan R J (2004) Neural systems supporting interoceptive awareness, *Nature Neuroscience*, 7(2), 189–195

Croxson, P L, Walton, M E, O'Reilly, J X, Behrens, T E and Rushworth, M F (2009) Effort-based cost-benefit valuation and the human brain, *Journal of Neuroscience*, 29(14), 4531–4541

Davidson, R J, Ekman, P, Saron, C D, Senulis, J A and Friesen, W V (1990) Approach-withdrawal and cerebral asymmetry: Emotional expression and brain physiology, *Journal of Personality and Social Psychology*, 58, 330–341

Dichter, G S, Damiano, C A and Allen, J A (2012) Reward circuitry dysfunction in psychiatric and neurodevelopmental disorders and genetic syndromes: Animal models and clinical findings, *Journal of Neurodevelopmental Disorders*, 4(19), 1–43

Falk, E B, Berkman, E T and Lieberman, M D (2012) From neural responses to population behavior: Neural focus group predicts population-level media effects, *Psychological Science*, 23(5), 439–455

Genevsky, A, Yoon, C and Knutson, B (2017) When brain beats behavior: Neuroforecasting crowdfunding outcomes, *Journal of Neuroscience*, 37(36), 8625–8634

Gu, X, Hof, P R, Friston, K J and Fan, J (2013) Anterior insular cortex and emotional awareness, *Journal of Comparative Neurology | Research in Systems Neuroscience*, 521, 3371–3388

Hartson, H (2012) The case for compulsive shopping as an addiction, *Journal of Psychoactive Drugs*, 44(1) 64–67

Johnson, S (1751) The usefulness of advice, *The Rambler*, No 155, 10 September

Kable, J W and Glimcher, P W (2007) The neural correlates of subjective value during intertemporal choice, *Nature Neuroscience*, 10, 1625–1633

Kahneman, D and Miller, D (1986) Norm theory: Comparing reality to its alternatives, *Psychological Review*, 93, 136–153

Kahneman, D, Knetsch, J and Thaler, R (1991) Anomalies: The endowment effect, loss aversion, and status quo bias, *Journal of Economic Perspectives*, 5, 193–206

Knutson, B and Greer, S (2008) Review: Anticipatory affect: Neural correlates and consequences for choice, *Philosophical Transactions of The Royal Society B: Biological Sciences*, 363(1511), 3771–3786

Knutson, B, Rick, S, Wimmer, G E, Prelec, D and Loewenstein, G (2007) Neural predictors of purchases, *Neuron*, 53(1), 147–156

Kucyi, A and Parvizi, J (2020) Pupillary dynamics link spontaneous and task-evoked activations recorded directly from human insula, *Journal of Neuroscience*, 40(32), 6207–6218

McClure, S M, Laibson, D I, Loewenstein, G and Cohen, J D (2004) Separate neural systems value immediate and delayed monetary rewards, *Science*, 306, 503–507

Menon, V and Uddin, L Q (2010) Saliency, switching, attention and control: A network model of insula function, *Brain Structure and Function*, 214(5–6), 655–667

Nielsen (2016) We're ruled by our emotions and so are the ads we watch, www. nielsen.com/us/en/insights/news/2016/were-ruled-by-our-emotions-and-so-are-the-ads-we-watch.html (archived at https://perma.cc/82DV-76ZQ)

Paulus, M P, Rogalsky, C, Simmons A, Feinstein, J S and Stein, MB (2003) Increased activation in the right insula during risk-taking decision-making is related to harm avoidance and neuroticism, *NeuroImage*, 19, 1439–1448

Prevost, C, Pessiglione, M, Metereau, E, Clery-Melin, M-L and Dreher, J-C (2010) Separate valuation subsystems for delay and effort decision costs, *Journal of Neuroscience*, 30(42), 14080–14090

Ramsøy, T Z, Skov, M, Christensen, M K and Stahlhut, C (2018) Frontal brain asymmetry and willingness to pay, *Frontiers in Neuroscience*, 12, 138

Ravaja, N, Somervuori, O and Salminem, M (2013) Predicting purchase decisions: The role of hemispheric asymmetry over the frontal cortex, *Journal of Neuroscience, Psychology, and Economics*, 6(1) 1–13

Reichelt, A C, Westbrook, R F and Morris, M J (2015) Integration of reward signaling and appetite regulating peptide systems in the control of food-cue responses, *British Journal of Pharmacology*, 172, 5225–5238

Samuelson, W and Zeckhauser, R J (1988) Status quo bias in decision-making, *Journal of Risk and Uncertainty*, 1, 7–59

Schmuck, D, Matthes, J and Naderer, B (2018) Misleading consumers with green advertising? An affect–reason–involvement account of greenwashing effects in environmental advertising, *Journal of Advertising*, 47(2), 127–145

Smith, M E and Marci, C (2016) From theory to common practice: Consumer neuroscience goes mainstream, *Nielsen Journal of Measurement*, 1(2), 3–11

Venkatraman, V, Dimoka, A, Pavlou, PA, Vo, K, Hampton, W, Bollinger, B, Hershfield, H E, Ishihara, M and Winer, R S (2015) Predicting advertising success beyond traditional measures: New insights from neurophysiological methods and market response modeling, *Journal of Marketing Research*, 52(4), 436–452

Vezich, S, Gunter, B C and Lieberman, M D (2017) The mere green effect: An fMRI study of pro-environmental advertisements, *Social Neuroscience*, 12(4), 400–408

Westbrook, A, Lamichhane, B and Braver, T (2019) The subjective value of cognitive effort is encoded by a domain-general valuation network, *Journal of Neuroscience*, 39(20), 3934–3947

Winkielman, P, Berridge, K C and Wilbarger, J L (2005) Unconscious affective reactions to masked happy versus angry faces influence consumption behavior and judgments of value, *Personality and Social Psychology Bulletin*, 31(1), 121–135

Yu, R, Mobbs, D, Seymour, B and Calder, A J (2010) Insula and striatum mediate the default bias, *Journal of Neuroscience*, 30(44), 14702–14707

Zajonc, R B (1980) Feeling and thinking: Preferences need no inferences, *American Psychologist*, 35(2), 151–175

04

The Force of Habit in Consumer Behavior

As we have seen, our brains are heavily weighted to prefer tried-and-true things that don't require much thought instead of experimenting with alternatives. A great deal of that bias depends on the development and exploitation of habitual responses to stereotyped opportunities with routinized action sequences. The study of how habits develop and guide behavior has been a central topic in experimental psychology for much of the existence of the field. William James noted in his foundational text *The Principles of Psychology* that "When we look at living creatures from an outward point of view, one of the first things that strike us is that they are bundles of habits." He further noted: "The more of the details of our daily life we can hand over to the effortless custody of automatism, the more our higher powers of mind will be set free for their own proper work" (James, 1890). As we will see in this and subsequent chapters, the existence of entrenched habits can be a potent source of cognitive friction in the shift to green consumption.

Consumer decision-making is sometimes characterized as a complex problem-solving activity, and in many situations it may well be a process of deliberate consideration. But for products that are regularly purchased as part of someone's routine market basket, consumers appear to spend little time or mental effort on deciding between alternatives (Hoyer, 1984). In response to a perceived need or other cue, most often you satisfy that need or respond to that cue by buying a favorite brand, or the cheapest alternative, or the most readily available good-enough option, based on your subjective judgment of best value and any trade-offs involved. This behavior doesn't usually require much thought unless there has been a prominent change in the buying situation.

Consumer habits form when products are purchased and consumed repeatedly, especially when contextual circumstances are held relatively constant. Diary studies have estimated that as much as 45 percent of most people's activities repeat almost daily and in the same or similar context (Wood et al, 2002)—exactly the type of scenario that encourages habit formation. Of course, part of this frequent repetition involves purchase and consumption activities. In product choice experiments involving repeat-purchase CPG products, consumers reliably display a strong preference for more familiar brands, independently from quality and price considerations (Hoyer and Brown, 1990; Macdonald and Sharp, 2000). Back in the real world, across shopping trips people most often frequent the same stores and buy the same brands of products in the same or similar quantities. And consumption of those products follows equivalent routines, with recurring food and drink choices, cleaning rituals, and personal care activities.

In coming chapters we will be considering a range of strategic interventions for shifting consumer behaviors, including product choices, in more sustainable directions. For non-habitual behaviors, informational campaigns can impact consumer attitudes and choice architectures can be designed to encourage greener selections. But under conditions where habits and preferences have already formed, behaviors can be markedly resistant to change—especially when the actor may not be particularly aware that a habit is in place and is guiding behavior. Let's then take a closer look at the neuroscience of habits, their development, and what it takes to change behavior in their presence.

Forms of Learning and Memory in the Brain

Habits are learned behaviors, so it is important to understand that organisms employ a variety of mechanisms to learn about the world and to effectively adapt behavior to environmental demands. At a species level, for any type of organism operating in a relatively stable environmental niche, much of that adaptation occurs slowly over generations through natural selection of behavioral repertoires or patterns of thinking that are instinctual but relatively optimal for that niche. But of course, as we have reviewed, the human niche is becoming much less stable, and we might not want to just wait and see how everything plays out many generations into the future.

Fortunately people have evolved a capacity to adapt behavior relatively flexibly and on the fly to a wide variety of environmental conditions through different processes by which information is stored in the brain. These processes help us to save time and energy and to better predict what might happen next, to have better and more current mental models, and thereby improve our odds of survival in the short term, even in a gradually changing world.

Broadly speaking there are two types of dynamic information storage in the brain—one that is fleeting and another that persists over time. The first includes "active," or "short-term," or "working" memory, and the second includes various forms of "long-term" memory. Working memory is just the stuff that is bouncing around in or near your focus of consciousness at any given moment. For example, your ability to read a phone number and then keep it active in your awareness long enough to call it, or your ability to add two numbers together in your head. With deliberate effort you can strategically keep ideas front of mind. This capability is severely constrained in capacity, requires the strategic focusing of cognitive resources, and often the willful suppression of distracting influences. As we discussed, people can find this a little stressful when this capacity is pushed beyond comfortable limits. That said, this capacity is extremely important for behavioral flexibility and critical for responding thoughtfully to unfamiliar or rapidly changing situations.

Working memory involves the temporary heightened activation of existing representations in the brain and allows those representations to be recombined in novel ways within the focus of awareness. Such novel combinations may themselves then be stored in more permanent form, or they may simply dissipate like a wave on the beach. Existing representations in the brain can also be in a heightened state of activation without reaching a threshold that brings them into conscious awareness. This can happen because they have been recently accessed, or because something they are associated with led to their activation.

The phenomena associated with such "priming" activations have been the topic of extensive study by memory researchers. Priming refers to a situation in which exposure to a stimulus influences a subsequent response to another stimulus, regardless of any conscious memory for the first stimulus or even conscious awareness that it occurred when you first saw it. It relies on automatic activation of an associative link in memory. For example, if I first flashed the word "fruit" on a screen and then asked you to decide whether or not a subsequent string of letters that spelt "banana" was a word or not, you would respond faster with a yes or a no than you would if the first word presented was instead "tool."

Such types of priming effects can inform market research and product design. As we previously considered, brands that promote sustainability claims tend to automatically activate the idea of "gentleness" more strongly than equivalent brands that don't promote pro-environmental bona fides (Luchs et al, 2010)—which could be a good thing or a bad thing depending on the particular product benefits you are trying to promote. Priming phenomena also extend beyond the activation of semantic associations to the activation of affective and behavioral responses. In particular, with respect to the types of automatically triggered habitual responses that we will discuss in coming pages, the environmental cues or prompts that can act as a trigger to the response can be viewed as a class of priming events.

The other type of memory, "long-term" memory, is of the more permanent type. It depends on lasting anatomical and functional changes between brain cells. In other words, it depends on "neuroplasticity," which involves persistent changes in the manner by which nervous system cell networks interact and changes in the ways in which one thought leads to another and in which one or another environmental cue leads to a behavioral response. It is critical for exploiting redundancies in the environment and for reducing the effort needed to respond to recurring situations. It is this plasticity and these more lasting changes in brain activity that we are most concerned with here. And within long-term memory there are key distinctions one needs to understand (Figure 4.1).

FIGURE 4.1   Types of Learning and Memory in the Brain

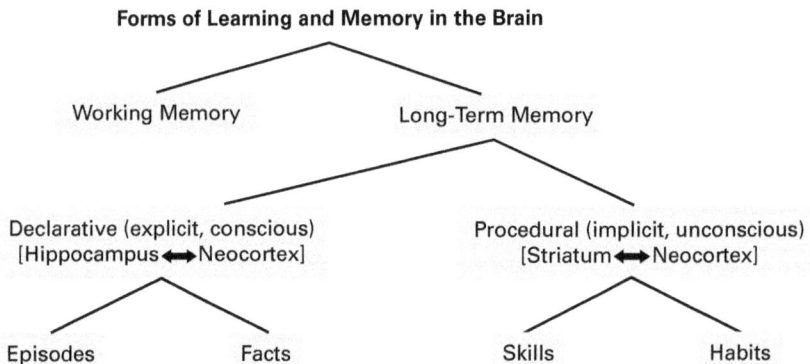

Forms of Learning and Memory in the Brain

Working Memory   Long-Term Memory

Declarative (explicit, conscious)   Procedural (implicit, unconscious)
[Hippocampus ⟷ Neocortex]   [Striatum ⟷ Neocortex]

Episodes   Facts   Skills   Habits

Declarative Memory

To the left side of the long-term memory tree presented in Figure 4.1, under the term "declarative memory," is what we most often think about when we think about memory. It includes memories for past experiences and general facts that can be recalled or brought to mind. It is sometimes alternatively referred to as "explicit memory" as it is subject to the conscious deliberate recollection of information learned from past experiences. Declarative or explicit memory can be further subdivided into episodic and semantic types.

Episodic Versus Semantic Forms of Declarative Memory

Episodic memory stores information about individual autobiographical events and semantic memory stores more general factual information organized into associative networks (Tulving, 1983). In a consumer context, episodic memory is responsible for storing information about specific purchase or usage occasions. For example, I remember that I bought breakfast cereal at the store yesterday and ate some of it this morning. In contrast, semantic memory stores generic facts and beliefs about product characteristics or usage occasions. For example, I also believe breakfast cereals labeled organic are less likely to contain pesticide residues than those without such labeling and I understand that, organic or not, it would be unusual to serve breakfast cereal to my dinner guests. Changing the contents of declarative memory is the aim of most informational marketing campaigns.

While the exact relationship between episodic and semantic memory has long been a topic of intellectual debate and vigorous research, the general notion is that episodic memory serves to encode exemplars of experiences and semantic memory is abstracted from the commonalities between those exemplars. This system is supported by interactions between medial temporal lobe structures such as the hippocampus (a small, seahorse-shaped structure deep inside the temporal lobe of the brain) and the broader neocortex (the superficial layers of the brain involved with higher-order processes including perception, reasoning, motor planning, language, and conscious thought) (Figure 4.2).

Damage to the hippocampus and surrounding structures has long been known to result in chronic amnesia, a permanent loss of the ability to encode new declarative memories and a loss of prior memories that were encoded in the recent past. Both basic neurobiological research and more theoretical computational studies (McClelland et al, 1995; O'Reilly and Norman,

FIGURE 4.2   Brain Structures Involved in Learning and Memory

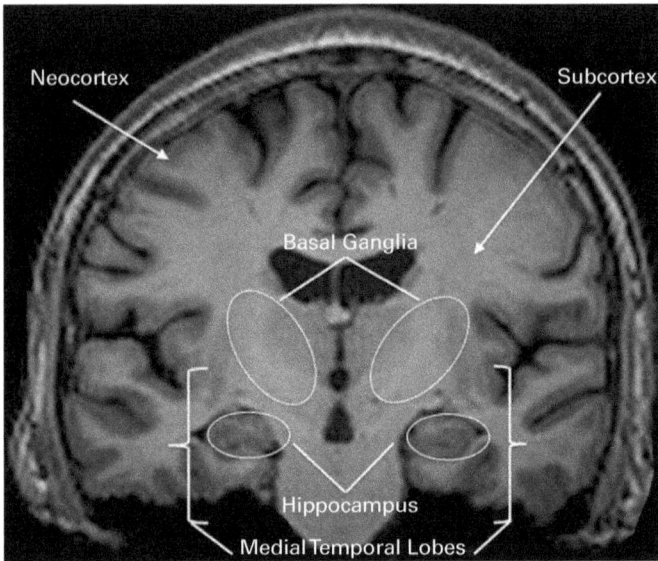

2002) suggest that connections between cells in the hippocampus can rapidly form in order to bind together the unique constellation of neocortical inputs that represent an individual experience, and that those plastic changes in the hippocampus can then serve to help reinstate a past pattern of neocortical activity. This allows you to recollect that past experience at a later date. Presumably plastic changes representing direct connections between neocortical neurons proceed more slowly and occur as past memories are reactivated and memories from similar experiences are accumulated, leading to the gradual growth of more generic knowledge about the world.

Procedural Memory Differs From Declarative Memory

An interesting thing has emerged in research about the way in which hippocampal damage impacts learning in the brain. While such damage has profound effects on explicit declarative memory, a variety of other types of learning can proceed relatively normally as revealed by more indirect or implicit means. Such "nondeclarative" types of adaptation include the formation of "procedural memories." Procedural learning involves the development of skills and habits as illustrated under the right-sided branch of the tree structure in Figure 4.1. Evidence of procedural memory is revealed by observing changes in the speed and accuracy of behaviors over time as a result of some past learning, but these changes can be expressed unconsciously and can even be observed completely in the absence of conscious declarative memory for the past experience that produced the learning (reviewed in Squire, 2004).

For one early example, a patient with severe amnesia subsequent to surgical removal of the hippocampus bilaterally was nonetheless able to improve performance on a new complex perceptual and motor skill (mirror drawing) after several days of practice, despite on each day having no declarative memory for having practiced the task in the past. Additional research demonstrated that this patient also displayed an ability to acquire a variety of other new perceptual and motor skills (Corkin, 1968), and a wide body of work by other investigators has provided convergent evidence for preserved skill learning in the absence of declarative memory in such patients. Such nondeclarative skill development is a category of behavior change that also includes habit formation.

Procedural learning involves the development of new associations in the context of learning how to do something new rather than explicitly knowing something occurred in the past. It is accomplished by repeating a complex activity enough times that all of the component neural networks involved come to work in coordination to produce the activity automatically and unconsciously. It is critical to performing any type of complex motor or cognitive act quickly, effortlessly, and competently, from tying your shoes to riding a bike to flying an aircraft using a stick and a rudder. As we will see later, procedural learning depends on a completely different neural system from declarative memory.

Other Forms of Nondeclarative Memory

A second type of implicit learning is "classical conditioning," which refers to simply pairing a biologically potent stimulus such as a reward or punishment (the unconditioned stimulus) with a previously neutral stimulus, and doing so enough times that a response elicited automatically by the reward or punishment comes to be elicited by the "conditioned" stimulus. Classical conditioning can lead to a learned emotional or motoric response to a stimulus, and the learning processes involved with such conditioned responses also appear to be mediated by different brain networks than those involved in declarative memory. You undoubtedly have already heard of the discoverer of this effect, Ivan Pavlov, the Russian physiologist who found that if he preceded a food reward with a bell enough times, he could train a dog to salivate in response to the bell itself.

This form of learning has been demonstrated in human amnesic patients as well. If you have ever had a test at an optometrist where they measured your intraocular pressure by having you fixate on a visual target and hold still while they at some point blast a puff of air on your cornea, you'll remember that it is somewhat unpleasant though innocuous, and that it causes you to immediately blink. If you pair this activity enough times with a preceding warning tone, eventually people come to blink to the warning tone alone, expecting an air puff. This learned response occurs whether the people are healthy control subjects or are neurological patients with dense amnesia for declarative information in general (Gabrieli et al, 1995). Whether depictions of your product make people automatically salivate or cringe might in some cases reflect the unconditioned rewards and punishments it has been associated with in the past.

A third type of nondeclarative memory is often referred to as non-associative learning or habituation. Pretty much all organisms display forms of non-associative learning. This class of phenomena includes a change in response to a novel stimulus that occurs after repeated exposure to the stimulus. For example, you may become sensitized to a stimulus after repeated exposure because it becomes more visually salient and easier to process. Or desensitized as it becomes less threatening on repeated exposure, so you become less negatively aroused when encountering it repeatedly. In some ways the "mere exposure" effect described in the previous chapter, which endows familiar stimuli with increased likability, might be viewed as a form of non-associative learning.

Habits: Actions Without Intentions

Now that we have worked our way down the learning tree, let's get back to considering the nature of habits. Closely related to the type of skill acquisition I mentioned above when introducing the notion of procedural memory, habit formation is sometimes also referred to as "instrumental learning" or learning that occurs as a consequence of a behavioral response being reinforced in some fashion. A great deal of research about the mechanisms and implications of habit learning has been conducted over the past few decades.

In a comprehensive review of the psychology of habit learning, Wood and Runger (2016) portray habit formation as an efficient alternative to the more resource-demanding conscious process of intentional goal pursuit.

A habit is formed when we learn associations between some environmental context and a behavior that is rewarded in it (Figure 4.3). Habits are created when an individual intentionally pursues a goal by repeating some type of behavior in a given context. They don't eliminate intentional goal pursuit and at times can work synergistically with it. But with sufficient repetition they become automated response patterns operating independently from intentions.

Given that thinking hard is costly, habits are one of the brain's mechanisms to reduce the resource demands of dealing with familiar situations by enabling reliance on a learned procedure rather than thinking things through. Eventually the strength of association between a contextual cue and a related response pattern can become great enough that they can even become "outcome insensitive" and dissociated from any subsequent reinforcement. That is, a cued behavior can continue to be triggered, at least for a while, even when the action is no longer effective at achieving some reward.

People in general tend to infer that their behaviors controlled by habits are fully intentional, yet, as we have seen, automatic behaviors are by definition "mindless," and their mechanisms are not introspectively accessible. That is, inferred intentionality is often just that: an after-the-fact inference about an action initiated without conscious intent. In any case, in the domain of consumer behavior, intentions appear to only control behavior when there is an absence of strong habits. And once established, a habit can take on a life of its own.

FIGURE 4.3   Trigger–Drive–Behavior–Reinforcement Cycle of Habit Formation

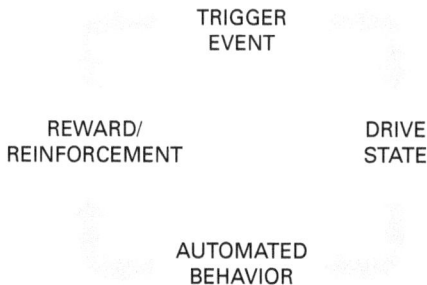

TRIGGER
EVENT

REWARD/
REINFORCEMENT

DRIVE
STATE

AUTOMATED
BEHAVIOR

Neuropsychological Dissociation of Habits From Declarative Memory

The category of procedural learning that includes habits extends the learning of perceptual and motor associations to emotional and cognitive dispositions and tendencies (such as expressed preferences and choices). Like skill development, habits can become ingrained even without explicit conscious recollection of past learning episodes. Neuroscientist Larry Squire and his colleagues at the University of California, San Diego have shown that amnesic patients have an ability to learn new associations through gradual trial-and-error learning without requiring contributions from the explicit declarative memory system that is based on plasticity in the medial temporal lobes.

Those researchers demonstrated that over days of repeated practice on an object discrimination task, patients with extensive medial temporal lobe lesions (which included the hippocampus) could gradually learn to identify "correct" (previously rewarded) objects when presented with eight pairs of two alternative objects to choose between. After weeks of training they came to be able to perform this discrimination with almost perfect accuracy, even though at the beginning of each test day they evinced no explicit memory of having gone through the test before and could not *a priori* describe the task they were to perform, the instructions, or the objects themselves. After having successfully picked the "correct" one from a pair of alternatives, when asked why they had chosen their preferred alternative they could offer no better reason than something like "it just felt right" (Bayley et al, 2005).

Similar results were observed in an earlier study with amnesic patients who learned to perform a probabilistic classification task (Knowlton et al, 1996). In that study participants performed a computer-based task that asked them to be a weather forecaster. On the screen appeared a sunny icon and a rain-cloud icon. On each trial of the task participants were presented with subsets of four cue stimuli, each of which appeared as a playing card type token with a number of arbitrary but distinctive geometrical items on them. Unknown to the participants each of the cue cards had an *a priori* probability of predicting sun or rain with a high, medium, or low predictive weighting. Thus, the complex task of the participants was to learn over trials to infer which of the choices was most likely given the joint probability of the different cue sets. After each trial of the task participants were given feedback as to whether their guesstimate was correct or not, and a cumulative score for correct responses was displayed. Of course, on early trials of the task, prediction of sun or rain was accomplished at no better than chance performance, and this was equally true for both a non-amnesic control group and for the amnesic patients.

Nonetheless, prediction performance gradually improved over trials for both groups, and by the end of the training both groups were performing well above chance levels, with about 70 percent correct predictions. After training, both groups were given a set of questions to assess their declarative memory for the task through multiple-choice factual questions about the cues, the layout of the computer screen, and the training episode. The non-amnesic control group did very well on this explicit memory task, scoring around 80 percent correct responses. And not surprisingly, the group of amnesic patients did very poorly and barely above chance levels.

Role of the Basal Ganglia in Procedural Learning

In an interesting twist to this latter study, though, another group of patients was also included, in this case patients with Parkinson's disease, and results from this group give us further insight into the brain mechanisms of habit formation. Parkinson's disease is a movement disorder that reflects neuro-degeneration in a region of the brain called the substantia nigra (SN). The SN in turn is a structure in the basal ganglia (Figure 4.2) and is a major source of dopaminergic neurotransmission in the brain—loss of SN cells causes dopamine levels to drop and a primary source of input to the striatum is reduced. You'll remember the basal ganglia and the striatum from the prior chapter where we considered the role of the NAcc in the ventral striatum in motivation and reward anticipation in the context of virtual shopping and other choice decisions.

Loss of dopaminergic input to the striatum appears to have consequences beyond just diminished motor control. It also impacts performance on the probabilistic category-learning task described above. Despite having had as much practice as the other groups, the Parkinson's patients that were tested displayed little improvement over trials in their ability to predict rain or shine, with the most severe patients never getting past chance levels of performance. This was despite their performance on the explicit memory post-training assessment about the testing episode and materials being every bit as accurate as that displayed by the healthy control group. This double dissociation between the patterns of task performance displayed by amnesic patients versus Parkinson's patients provides especially compelling evidence for a neurological distinction between declarative and procedural memory systems.

The way in which habits tend to be established in the procedural memory system is becoming increasingly well understood. While a deep dive into the neurobiology of this process is outside our current scope, a high-level summary will be useful for understanding some of the challenges that habits pose for efforts toward behavior change, including the development of more sustainable consumer behaviors.

Briefly, then, the striatum plays an important role in motor control and mediating rewarding experiences (see Amaya and Smith, 2018; Yin and Knowlton, 2018). The dorsal portion of the striatum is one of the main input regions for the basal ganglia. It receives inputs from many regions of the neocortex, including both sensorimotor regions and prefrontal and parietal regions involved with cognitive control and in formulating and pursuing goals. In goal-directed behavior, inputs to the basal ganglia include information about the desired goal itself.

Some regions of the basal ganglia support goal-directed behaviors by helping to select action plans suitable for achieving the goal, triggering and motivating the motor activity necessary for it, and inhibiting other movements that might compete with it. Not surprisingly, then, motor control abnormalities, including a paucity of movements overall and slowness to initiate those which occur, are hallmark symptoms of Parkinson's disease.

During habit development the brain learns goal-directed actions by modifying how the basal ganglia responds to goal-related inputs from the cortex. In particular, when sequences of actions are repeated in some recurring context in the pursuit of rewards or goals, some of the cells in the dorsal striatum combine those sequences into something like a script that represents the overall activity from beginning to end.

The NAcc in the ventral part of the striatum is involved with learning the relationship between cues and anticipated rewards and is important for the reinforcement and fine-tuning of such a script (Gale et al, 2014). With practice the script becomes increasingly ingrained and eventually will be executed automatically in response to a contextual cue or when activated by a deliberately initiated goal pursuit activity. While dense reciprocal connections with prefrontal cognitive control regions allow for an over-ride of these scripts and preserves an option for behavioral flexibility (Mukerji and Caroni, 2018), superseding the automated route requires effort and becomes less likely if the individual in question is distracted or has depleted mental reserves for expending effort.

Pathological Habits

Habitual patterns of responding can persist even once they have become maladaptive. As noted in in the last chapter, cue- or context-triggered habitual actions are problematic for eating disorders, a variety of substance abuse disorders, and a variety of disorders involving behavioral compulsions and a lack of control over impulsivity. Interestingly, although untreated patients with Parkinson's disease are slow to initiate actions, patients treated with medications that serve as dopamine precursors or dopamine agonists (that are intended to replace the loss of dopaminergic input from the SN in an effort to improve their motor symptoms) not infrequently also develop impulse control disorders and behavioral compulsions.

Such patients may be at over three times greater risk than untreated patients for developing pathological behaviors such as binge-eating, compulsive sexual activity, compulsive gambling, and, yes, compulsive shopping (Voon, 2006; Weintraub et al, 2010). Usually people who suffer from a compulsive disorder involving shopping tend to purchase relatively mundane everyday things, items like clothes, shoes, jewelry, cosmetics, or household items. In general, the individual items are not expensive, and when questioned such patients typically report that they made a purchase because of the item's attractiveness or that they thought it was bargain priced (Christenson et al, 1994).

But sometimes the compulsive purchaser's desires can be quite specific and highly repetitive. For example, in one noteworthy case report, a woman in South Korea who had been diagnosed with Parkinson's disease was initiated on dopamine replacement therapy. She then developed a general impulse control disorder that included a compulsive shopping component of a unique type. According to the case study her husband reported the onset of compulsive shopping since her medication was initiated. And complained that:

> ...she bought rabbits every day at a market like an addiction and so there were so many rabbits in our house. She has liked rabbits since she was young but never raised one. Usually she didn't spend much money for shopping. But... she just wanted to buy a rabbit and acted out without considering. She felt guilty after shopping (Cho et al, 2008).

Habits of Visual Attention

While we have considered how actions can become habitual and automated, it is also the case that habit formation can change how you see the world.

Habits can influence what you notice and what you automatically focus your attention on. We considered this issue briefly before when discussing the fact that a stimulus that has come to be associated with emotional significance, or rewarded in some way or otherwise assigned a relatively high value, can then preferentially pop into awareness when one scans the environment one is working in, at least relative to relatively unfamiliar competitors. People are quicker to turn their eyes to such stimuli in a distracting array, to look at them longer, and to remember them better.

There is growing evidence that this visual phenomenon is also mediated by the habit system. Recent research is leading to the emergence of a view that habits are not limited to just the automatic execution of over-learned stimulus–response sequences. Habit-learning also influences how the visual system automatically directs attention in order to prioritize the processing of some stimuli over others (Anderson, 2016; Le Pelley et al, 2016).

When participants are pre-trained to associate a stimulus with a subsequent reward, that stimulus will automatically capture attention even if it is irrelevant to the current task at hand and thus in the absence of intentional search (Anderson and Yantis, 2012), and especially if the task context resembles that in which the association was originally learned (Anderson, 2014). Such responses are highly persistent—they can be observed days or even months after they have been acquired (Anderson and Yantis, 2013).

Moreover, just as dopamine signaling in the dorsal striatum is involved with the execution of motor habits, it appears to also be involved with these visual habits (Anderson et al, 2016). And the impact of habit learning on the brain's prioritization of previously rewarded stimuli occurs at very early stages of processing—electrophysiological studies of the visual system have demonstrated that enhanced responses to automatically attended stimuli that are associated with visual salience occur within 1/10 of a second after such prioritized stimuli appear (Luque et al, 2017; MacLean and Giesbrecht, 2015). What pops out at you in the world appears to depend on your visual habits.

Visual Habits Can Affect Market Dynamics

Visual habits might be critical for marketers to understand, as they likely benefit established brands and pose a barrier to introducing new brands. Products with visually distinctive brand assets that activate emotional associations, and that have previously been rewarded by product benefits, visually tend to leap off the shelf from the perspective of the consumer, at least relative to less distinct members of its competitive set. This fact suggests that package updates can be a particularly risky marketing tactic, especially if an update disrupts the perceptual habits that brand's consumers have developed.

This possibility was vividly illustrated over a decade ago when a package design for a major orange juice brand was introduced (Young and Ciummo, 2009). That redesign was sufficiently radical that brand loyalists could no longer easily find their desired product on the shelf and had an aversive emotional reaction to the changes when they did. And after losing 20 percent of normal sales over the ensuing few months, the brand marketer reverted to the traditional package design. The brand quickly regained its prior market share, but between the missed sales and the redesign costs, tens of millions of dollars were forfeited.

Visual Habits and Package Design

Understanding the role of visual habits can also be important for designing packages that successfully signal sustainability benefits, and for explaining some related anomalous results. For example, in 2018 there was a widely publicized research study result in the packaging industry (Quad Packaging & Package Insight, 2018). The study was conducted in a marketing lab that included a simulated grocery store environment, and a representative sample of retail shoppers. A decent subset of the shoppers reported that sustainability issues were important considerations for them when making purchase decisions.

Those shoppers completed a shopping task where they were given a grocery list and were required to fill a basket by deciding among competing alternatives. The research team created a sustainability logo with an associated grade (A—Sustainable, B—Efficient, and C—Average) and created packaging designs for products in diverse categories such as frozen food, snacks, pasta, and over-the-counter medical supplies. Some of those packages were affixed with the sustainability logo to signal each item's relative environmental sustainability.

Before sending them on their respective journeys, the researchers fixed head-mounted eye-tracking devices on the shoppers' heads so they could collect data on the shoppers' direction of gaze while inspecting shelves and packaging. And then they set the participants off to shop. The researchers were thus able to measure whether the sustainability logos were an object of gaze fixation during the shopping adventure, and in turn infer whether those logos may have impacted purchase decisions.

The headline that was promoted in conjunction with the results obtained in the study was not subtle: "Consumers don't notice on-pack sustainable messaging, study finds more education needed around sustainability claims" (PR Newswire, 2018). The researchers reported that they found that 92 percent of participants never fixated on the sustainability logos when examining packages in the store, nor did those logos disproportionately affect participants' rate of first fixation, nor did they affect purchase decisions.

Are these findings surprising? A survey across the EU that evaluated the explicitly stated attitudes of consumers toward such labels found that "sustainability labels currently do not play a major role in consumers' food choices, and future use of these labels will depend on the extent to which consumers' general concern about sustainability can be turned into actual behavior" (Klaus et al, 2014). Other survey-based research studies have suggested that consumers who claim to have environmentally friendly attitudes claim they do not rely on such cues in the marketplace when they are unfamiliar and that most consumers are price-sensitive and don't want to pay more for products with sustainability-related labeling (Kaczorowska et al, 2019).

More Familiar Sustainability Symbols on Packages Can Be Impactful

What are we to make of such findings? That logos suggesting product sustainability may be worthless? That conclusion may be premature—other results indicate that there is more going on than such disheartening outcomes suggest. For example, there is the fact that leading brands tend to be more accessible in mind. And that symbols that are familiar and that especially those that have been reinforced tend to be preferred and to automatically capture attention. And additionally that a great deal of purchasing decisions end up being automatized and habitual. And then in contrast we must also consider that the shopping journey that was created in the eye-tracking study described above was one involving purchasing decisions in an unknown store, made for unknown products, on which previously unknown sustainability symbols had been affixed. That situation is not reflective of the world we live and habitually shop in.

But is there any contra-evidence that sustainability symbols can actually automatically capture attention and engage consumers? Yes, apparently there is. Consider a study that examined consumers' brain activity when they were evaluating products that were or were not labeled with an "organic" logo (Linder et al, 2010). The investigators found that the sustainability context that food items were presented in had a large effect on both consumer decisions and brain activity. Food products that were labeled with a highly familiar emblem for organically sourced food products first elicited a greater level of activation in the NAcc of the reward network when they were presented, and then on average were preferred in choice decisions over alternatives lacking such logos. Moreover, these brain activity differences were greater in participants who reported greater actual day-to-day organic food consumption, suggesting that the symbols may have been particularly salient and relevant to them.

A similar follow-up study examined the impact of "fair-trade" logos on the value the brain calculates for products (Enax et al, 2015). The researchers found that highly familiar fair-trade logos increased NAcc activation when they were initially presented. Items which also elicited an increased willingness to pay were additionally associated with greater activation of the vMPFC, which, as we have seen, can be related to the engagement of processes of subjective valuation. Such results provide compelling evidence that when familiar sustainability symbols are placed on familiar products, they may in fact help to trigger positive associations and increase engagement in the minds of consumers.

So far we've seen that habits can produce both actions and visual attention without intention. In the next chapter we'll also see how habits can be responsible for keeping intentions from producing actions. Habits can actively interfere with attempts to change course, and that can be an impediment for efforts to encourage more sustainable patterns of consumer behavior. We'll also begin to consider strategies to compensate for such cognitive barriers to change.

---

1   The brain systems involved with encoding and storing facts about the world differ from the brain systems involved with learning skills and developing habits. While factual information can be a focus of conscious reflection, habits can form and unfold below the level of awareness.

2 When a course of action has been reinforced in the past, environmental cues can subsequently automatically prime or trigger reward anticipation and habitual response patterns outside the scope of volitional goal direction. Under normal circumstances this process can make life more efficient, but it can also interfere with efforts to change consumer choices.

3 Habit-learning is not limited to acquisition of automated behavioral sequences. It also extends to our actual visual perception of the world around us. Things that have been previously associated with some reward enjoy privileged access to visual search processes and can "pop out" from a display and lend an advantage to familiar brands and disadvantages new brands and package refreshes.

4 Familiar sustainability logos might facilitate habitual visual search and allow the packages they are placed on to better automatically activate positive emotional responses.

References

Amaya, K A and Smith, K S (2018) Neurobiology of habit formation, *Current Opinion in Behavioral Sciences*, 20, 145–152

Anderson, B A (2014) Value-driven attentional priority is context specific, *Psychonomic Bulletin and Review*, 22(3), 750–756

Anderson, B A (2016) The attention habit: how reward learning shapes attentional selection, *Annals of the New York Academy of Sciences*, 1369, 24–39

Anderson, B A, Kuwabara, H, Wong, D F, Gean, E G, et al (2016) The role of dopamine in value-based attentional orienting, *Current Biology*, 26, 550–555

Anderson, B A and Yantis, S (2012) Value-driven attentional and oculomotor capture during goal-directed, unconstrained viewing, *Attention, Perception, and Psychophysics*, 74, 1644–1653

Anderson, B A and Yantis, S (2013) Persistence of value-driven attentional capture, *Journal of Experimental Psychology: Human Perception and Performance*, 39, 6–9

Bayley, P J, Frascino, J C and Squire, L R (2005) Robust habit learning in the absence of awareness and independent of the medial temporal lobe, *Nature*, 436, 550–553

Cho, H, Kwan, J-h, and Seo, H-j (2008) Compulsive shopping in Parkinson's disease: A case report, *Journal of Movement Disorders*, 1(2), 97–100

Christenson, G A et al (1994) Compulsive buying: Descriptive characteristics and psychiatric comorbidity, *Journal of Clinical Psychiatry*, 55, 5–11

Corkin, S (1968) Acquisition of motor skill after bilateral medial temporal-lobe excision, *Neuropsychologia*, 6(3), 255–265

Enax, L, Krapp, V, Piehl, A and Weber, B (2015) Effects of social sustainability signaling on neural valuation signals and taste-experience of food products, *Frontiers in Behavioral Neuroscience*, 29, 1–15

Gabrieli, J D E, McGlinchey-Berroth, R, Carrillo, M C, Gluck, M A, Cermak, L S and Disterhoft, J F (1995) Intact delay-eyeblink classical conditioning in amnesia, *Behavioral Neuroscience*, 109(5), 819–827

Gale, J T, Shields, D C, Ishizawa, Y and Eskandar, E N (2014) Reward and reinforcement activity in the nucleus accumbens during learning, *Frontiers in Behavioral Neuroscience*, 8, 1–10

Hoyer, W D (1984) An examination of consumer decision-making for a common repeat purchase product, *Journal of Consumer Research*, 11, 822–829

Hoyer, W D and Brown, S P (1990) Effects of brand awareness on choice for a common, repeat purchase product, *Journal of Consumer Research*, 17, 141–148

James, W (1890) *The Principles of Psychology*, Henry Holt and Company, New York

Kaczorowska, J, Rejman, K, Halicka, E, Agata Szczebyło, A and Górska-Warsewicz, H (2019) Impact of food sustainability labels on the perceived product value and price expectation of urban consumers, *Sustainability*, 11, 1–17

Klaus, G, Grunert, K G, Hieke, S and Wills, J (2014) Sustainability labels on food products: Consumer motivation, understanding and use, *Food Policy*, 44, 177–189

Knowlton, B J, Mangels, J A and Squire, L R (1996) A neostriatal habit learning system in humans, *Science*, 273, 1399–1402

Le Pelley, M E, Mitchell, C J, Beesley, T, George, D N and Wills, A J (2016) Attention and associative learning in humans: An integrative review, *Psychological Bulletin*, 142, 1111–1140

Linder, N S, Uhl, G, Fliessbach, K, Trautner, P, Elger, C E and Weber, B (2010) Organic labeling influences food valuation and choice, *NeuroImage*, 53, 215–220

Luchs, M G, Walker-Naylor, R, Irwin, J R and Raghunathan, R (2010) The sustainability liability: Potential negative effects of ethicality on product preference, *Journal of Marketing*, 74(September), 18–31

Luque, D, Beesley, T, Morris, R W, Jack, B N, et al (2017) Goal-directed and habit-like modulations of stimulus processing during reinforcement learning, *Journal of Neuroscience*, 37(11), 3009–3017

Macdonald, E K and Sharp, B M (2000) Brand awareness effects on consumer decision-making for a common, repeat purchase product: A replication, *Journal of Business Research*, 48, 5–15

MacLean, M H and Giesbrecht, B (2015) Neural evidence reveals the rapid effects of reward history on selective attention, *Brain Research*, 1606, 86–94

McClelland, J L, McNaughton, B L and O'Reilly, R C (1995) Why there are complementary learning systems in the hippocampus and neocortex: Insights from the successes and failures of connectionist models of learning and memory, *Psychological Review*, 102(1), 419–457

Mukerji, A and Caroni, P (2018) Infralimbic cortex is required for learning alternatives to prelimbic promoted associations through reciprocal connectivity, *Nature Communications*, 9, 1–14

O'Reilly, R C and Norman, K A (2002) Hippocampal and neocortical contributions to memory: Advances to the complementary learning systems framework, *Trends in Cognitive Sciences*, 6(12), 505–510

PR Newswire (2018) Consumers don't notice on-pack sustainable messaging, study finds more education needed around sustainability claims, www.prnewswire. com/news-releases/consumers-dont-notice-on-pack-sustainable-messaging-study-finds-more-education-needed-around-sustainability-claims-300635487.html (archived at https://perma.cc/RH3T-WN7R)

Quad Packaging & Package Insight (2018) Sustainability packaging and brand image, Part 1: Understanding how sustainable messaging influences consumer decisions, www.quad.com/resources/documents/sustainable-packaging-brand-identity-part-1/ (archived at https://perma.cc/KYN4-XEXG)

Squire, L R (2004) Memory systems of the brain: A brief history and current perspective, *Neurobiology of Learning and Memory*, 82, 171–177

Tulving, E (1983) *Elements of Episodic Memory*, Clarendon Press, Oxford

Voon, V (2006) Prevalence of repetitive and reward-seeking behaviors in Parkinson disease, *Neurology*, 67, 1254–1257

Weintraub, D et al (2010) Impulse control disorders in Parkinson disease: A cross-sectional study of 3090 patients, *Archives of Neurology*, 67(5), 589–595

Wood, W, Quinn, J and Kashy, D (2002) Habits in everyday life: Thought, emotion, and action, *Journal of Personality and Social Psychology*, 83, 1281–1297

Wood, W and Runger, D (2016) Psychology of habit, *Annual Review of Psychology*, 67, 289–314

Yin, H H and Knowlton, B J (2018) The role of the basal ganglia in habit formation, *Nature Reviews Neuroscience*, 7, 464–476

Young, S and Ciummo, V (2009) Managing risk in a package redesign: What can we learn from Tropicana?, www.packagingstrategies.com/articles/91264-managing-risk-in-a-package-redesign-what-can-we-learn-from-tropicana (archived at https://perma.cc/2CDP-4HY4)

05

Green Intentions Are Not Enough

In the 1600s Rene Descartes promulgated a dualist theory of mind premised on the notion that thoughts are immaterial in nature, part of a "soul," and separate from the physical body itself. A central problem with this view is formalizing how these two different things interact—after all, one can think about moving one's hand and then physically move it, and one can feel a physical sensation and think about whether it feels good or bad. Not exactly an empirical neuroscientist, Descartes' solution to this problem was to just make stuff up. In particular, he posited that a tiny structure in the middle of the brain, the pineal (pine cone) gland, was the locus of this interaction. He viewed it as the temporary seat of the immaterial soul, and that all thoughts occurred in it, and that it was through this nexus that the soul controlled the meat-puppet body and observed changes in it. This notion wasn't even consistent with how his contemporary anatomists and physiologists viewed brain function at the time.

Three centuries later the British philosopher-of-mind Gilbert Ryle somewhat acerbically dismissed the idea as incoherent, labeling it as the mythical "dogma of the *Ghost in the Machine*" (Ryle, 1949). We now know that the pineal gland is a part of the endocrine system and produces a hormone that helps to regulate sleep–wake cycles. We also know that whatever thinking is, it is clearly distributed in the brain. You can rely on your own intuitions about where your soul resides and how it interacts with the rest of you.

The notion of an "intention" also has similar ghost-like qualities. Descartes would have placed it definitively in the mind or soul rather than in the physical body. Regardless of whether it is used colloquially as a folk-psychology concept or more formally by academic psychologists, the term intention is understood to refer to some sort of mental object that is the product of planning and forethought, that is accessible to consciousness, and that represents a person's decision to carry out some future goal-directed action. This idea is equivalent in some ways to the mysterious notion of "the force" in the *Star Wars* universe. In our more pedestrian universe, we are supposed to wield ghostly intentions as some motive power, invisible but sometimes needed to take action and get things done. In the statistical modeling pocket of our universe, an intention is a type of underlying "latent variable" that cannot be directly observed but is inferred to exist because it can explain a significant amount of variance in other directly measurable or observable variables.

Whether or not an "intention" is a real thing that resides in your head or just a convenient shorthand metaphor for something much more complex, given the pervasiveness of the notion we need to continue to consider it. The notion of intention is central to several major theories about behavior change. We will be considering a variety of views on the factors that lead to behavior change in coming chapters. But for now let's focus on one perspective that has been particularly influential in stimulating a great deal of research on motivated behavior in general, and research on issues related to environmental psychology and green consumer choices in particular.

Green Purchase Intentions

The American social psychologist Icek Ajzen developed his theory of planned behavior (TPB) as an evolution of prior research that he and his collaborator Martin Fishbein conducted on how thoughts and beliefs led to action (Ajzen, 1985, 1991). They considered reasons for why much of the prior research on the attitudes that individuals held, and the actual behaviors of those individuals, often were incongruent (Ajzen and Fishbein, 1977). They marshaled evidence that it wasn't that attitudes were unimportant, but rather that they were just one part of a constellation of personal factors and social influences that contribute to an individual's ability to change the way they act. In Ajzen's TPB, overt behaviors depend on (ghostly) "behavioral intentions" (Figure 5.1), and those intentions are in turn mediated by a variety of beliefs about the behavior. The stronger that a behavioral intention is activated by relevant beliefs, the more motivated an individual will be to act on the intention, and the more likely a related behavior will occur.

FIGURE 5.1 Summary of the Theory of Planned Behavior

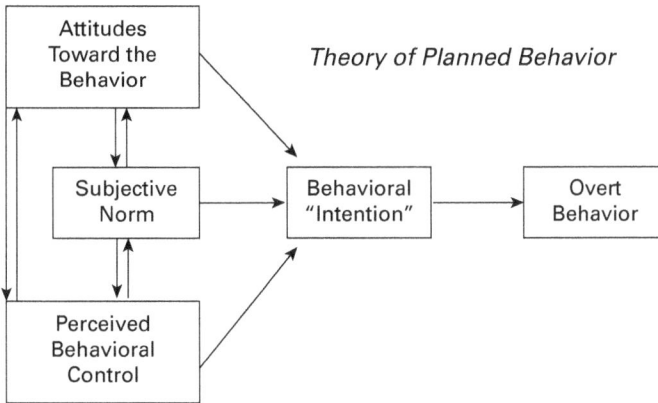

SOURCE Adapted from Ajzen (1991).

Beliefs Underpinning Behavioral Intentions

One of those types of beliefs relates to the individual's personal attitude towards the behavior, and in particular the degree to which the individual views the target behavior itself and its expected result favorably or unfavorably. A second type of belief is what the potential actor's *subjective norm* is about the behavior—a belief about whether or not the people most important to the actor would approve of the behavior, and the potential actor's understanding of what the broader normative imperative is concerning the behavior and its anticipated outcome (the impact of social cognition on sustainable decision-making will be considered at length in the next chapter).

A third type of belief incorporated into the TPB built on a stream of contemporaneous research indicating that a feeling of self-efficacy is a key determinant of behavior change (Bandura, 1977). Does the potential actor have knowledge of factors that may promote or prohibit their ability to perform the behavior successfully—that is, do they have *perceived behavioral control*? Such perceptions of behavioral control derive from the actor's perception of the relative ease or difficulty of performing the behavior and their judged likelihood of it leading to a preferred outcome given situational factors.

Collectively this constellation of beliefs serves to essentially define important aspects of the individual's "mental model" of the situation at hand. The relative weighting or motivational impact on a behavioral intention for each

of these types of beliefs can vary depending on individual personality differences and the unique set of contextual constraints a given situation imposes,
but in general "the more favorable the attitude and subjective norm and the
greater the perceived control, the stronger should be the person's intention
to perform the behavior in question" (Ajzen, 2002). Across individuals and
situations, the TPB has a track record of success at predicting either strength
of subjective behavioral intentions or actual behavioral outcomes in a wide
variety of behavioral change settings.

Consumer Decision-Making and the TPB

A variety of studies related to sustainable consumer decision-making have
been explicitly inspired at least in part by Ajzen's TPB and have provided
findings convergent with it. For example, one early meta-analysis of studies
that had examined psychological factors that contribute to environmentally
friendly behaviors found that both attitudes and a sense of behavioral
control were important predictors of behavioral outcomes across many of
the studies examined (Hines et al, 1987). A more recent literature review of
factors driving consumer purchasing of green products found that the TPB
framed many studies, and that "an individual's pro-environmental attitude
has a significant positive influence on the consumer's intention to purchase"
(Popovic et al, 2019).

Other studies have employed a formal structural equation modeling
approach to better characterize both the observed interactions between the
different constructs in the TPB and other hypothesized factors, as well as the
directionality of their effects. Structural equation modeling is a widely used
technique that combines statistical methods from confirmatory factor analysis, multivariate regression, and path analysis among other fields in an
attempt to fit theoretical constructs to patterns of multivariate empirical
data obtained from surveys and other sources. This approach essentially
tests whether, across respondents, the type of imputed mental model implied
by the TPB can actually explain the data at hand.

One early study of this nature (Chan, 2001) was conducted in the major
cities of Beijing and Guangzhou in China. The author used a survey instrument to gauge the attitudes and self-reported behaviors of Chinese consumers
related to environmental concerns. Questions gauged the degree to which
respondents felt like they were part of the natural environment and the
degree and direction of their feelings about the environment. Such measures

of their attitudes were used to gauge any association with a pro-environmental behavior of interest. They also sought to gauge the degree to which respondents held a sense of "collectivism," which is similar to the aspect of the TPB concerned with sensitivity to subjective norms. The survey instrument further incorporated questions designed to get at a latent variable of "green purchase intent," any self-reported actual propensity to choose products perceived to be more environmentally friendly, and a follow-up validation step designed to verify those self-report responses.

While no measures of something analogous to "perceived behavioral control" were included, the author did find that a structural equation model applied to the survey results provided a significant fit to the data, supporting the general notion that the latent variable structure was predictive of shopping behavior. Similarly, a study of Finnish consumers (Tarkiainen and Sundqvist, 2005) also found that both attitudes and subjective norms significantly contributed to consumer intentions to purchase organic food as well as self-reported actual purchase behaviors. A decade later a study conducted in India additionally demonstrated that attitudes that include concern about the environment also mediated "green purchase intention" (Paul et al, 2016).

Many other studies have addressed the broader issue we are concerned with here. For example, a study conducted in Lebanon (Dagher and Itani, 2014) found a significant relationship between reports of "green purchase behavior" and attitudes relating to the seriousness of environmental problems and the respondent's perceived responsibility for them, as well as the social construct of their self-image with respect to environmentalism. More explicitly examining the tenets of the TPB, Masud and colleagues (2015) conducted a study in Malaysia to "examine whether attitudes toward climate change, subjective norms, and perceived behavioral control have significant associations with behavioral intention to adapt to climate change and adopt pro-environmental behavior." While the results may have been influenced from pro-social biases, the researchers nonetheless found significant associations with their latent construct of behavioral intention as well as significant associations between self-report of engaging in pro-environmental behaviors and all of the key factors described in the TPB.

More recent work has continued along this tradition. Jaiswal and Kant (2018) applied structural equation modeling to characterize survey results collected in major cities within Uttar Pradesh, the most populous state of India. The researchers found that a construct of "green purchase intent" was significantly influenced by stated attitudes toward green products as well as perceptions of consumer efficacy in terms of their product choices, and that green purchase intent was a significant, and the highest overall, predictor of "green" product choices. That is, it appeared to be an efficacious ghost-in-the-machine.

Limitations of the TPB

Findings such as these appear to be broadly consistent with the outlines of the TPB. But it is important to also consider some of the things that the studies leave out. None of them examined physical factors that might undermine perceived control, down-regulate "green purchase intent," and constrain actual green purchase behavior. For example, in a study conducted in Belgium that examined factors driving sustainable food consumption, researchers found that while social norms and attitudes were predictive of intentions to buy sustainable food products, a perceived lack of availability of those same products had a negative impact on consumer intentions (Vermeir and Verbeke, 2006). Similarly, physical constraints rather than attitudes or intentions have been found to be a limiting factor for consumer engagement with other types of environmentally friendly behaviors (Tanner, 1999). And both situational factors and product functional attributes have been found to be important determinants of green purchase behavior above and beyond just psychological factors intrinsic to the individual green decision-maker (Joshi and Rahman, 2015).

Premium pricing for green products might also further widen the gap between green attitudes and shopper behavior. One recent study examining the influences on sustainable purchasing in China found that attitudes related to environmental concerns and notions of personal responsibility over environmental impacts were positively related to self-report of green consumption behaviors and green consumption intent (Yue et al, 2020). But the authors also found that a construct of price sensitivity negatively impacted this influence for both intention and action. That is, the people in their study really didn't want to, or perhaps felt that they couldn't, pay more for more sustainable options.

This finding is probably not at all an outlier. And as we reviewed earlier, subjective valuation of options is also weighted not just by price but also by the expected cognitive effort required by an action—yet none of these studies gauged any adverse impacts of the additional mental effort sometimes required to make "green" choices above and beyond the effort required to just go with the flow and repetitively purchase products that may not be green but that are easy to understand and comfortingly familiar.

Best-Laid Plans: Actions Impervious to Intentions

In the previous chapter we saw that while some actions may initially result from thoughtful consideration of the world and are guided by explicit conscious intentions, as they are repeated in particular contexts actions can become habitual and automatic and unfold in the absence of intentions. They just become behaviors following scripts that are acted out unconsciously in response to the contextual cues that activate them (Ouellette and Wood, 1998; Wood and Neal, 2007). Not everyone agrees with this view. One such individual is Icek Ajzen himself, who has argued vociferously that intentions continue to be important even in repetitive behavior. He claimed that activations of intentions from beliefs and their translation into action became more efficient with practice, but that both repeated and newly planned actions depended on "attitudes and intentions that are available to introspection" (Ajzen, 2002). In homage to Gilbert Ryle, we can describe this as the "dogma of the *Intention in the Machine.*"

Contraposed to this notion is the idea that intentions become increasingly irrelevant in repetitive circumstances: that once they are ingrained as automatically triggered and well-practiced responses to recurring situational circumstances, they exist as procedural memories that are activated and acted upon when people once again encounter those situations, often without any intervention from a latent variable like conscious intention *per se*. For example, a busy parent with young children at home may automatically add a carton of milk to their grocery cart without giving it much deliberative thought or trying to remember whether there was already milk in their refrigerator.

Among other evidence for this view is the fact that when measures of habit strength are incorporated into predictive models, such as those described above, such measures can directly predict behavioral outcomes and/or modulate the impact of a latent intention construct on overt behavior (Ouellette and Wood, 1998). This sort of situation is described in Figure 5.2, which depicts a hypothesized interaction effect between habit strength and behavioral intention. For weak habits, a strong intention might increase the frequency of a related behavior, whereas for strong habits the strength of intention alone is unlikely to have much of an effect on behavior frequency beyond that dictated by the habit.

FIGURE 5.2   Interaction Between Behavior Intention and Habit Strength

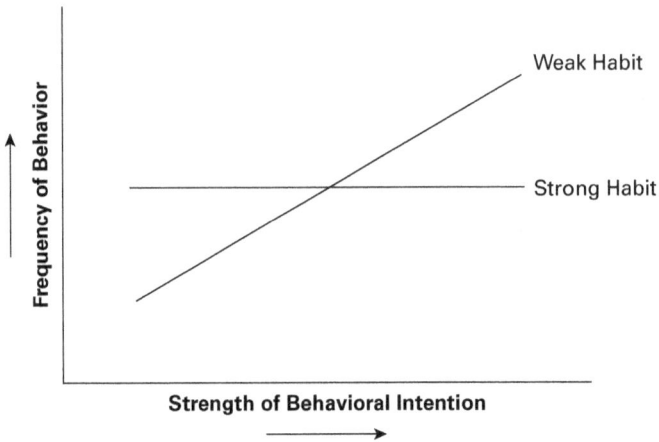

Evidence That Habits Can Override Intentions

The distinction between this latter notion and the view of the supremacy of intentionality-guided consumer behavior has been explicitly and cleverly evaluated (Ji and Wood, 2007). Part of the problem that has to be overcome in such research is the fact that the strength of a habit is defined in part by the frequency of a past behavior in a recurring context, but frequency of a past behavior is also closely correlated with the degree to which individuals rate their intentions to execute the behavior in the future as strong and confidently held.

To address this issue the investigators first sought to gauge the strengths of participants' existing habits and intentions having to do with common consumer behaviors, including those related to fast-food consumption, using public transportation (bus riding), and media consumption (watching the evening news). On an initial meeting, participants first indicated how frequently over the course of a week they engage in the target behavior, and then their basis for making that estimate. They were then required to rate on a number of scales how stable the context was in which the behavior took place (i.e., location, time of day, people it occurred with, and characteristic mood). A habit strength score was then calculated for each participant for each behavior by multiplying the frequency of the behavior by the ratings of contextual stability. That proxy habit strength measure was in turn based on the notion that habits develop when a behavior is repeated in a particular environmental context.

Participants then completed separate scales concerning the strength of their subjective intention to engage in the behavior in the future, the likelihood that they will actually do so in the coming week, and their level of confidence in their ratings. These measures were then combined into a score for the strength of subjective intention for that behavior for each person in the study. The participants then went about their daily lives for a week, and at the end of each day they updated a standardized electronic diary indicating if they had engaged in the target behavior that day and, if so, described when, where, and with whom they had done so. This enabled the researchers to calculate the frequency of target behaviors for each type of action that occurred over the course of the study for each participant.

Of course, not surprisingly, for each of the three behaviors individuals with either strong intentions or strong habits on average tended to engage in the target activities more frequently during the diary study period. But when participants were stratified into groups scored as having weak, moderate, or strong habits in each of the domains (based on the frequency of the behavior and the stability of the context it occurred), interesting interactions emerged consistent with the type of hypothetical relationship described in Figure 5.2.

In particular, strength of intention in a domain of behavior was a significant positive predictor of the observed frequency of the behavior of interest in the group with the weakest related habits. In a group with moderately strong habits, this positive correlation between intention strength and behavior frequency was still significant but reduced in magnitude. But for the group of participants with the strongest habits in each domain, strength of intention was not at all predictive of actual frequency of occurrence of the behavior of interest. That is, in the absence of strong habits, subjective intentions are predictive of the likelihood of future performance. But once a strong habit develops in a stable performance context, intentions to do something (or not do something) in the future become largely irrelevant for predicting what will actually come to pass. This pattern is of course familiar to anyone who has struggled with the types of habits that become addictions.

Other researchers evaluating the implications of habits for the TPB framework have also observed that the existence of habits can undermine the association of intentions with actual behavior change (Danner et al, 2008; Norman and Conner, 2006). This type of result has clear, if somewhat disheartening, implications for efforts to shift consumer choices in more sustainable directions. Despite whatever belief structures might yield a "green purchase intent," that intention on its own may not lead to much real-world action in the broad domains of day-to-day life where purchase and consumption choices are made in largely habitual ways. As we all know, deliberately forming new habits can be hard at best and can result in failures more often than successes. As we also all know, deliberate intentional self-control is both hard to exercise at the best of times and becomes more so under conditions of stress and distraction (Baumeister et al, 2008).

Barriers to Sustainable Consumption

Habits provide savings in terms of reduced effort and reduced errors in decision-making and actions when circumstances are held reasonably constant. Exploring the new requires overcoming a great deal of status quo inertia and resistance to change in existing behavior patterns, and thus habits can serve as a source of cognitive friction and as barriers to change (Polites and Karahan, 2011). Shifting consumers towards more sustainable forms of marketplace behavior requires working around this source of friction, at least when it comes to expanding the consideration set beyond an incumbent choice.

Of course, entrenched patterns of behavior are only one type of barrier to more sustainable consumer behaviors. More systematic research has documented a variety of factors that aspiring green consumers feel work against them and that can undermine their good intentions—or that can serve as points of evidence defensively supporting suspicions of green products on the part of people who lack green purchase aspirations.

Survey methods have been used to probe the perceived barriers consumers report towards making green consumption choices (Gleim et al, 2013). Such barriers, ranked roughly from most to least problematic, include:

- high prices relative to alternatives;
- lack of expertise to choose among alternatives;
- perceived value relative to alternatives;
- general inertia due to existing habits;
- unknown quality of products;
- lack of availability of products;
- unwillingness to comply with social norms;

- lack of trust in the manufacturer;
- lack of awareness of options;
- lack of a personal norm to seek out green options;
- lack of trust in advertising claims;
- lack of belief in personal efficacy in making a difference;
- lack of a prevailing social norm to support the choice.

This listing is entirely consistent with other work in this area. For example, a global survey of consumer attitudes conducted by the management firm McKinsey & Company (Bonini and Oppenheim, 2008) identified five key barriers inhibiting consumer adoption of sustainable products and services: lack of awareness of green options, high prices, low availability, negative perception of benefits, and distrust of green claims. Similarly, in research on consumers in the US and China conducted by Ogilvy (Bennett and Williams, 2011), pricing issues, consumer lack of knowledge and confusion, and a mistrust of green claims were identified as some of the major barriers to transitioning the market for sustainable markets from a niche to mainstream.

Using cluster analysis, Gleim and colleagues (2013) were able to successfully segment their sample into subgroups based on their survey responses. At one extreme was a group of about one-fifth of the total sample that were defined as "green" consumers who scored highest on their degree of satisfaction with past purchases of sustainable products and highest on expressed intent to purchases such products in the future. At the other extreme was a smaller group of consumers who scored lowest on both satisfaction and purchase intent. And in the potentially persuadable middle was everyone else. Predictably, the group with the greatest dissatisfaction and lowest purchase intent tended to rate all of the barriers as being more extreme problems than did the group of "green" consumers. Yet despite this significant difference in magnitude of grievance between the groups, the actual rank ordering of the seriousness of the barriers did not vary much between the clusters. Instead, price sensitivity, limits of knowledge, and questions about product value ranked in the top concerns among participants in all clusters.

Virtually all of the top barriers are potentially amenable to being addressed by providing consumers with reliable information and conducting marketing campaigns, implementing competitive pricing, and engaging in other brand-building exercises that inform consumers and increase their sense of value and trust. Accordingly, in a related final follow-up to their survey results, Gleim and colleagues also presented evidence from an experimental study investigating how to best inform consumers about green product benefits and found that the type and form of informational cues used to describe a green product had a significant impact on stated purchase intent for that product. In brief, they found that more information increases purchase intent for a green product if that information was presented verbally. But if that same information was instead presented in numeric form, having more of it actually reduced purchase intent! As we saw earlier, people don't like to have to think too hard about everyday decisions, so as a practical marketing rule of thumb, making things easy for them to understand is generally the right approach.

Increasing awareness, knowledge, and availability of green products can also be addressed with technological solutions. For example, the ecommerce giant Amazon has recently announced a "Climate Pledge Friendly" program that labels products, all searchable and available for online ordering, with one of 19 certifications for sustainability that can aid environmentally motivated consumers in identifying products from brands that have worked to reduce their carbon footprint and make other progress towards sustainable operations (Amazon, 2020). Other barriers may be relatively intractable. For example, the fourth item on the overall hierarchy of perceived barriers, habit-based inertia, may be more challenging to address with traditional marketing tactics. So, let's take a closer look at what works to overcome it and some of the other items on the list.

Strategizing for Change

In terms of brand marketing, what does one do to adjust to growing intentions to shop more green, especially in a world that is not a blank slate but rather one in which there are entrenched market participants that dominate their categories? And, what does one do to adjust to the fact that there is a growing social imperative for more sustainable corporate behavior? After all, the McKinsey & Company study mentioned above also found that consumers feel that it is largely the responsibility of companies and governments to reduce barriers to green consumption, as many of those barriers are not within the scope of the personal "behavioral control" of consumers but rather fall under the management control of companies and regulatory policies. If a shift in marketplace behavior towards more sustainable forms of consumption is increasingly a social imperative, how can we leverage what is known about the mind of the consumer to help enable that shift?

Different Strategies for Product Leaders Versus Challengers

The answers to these questions depend in part on where your product's market position sits on the broad spectrum of habitual consumerism. Momentarily we'll consider the more difficult problem of the barriers that new innovative entrants or otherwise minor members of the competitive set must confront. But first, let's consider the advantages which accrue to entrenched market leaders.

If you are in that position, you are already enjoying all the advantages that Byron Sharp (2010) documented with respect to your product's mental and physical availability. That is, your option readily comes to mind for the consumer when a relevant need state arrives, and your product is easy enough for the consumer to find when it is needed. So that alone provides you with an advantage. You wouldn't be in this exalted position if your customers didn't already at some level believe in your product benefits, and trust your organization, and think your pricing was acceptable.

You also have the distinct advantage of built-in habits that have developed from your customers repetitively making the same choices in similar contexts to continue to buy your product. That is, your customers find it easy, thoughtless, and comfortable to stick with past choices. So, you currently benefit from status quo and familiarity biases. But can you ignore the growth in both the numbers and the increasing concern level of green consumers? Well, you could take comfort in the fact that there is also a group of consumers who are either highly skeptical about the benefits or value of green products, and a bigger group of consumers who are just complacent and don't think too much about the issue.

That would be a great approach if your strategy is to gradually whittle away market share as consumer preferences shift and new product alternatives come to market. It is worthwhile here to remember that the dominant market position that leaders in the photography industry long enjoyed was rapidly degraded when they failed to innovate while their film offerings were being outmoded by the advent of digital cameras—which, in addition to being more convenient, are also dramatically more environmentally friendly in that they eliminate the chemicals and heavy metals involved in film processing, the canisters that contain the film, the film itself, in many cases the materials needed to make prints, and all the vehicle miles traveled to drop film off to be developed and to pick up the results.

A different approach is to get ahead of the situation and work towards reducing any motivation that a growing subset of your existing customers may have about committing to a more sustainable future with another product—especially given that your dominant market share may also be at risk for being more whittled away by demographic shifts, including the maturation of younger shoppers who may be less brand-allegiant and more attuned to green concerns. And, sadly, it may suffer from the inevitable reduction in the number of older shoppers. That is, those who may depend more on habits and less on abstract longer-term environmental concerns. And not least, despite the benefits of habitual consumption, your brand may become imperiled by a growth in environmental concerns about your offerings.

If you are lucky enough to manage brands that are within the top tier of your category with respect to revenue or market share, you have a pretty easy job to do. Just don't give the growing segment of your customers who are sensitive to environmental issues a reason to defect to a competitor, or give policymakers or other potential influencers a reason to object to your environmental impact. For example, the major global CPG brand manufacturers have in recent years publicly worked towards increasing their commitment to including recycled materials in their packaging, including environmentally friendly ingredients in their product formulations, reducing or eliminating their carbon emissions and water use, and in some cases committing to developing closed-loop processes consistent with a more circular-economy future. This only makes sense—they have everything to lose, and given their established category-leading brands, they are in an especially privileged position to gain from the growing imperative of increasing green consumption. In fact, as an added bonus, empirical research has indicated that environmentally friendly extensions of existing brands enjoy a significantly higher "green purchase intention" than that accorded to new-entrant green brands (Lopes and Veiga, 2019).

Gaining Acceptance for New-Entrant Green Underdogs

As we've seen, when a behavior becomes more practiced and relies less on overt effort, it eventually depends less on motivation—and thus can instead be more easily activated by cues in the environment it routinely takes place in. Figure 5.3 depicts the situation of a consumer having to choose between

FIGURE 5.3   Moving Green Product Entrants Into the Consideration Set

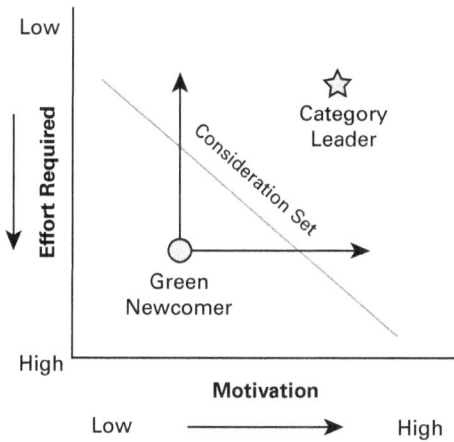

an entrenched, habitually purchased, conventional product offering over that of a less widely adopted green competitor. When prompted by situational cues, the choice or action of picking the conventional incumbent (represented by the star) is very easy to do, and since it has satisficed a need in the past there is some reward anticipation serving as a motivational force driving choice towards it. Together those two factors can conspire to once again push that option above the consideration set threshold and likely into your shopping basket. Whereas the green alternative new entrant languishes below that threshold, being unprompted, inadequately motivated, and relatively hard to think about (and likely hard to even notice or access given that infrequently purchased brands usually are relegated to unfortunate shelf positions).

So what is one to do? You could either short-circuit the existing habitual purchase by changing the situational context and thus the behavioral prompts that elicit the habit. Or you could make the choice of the alternative easier in some way, such as through price promotions or other point-of-sale interventions. Or you could try to increase motivation, perhaps through informational efforts designed to clarify benefits and increase their perceived value and personal relevance. All of the above could be useful for at least trying to get the new entrant into the shopper's consideration set.

Similar alternative approaches to disrupting old habits and developing new ones have been proposed by experts concerned with the role that habits play in human behavior and their implications for behavior change efforts.

Verplanken and Wood (2006) note that while policy-guided attempts to change people's behaviors often focus on informational campaigns intended to modify people's beliefs and intentions, such campaigns often fail when attempting to change behaviors when they are driven by habits. They described two alternative approaches to behavior change that have more promise for being effective in the face of habit-driven behaviors.

An "upstream" approach includes interventions for modifying situational factors that interfere with the habits being triggered in the first place—by eliminating associated environmental cues and establishing new ones in their place. This strategy can be contrasted with a "downstream" approach where information can be targeted at individuals when their environments are changing anyway, such as when they move to a new city or start a new job or divorce their spouse or attend a new school. This latter approach is based on the notion that their existing environmental triggers have been eliminated or drastically diminished in some way anyway: consumers might be more susceptible to outside influences before they have established new routines.

"Upstream" Approaches to Shaping Sustainable Behavior

The "upstream" approach can be illustrated by case studies from the food industry. There is good evidence that reducing meat consumption overall is important for reducing the environmental impacts of consumption, including climate change, water use, deforestation, and biodiversity loss. As an additional, more personal benefit, it may be healthier. In the retail environment grocery stores can serve as test beds for exploring changes in the immediate situational cues that can lead to habitual product selections, and in the process help to shift dietary choices.

Traditionally, refrigerated food products targeting vegetarian audiences were isolated in cooler or freezer sections of stores that non-vegetarian audiences seldom if ever visited. Instead, they habitually navigated directly to the meat cooler for servicing their protein needs. Even so, while the segment of people who self-identify as vegetarian is small, a larger proportion of the population might be willing to try plant-based protein products on at least some occasions. They just seldom get around to it. Disrupting the existing routines of protein shoppers thus has the potential for increasing green choices in this category. In one recent study (PBFA, 2020), plant-based food products were placed in the meat cooler of test stores in a prominent fashion with associated point-of-sale displays and in direct competition with meat-based alternatives. Meat shoppers who had consumption habits that would normally mean that they never even see plant-based alternatives suddenly had the opportunity to consider a more sustainable alternative. And trial of those plant-based alternatives rose 23 percent over that observed in the control stores of the same national grocery retailer during the course of the study period.

Moving out of the grocery store and into restaurants, a similar dynamic is observed in terms of how consumers routinely assess restaurant menus. Most mainstream formal restaurants (at least in OECD countries) have traditionally included mainly meat-based entrées, and possibly a few vegetarian options. These latter alternatives have often been placed in a demarcated menu subsection for those inclined to explore such options—a section that other diners habitually ignore if they are primarily interested in a meat-based choice.

But large differences in choice behavior can be seen if that contextual cue is eliminated. In a consumer choice study conducted by researchers at the London School of Economics (described in Holzer, 2017), participants who normally ate animal or fish protein when making restaurant choices were presented with one of two different versions of a menu. A conventional "control" menu contained a separate "vegetarian" section with a few meatless entrées, as well as a section with a larger variety of meat-based options. In contrast, an experimental menu included all of the same entrée options worded in the same way as on the conventional menu, but it eliminated the separate categories of entrée options. This simple change in menu design led to 13.4 percent of the participants selecting a vegetarian option from the menu without a separate section for "vegetarian" items, whereas less than half as many (5.9 percent) chose a meatless option when the menu explicitly circumscribed vegetarian entrées.

In the language of behavioral economics, these sorts of "upstream" non-coercive interventions are described as "nudges"—changes made in some aspect of a "choice architecture" in a way that predictably modifies behavioral outcomes without limiting or forbidding choices or altering the economic incentives associated with making them (Thaler and Sunstein, 2008). We'll be considering additional nudges in coming chapters.

"Downstream" Approaches Toward Shaping Sustainable Behavior

A good example of a more "downstream" approach that takes advantage of a natural change in environmental setting was described in a study evaluating the "discontinuity hypothesis" of habit modification, the notion that "behavior change interventions are more effective when delivered in the context of life course changes" (Verplanken and Roy, 2016). In that ambitious study the researchers looked carefully at how a major life change might help engender consideration of, and acting upon, more sustainable consumer choices.

To evaluate this notion, the self-reported frequencies of a large number of environmentally friendly behaviors and their related habit strength was measured at baseline in a population of participants living in Peterborough, a city close to the North Sea in the east of England. They then compared those responses with a post-intervention assessment.

The participants included both people who had recently relocated to the area and thus had disrupted their normal consumer habits, and a sample of long-time residents matched on socioeconomic variables and other criteria. In a subset of both groups an informational intervention was conducted in which each group was provided with (1) information about sustainable choices in the context of a face-to-face encounter, (2) samples of sustainable products, (3) a guide to local options to support sustainable behavior, and (4) a community newspaper communicating sustainable options and implying local social norms. While both the new arrivals and the established residents who received the intervention self-reported to have increased their related sustainable consumer behaviors in the post-intervention phase relative to their baseline measurement, this effect was observed to be significantly larger in the new residents than in the more established residents.

While it is relatively difficult to conduct such community-based work compared with laboratory studies, and even harder to attempt it with actual measured behavior change instead of self-reported change, this type of exercise provides compelling evidence for the strategy of taking advantage of real-life habit disruption as an opportunity to introduce new ways of thinking and to create the opportunity for people to develop new, more sustainable, habits.

1 Beliefs and attitudes impact green purchase decisions. Such decisions are more likely in individuals who are knowledgeable about and care for the environment, believe that making green choices is in line with their personal and prevailing societal norms, and who believe that their personal decisions can be impactful. But price sensitivity can negatively impact green purchase intent.

2 Strong existing habits may make such intentions moot. They can drive behavior in the absence of any intention *per se*, and often subvert the impact of weak intentions that are inconsistent with them.

3 Category leaders that benefit from strong existing brand preferences can take advantage of this fact by making their products more environmentally friendly, reducing any motivation committed consumers might have to consider alternatives.

4 New green entrants into a product category must work to change the shopping context by providing additional prompts, by appealing to less committed consumers, by educating potential customers in order to increase their motivation, and by reducing barriers (such as high prices or a difficult-to-comprehend product promise) to consideration.

References

Ajzen, I (1985) From intentions to actions: A theory of planned behavior, in *Action Control: From cognition to behavior*, eds J Kuhl and J Beckmann, pp 11–39, Springer-Verlag, Berlin, Heidelberg, New York

Ajzen, I (1991) The theory of planned behavior, *Organizational Behavior and Human Decision Processes*, 50, 179–211

Ajzen, I (2002) Residual effects of past on later behavior: Habituation and reasoned action perspectives, *Personality and Social Psychology Review*, 6, 107–122

Ajzen, I and Fishbein, M (1977) Attitude-behavior relations: A theoretical analysis and review of empirical research, *Psychological Bulletin*, 84, 888–918

Amazon (2020) Amazon launches "Climate Pledge Friendly" to make it easier for customers to discover and shop for sustainable products, www.businesswire.com/news/home/20200923005297/en/ (archived at https://perma.cc/9BHA-MPA8)

Bandura, A (1977) Self-efficacy: Toward a unifying theory of behavioral change, *Psychological Review*, 84(2), 191–215

Baumeister, R F, Sparks, E A, Stillman, T F and Vohs, K D (2008) Free will in consumer behavior: Self-control, ego depletion, and choice, *Journal of Consumer Psychology*, 18(1), 4–13

Bennett, G and Williams, F (2011) Mainstream green: Moving sustainability from niche to normal, assets.ogilvy.com/truffles_email/redpaper_june2010/MainstreamGreen.pdf (archived at https://perma.cc/HP76-KD8Z)

Bonini, S and Oppenheim, J (2008) Cultivating the green consumer, *Stanford Social Innovation Review*, 6(4), 56–61

Chan, R Y (2001) Determinants of Chinese consumers' green purchase behavior, *Psychology and Marketing*, 18(4), 389–413

Dagher, G K and Itani, O (2014) Factors influencing green purchasing behaviour: Empirical evidence from Lebanese consumers, *Journal of Consumer Behaviour*, 13, 188–195

Danner, U N, Aarts, H and de Vries, N K (2008) Habit and intention in the prediction of behaviors: The role of frequency, stability and accessibility of past behavior, *British Journal of Social Psychology*, 47(2), 245–265

Gleim, M R, Smith, J S, Andrews, D and Cronin, J (2013) Against the green: A multi-method examination of the barriers to green consumption, *Journal of Retailing*, 89(1), 44–61

Hines, J M, Hungerford, H R and Tomera, A N (1987) Analysis and synthesis of research on responsible environmental behavior: A meta-analysis, *Journal of Environmental Education*, 18(2), 1–8

Holzer, J (2017) Don't put vegetables in the corner: A Q&A with behavioral science researcher Linda Bacon [blog], 12 June, www.wri.org/insights/dont-put-vegetables-corner-qa-behavioral-science-researcher-linda-bacon (archived at https://perma.cc/P4BA-5YH8)

Jaiswal, D and Kant, R (2018) Green purchasing behaviour: A conceptual framework and empirical investigation of Indian consumers, *Journal of Retailing and Consumer Services*, 41, 60–69

Ji, M F and Wood, W (2007) Purchase and consumption habits: Not necessarily what you intend, *Journal of Consumer Psychology*, 17(4), 261–276

Joshi, Y and Rahman, Z (2015) Factors affecting green purchase behaviour and future research directions, *International Strategic Management Review*, 3, 128–143

Lopes, E L and Veiga, R T (2019) Increasing purchasing intention of eco-efficient products: The role of the advertising communication strategy and the branding strategy, *Journal of Brand Management*, 26(5), 550–566

Masud, M M, Al-Amin, A Q, Junsheng, H, Ahmed, F, Yahaya, S R, Akhtar, R and Banna, H (2015) Climate change issue and the theory of planned behaviour: Relationship by empirical evidence, *Journal of Cleaner Production*, 113, 613–623

Norman, P and Conner, M (2006) The theory of planned behaviour and binge drinking: Assessing the moderating role of past behaviour within the theory of planned behaviour, *British Journal of Health Psychology*, 11(1), 55–70

Ouellette, J A and Wood, W (1998) Habit and intention in everyday life: The multiple processes by which past behavior predicts future behavior, *Psychological Bulletin*, 124, 54–74

Paul, J, Modi, A and Patel, J (2016) Predicting green product consumption using theory of planned behavior and reasoned action, *Journal of Retailing and Consumer Services*, 29, 123–134

PBFA (2020) PBFA and Kroger plant-based meat study, plantbasedfoods.org/marketplace/pbfa-and-kroger-plant-based-meat-study/ (archived at https://perma.cc/9EQS-Z669)

Polites, G and Karahan, E (2011) Shackled to the status quo: The inhibiting effects of incumbent system habit, switching costs, and inertia on new system acceptance, *Management Information Systems Quarterly*, 36(1), 21–42

Popovic, I, Bossink, B A G and van der Sijde, P C (2019) Factors influencing consumers' decision to purchase food in environmentally friendly packaging: What do we know and where do we go from here?, *Sustainability*, 11(7197), 1–22

Ryle, G (1949) *The Concept of Mind*, Hutchinson, London

Sharp, B (2010) *How Brands Grow: What marketers don't know*, Oxford University Press, Oxford

Tanner, C (1999) Constraints on environmental behaviour, *Journal of Environmental Psychology*, 19(2), 145–157

Tarkiainen, A and Sundqvist, S (2005) Subjective norms, attitudes and intentions of Finnish consumers in buying organic food, *British Food Journal*, 107(11), 808–822

Thaler, R H, and Sunstein, C (2008) *Nudge: Improving decisions about health, wealth, and happiness*, Yale University Press, New Haven, CT

Vermeir, I and Verbeke, W (2006) Sustainable food consumption: Exploring the consumer "attitude–behavioral intention" gap, *Journal of Agricultural and Environmental Ethics*, 19(2), 169–194

Verplanken, B and Roy, D (2016) Empowering interventions to promote sustainable lifestyles: Testing the habit discontinuity hypothesis in a field experiment, *Journal of Environmental Psychology*, 45, 127–134

Verplanken, B and Wood, W (2006) Interventions to break and create consumer habits, *Journal of Public Policy and Marketing*, 25(1), 90–103

Wood, W and Neal, D T (2007) A new look at habits and the habit–goal interface, *Psychological Review*, 114, 842–862

Yue, B, Sheng, G, She, S and Xu, J (2020) Impact of consumer environmental responsibility on green consumption behavior in China: The role of environmental concern and price sensitivity, *Sustainability*, 12(2074), 1–16

06

Leveraging the Social Imperative

This is a good point at which to share another personal anecdote. My home sits on the northwest corner of an intersection, and my street extends to the west for a short block before it ends in a cul-de-sac. I've lived here for seven or eight years. Shortly after I moved in, I observed solar panels being installed on the roof of one of the houses across the street from me, second to the west from the opposite corner and the first house on my cul-de-sac to have them. The house I moved into was older and needed new roofing, so I had to get it re-shingled before our next rainy season. While doing so I decided that my neighbor had made a prudent choice in getting their solar array. I also possess some degree of "green purchase intent," so I went ahead and contracted to get a similar array added to my roof. On reflection it's been a great deal as between the legislated incentives for installing it and the electrical usage savings I have since accrued it has already paid for itself. And it will provide free clean energy in future years. As an added benefit I feel somewhat virtuous about minimizing my need to draw from our polluting electrical grid. So it is both financially and intrinsically rewarding.

But that is not the point of this story. The actual point is that, within a year of completing my solar installation, the neighbor on this side of the street directly to the west of me also installed solar panels. And last year while my newer neighbor directly across the street was doing some remodeling, they also installed panels, without any explicit encouragement from the folks around them. So all of the nearest-neighbor houses on my end of the cul-de-sac now benefit from distributed solar energy production. As of this writing this spreading development has not migrated further west down the street, or into the houses on the opposite corner to the east of me. Not yet, anyway.

More recently, in the year after we replaced an older car with an electric vehicle, our nearest neighbor to my west on my side of the street did as well. We've since chatted about the heat pump they have also installed to obviate the need to add air conditioning. So now I'm eager to get one of those installed in my home as well, as our formerly comfortable coastal summers are definitely getting hotter. As we will see later, this social propinquity effect is one of the typical patterns by which sustainable innovations spread.

The Social Brain

Back in the introduction I proposed that Adam Smith's view of interpersonal behavior (Smith, 1759) was very similar to that espoused by more modern social psychology theorists in that it incorporated the somewhat obvious view that people have a "theory of mind" (TOM) about both themselves and other people. In recent decades this idea has become somewhat of a cornerstone in the empirical and theoretical understanding of interpersonal behavior. An imputed TOM refers to the apparent ability that people have to be able to understand that both they themselves and other people know things, believe things, feel things, and intend to do things. That the mental states attributed to others may be congruent or incongruent with one's own mental state in the same or similar circumstances. And that such knowledge can be strategically useful to the individual. That is, such understanding is assumed to bestow some advantages on the entities that possess it.

Evolution of the Ability to Have a TOM

A TOM appears to also exist to some degree in our close relatives such as chimpanzees and other great apes (Premack and Woodruff, 1977; Krupenye et al, 2016), and in a rudimentary form in monkeys and perhaps in other creatures as well. I think my dog has one, however crude. But it seems pretty clear that the intricacies of a TOM have evolved to a radically new, and perhaps qualitatively different, level in the human brain. After all, we invented poker and other games that depend in large part on having sophisticated social information processing skills and thus being able to "read" people and to infer deception (Leonard and Williams, 2015).

Some have argued that the cooperative and competitive advantages that this growing ability endowed upon our early hominid ancestors were key evolutionary drivers of the success of our big-brained species (Dunbar, 2009). Or, at least, they have been drivers of our success to date as we enter the *Anthropocene*. Others have referred to this explosive brain expansion in response to increasing social demands as the *Machiavellian hypothesis* (Byrne and Whiten, 1988), emphasizing more strategic advantages that are bestowed on those with a more sophisticated understanding of the motivations of others.

Social Norms and the Drive to Conform to Them

The desire to belong to a group has been characterized as a fundamental human motivation (Baumeister and Leery, 1995), and satisfying the drive for such belonging requires that individuals learn the rules of that game. One notion that seems to be represented in the TOM that resides in the brain of *homo sapiens* is the idea that people are concerned about "social norms," the implicit or explicit assumptions that govern the groups they operate in. We automatically activate expectations about how people will likely feel, think, and act, when we are in particular stereotypical social situations. In large part because of the way in which we are intrinsically wired, our brains are exquisitely tuned towards detecting whether we ourselves, or others we interact with, sometimes violate such expectations.

One stereotyped cultural idiom that is frequently applied to this notion is often communicated by the Japanese phrase: "the nail that sticks out gets hammered down." While astute, this notion is by no means culture-specific. Given a common understanding of the idea, if one complies with the perceived prevailing social norms, at a minimum few or any bad outcomes would be expected from such compliance in the absence of any norm violations. And in some scenarios, such docile behavior might be incrementally rewarded. On the other hand, if one doesn't conform to a perceived group norm, one could be disciplined or ostracized or worse. So the reward mechanisms we have discussed in prior chapters also apply here. And as we saw earlier, people are risk-averse and biased towards "status quo" behavior—which tends to align with prevailing social norms.

Past research has shown that perceptions about either injunctive or descriptive social norms can play a role in guiding individual behavior. Injunctive norms in this context reflect perceptions of whether a behavior might be viewed with approval or disapproval by others. In contrast, descriptive norms just refer to the relative typicality of different behaviors among some peer group.

The Value–Belief–Norm Theory of Pro-Environmental Behavior

When reviewing the TPB we saw how an actor's normative beliefs about whether or not others would approve of a behavior was predictive of both green purchase intentions and associated actions, a finding confirmed by multiple research studies conducted across the globe and a wide variety of consumer behaviors. An alternative perspective on the psychological factors that predict pro-environmental behaviors, Stern's value–belief–norm (VBN) theory (Stern, 2000), is less explicit in terms of the degree to which beliefs about perceived social norms influence such behaviors. Instead, VBN posits a separate daisy chain of mental processes that are precursors to green intentions and behaviors (Figure 6.1). This chain begins with the individual's personal values (altruistic values, biospheric values, egocentric values, etc.), and views those values as the precursors to beliefs. For example, if one values the biosphere and values altruism, then one might want to preserve the living world and its inhabitants. But if one's values are instead strongly egoistic, that might be less of a priority.

Beliefs such as a worldview in which people are part of the broader ecology, beliefs that some actions have adverse consequences for that ecology,

FIGURE 6.1   The Value–Belief–Norm Theory of Pro-Environmental Behavior

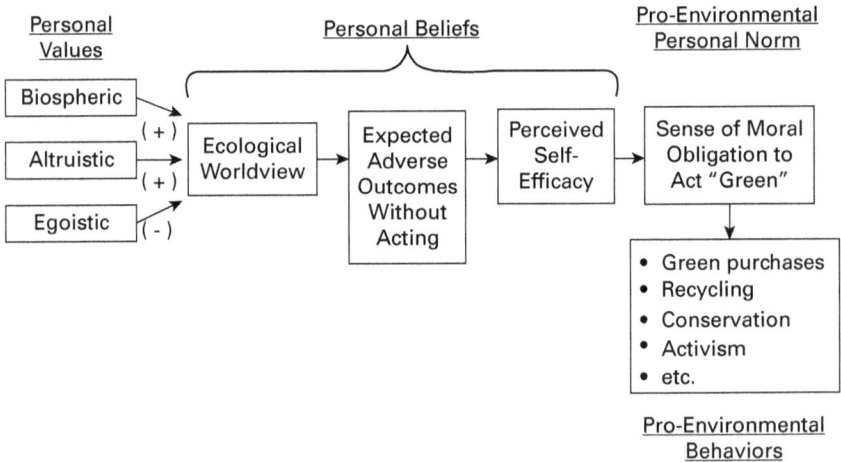

SOURCE   Adapted from Stern (2000).

and beliefs about one's personal ability and responsibility for addressing such threats, are assumed to weigh on the individual. Those beliefs in turn can lead to the development of a related personal or moral norm; that is, a sense of personal responsibility to engage in pro-environmental behaviors. According to the VBN theory, this sense of personal responsibility is the proximal cause of things like green purchase or recycling intentions or related actual real-world behaviors.

Results from studies in both European and US participants, using both survey and laboratory methods and a variety of outcome measurements (Martin and Czellar, 2017), have shown that a sense of being part of nature can in fact help predict preferences for eco-friendly products through mediation by a latent variable measuring biospheric values. Related research (Wang et al, 2019) conducted in China has shown that experiences which elicit the self-transcendent feeling of "awe" in response to natural scenery increases green purchase preference, both directly and by increasing one's feelings of being directly related to nature. From such studies a picture is emerging (Figure 6.2) which suggests that interventions that increase empathy with the natural environment might also serve to drive more sustainable consumption behavior.

Presumably one's understanding of prevailing social norms could also influence one's values, or beliefs, or one's sense of personal responsibility, but no such factor was directly represented in the original VBN model. So it is of interest that recent efforts to predict pro-environmental behaviors using this model have found that a better fit to data on real-world behaviors can be made by explicit inclusion of a perceived social norm factor as a mediating variable. For example, Fornara and colleagues (2020) found that an

FIGURE 6.2 Biospheric Values Mediate Green Purchase Preference

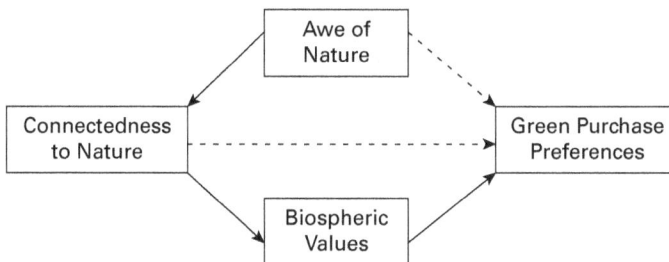

injunctive social norm mediated factors related to beliefs about pro-environmental behaviors and perceived behavioral control when predicting the frequency of individual actions by European participants related to wildlife and biodiversity protection. In this case the latent variable associated with an injunctive social norm was derived from questionnaire responses to items such as "Most people who are important to me think that I should act for nature and biodiversity."

Another recent study conducted in China and Malaysia found that extending the VBN theory to include an explicit perceived social norm construct which was a composite of injunctive and descriptive normative perceptions improved the ability of a related statistical model to predict individual differences in a variety of pro-environmental behaviors, from purchasing green products to recycling behavior (Ghazali et al, 2019). Increasingly such predictive models are growing to resemble a hybrid between the traditional TPB and VBN approaches, with a key role for perceived social norms as an important predictor of whether or not people decide to make green choices.

The Social Brain in Action

There are at least two distinct parts to the processing of social information in the human brain—thinking about your "self" and thinking about others. When thinking about your self-concept, how do you calculate what is implied in the prevailing social dynamics for you on a personal level? How do you evaluate an interpersonal opportunity with respect to your self? And do people you know like you or not? Do they judge you or not? How do their own attitudes amplify those feelings?

Then there are more general, less immediate issues having to do with your understanding of how people think and act and what you know about that. Are those perceived attitudes on the part of some actors congruent with yours? If they are not congruent with how you think, how, if at all, do you need to modify your attitudes and behaviors in response? Do you at all trust those other people and the attitudes you suppose they have? What if they pretend to have attitudes congruent with yours just so they can con you into an attitude or behavior not aligned with your own self-interest? We all have to deal with these questions on a day-to-day basis.

Imaging the Social Brain

To gain further insight into the distinction between these two types of social information processing, let's go back into that functional MRI scanner suite and perform some more tasks. In one sort of task you will see a list of adjectives that can be used to describe people (e.g., smart, anxious, funny, tiresome...) presented one at a time. For each word your task is to press one key if the meaning of that word to you reflects a positive trait, or a second key if it is judged negatively. In another version of the task, you see the same list of words, but your task is to press one key if you think the word applies to you personally and the other if it doesn't. If we look at the differences in brain activation observed between the task that required an "appraisal of self-relevance" and the first task, which didn't require such an appraisal, we would likely see increased activity in the ventral medial prefrontal cortex (vMPFC, Figure 6.3). In fact, across a very wide range of task conditions that involve some form of appraisal of the self-relevance of information, this same pattern of activation in the vMPFC is seen (Schmitz and Johnson, 2007; Amodio and Frith, 2006).

As we reviewed earlier, activation of this region is also seen in simulated shopping or gambling tasks, where it is activated by judgments related to

FIGURE 6.3 The Medial Prefrontal Cortex

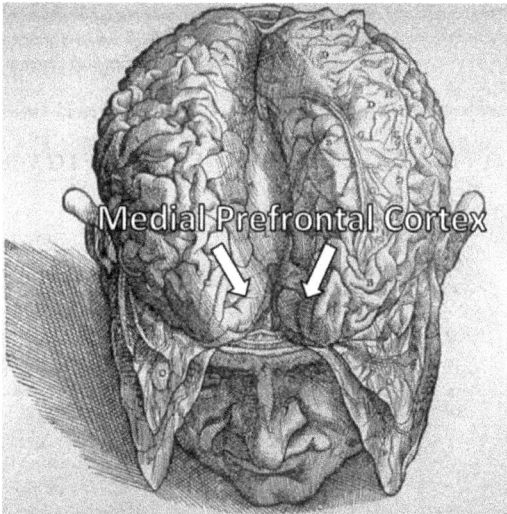

SOURCE Adapted from Vesalius (1543).

the subjective value of options, and in fact this area tends to be activated so routinely across many types of tasks that it has been referred to as part of a "neural common currency of choice" (Levy and Glimcher, 2012). It is not so much a marker of a thing's absolute value, but rather a marker of how valuable that thing is to you, personally, given your preferences, current state, and other situational factors—like what you think other people think about the situation you are in.

That is, it appears that such computations of value are subject to social influences. For example, the vMPFC (as well as reward-related areas such as the NAcc) is involved in person perception and the value you may assign to others, at least on a general attractiveness dimension. When heterosexual research participants have been asked to rate the attractiveness of pictures of the faces of members of the opposite sex, pictures that receive higher ratings tend to elicit more activation in these regions (Aharon et al, 2001; Cloutier et al, 2008). But apparently such person valuations can succumb to peer pressure and conform to a social norm. In another study participants first rated the attractiveness of a series of face pictures, and then after each rating they were provided feedback in the form of an ostensible average rating from a purported peer group (Zakiet al, 2011). The feedback was designed to be either higher than the individual's rating, lower than that rating, or in agreement with it. The participants then again rated each picture as their brains were scanned.

Behaviorally, on the second rating the participants tended to conform to group norms because their attractiveness rating shifted towards the direction indicated by the purported peer group average—that is, participants rated facial attractiveness higher than they originally had scored it for those faces that had received higher normative feedback relative to their own scoring, and they rated faces lower in attractiveness than they had originally for those faces that had received lower normative feedback. And for faces that were matched in attractiveness on their initial ratings, activity in the vMPFC and the NAcc was greater for those faces that had been associated with higher-rated peer feedback than for those that had been associated with lower-rated peer feedback.

While clearly implicated in judgments of value and self-relevance, the vMPFC also appears to be involved with judgments about how others would feel in particular circumstances, suggesting perhaps that when making such judgments we think about how we ourselves would feel when confronting that same circumstance. In one study (Oschner et al, 2004), the brain activity of participants was monitored while they watched pictures of people in the context of scenes that depicted things with a good, bad, or neutral emotional valence. In different trials participants rated their own personal affective response to the scene, or their assumption of what the affective response would be for the person in the scene, or simply whether the scene depicted an indoor or outdoor event. The subsequent judgments of the participant's own affective response (compared with the indoors versus outdoors comparative task judgment) was observed to activate the vMPFC. But this region also lit up when evaluating the potential emotional impact of the person in the scene. So while this region seems to play a key role in assessing the subjective value or self-relevance of things, it may also be involved when we think about the likely emotional relevance of things to other people. That is, as in Adam Smith's framework, it may help enable empathy.

The Social Brain and the Mentalizing System

The vMPFC appears to be just one node in a distributed network involved with the metacognitive process of thinking about the feelings and intentions of oneself and others. During self-appraisal tasks the vMPFC has been shown to interact with other structures involved in emotion and motivation including the NAcc, the anterior insula, and the amygdala (Schmitz and Johnson, 2006), which appear to transiently interconnect into a functional network for assessing self-relevance. A separate functional network emerges in such tasks that involves a transient coupling between more dorsal regions of the MPFC, lateral regions of the prefrontal cortex involved with more deliberately controlled cognitive processes, and the hippocampus. This additional network may be recruited to monitor, evaluate, and act on (or inhibit if necessary), any response biases automatically induced by a stimulus event signaling subjective value, perhaps in order to better adapt an initial feeling of approach or avoidance to one's immediate context and longer-term goals (Northoff and Bermpohl, 2004).

More broadly the MPFC serves as a node in a generalized network of structures frequently referred to as the "mentalizing system" (Frith and Frith, 2006; Van Overwalle and Baetens, 2009). The term mentalizing is made in reference to our ability to consider the mental states of others, to imagine their perspective on the world and to infer their likely beliefs and intentions. Beyond the MPFC itself, meta-analyses indicate that tasks with a social component tend to also strongly co-activate the temporal parietal junction (TPJ), a cortical region involved with integration of information from multi-

FIGURE 6.4 Additional Anatomical Regions Involved in "Mentalizing"

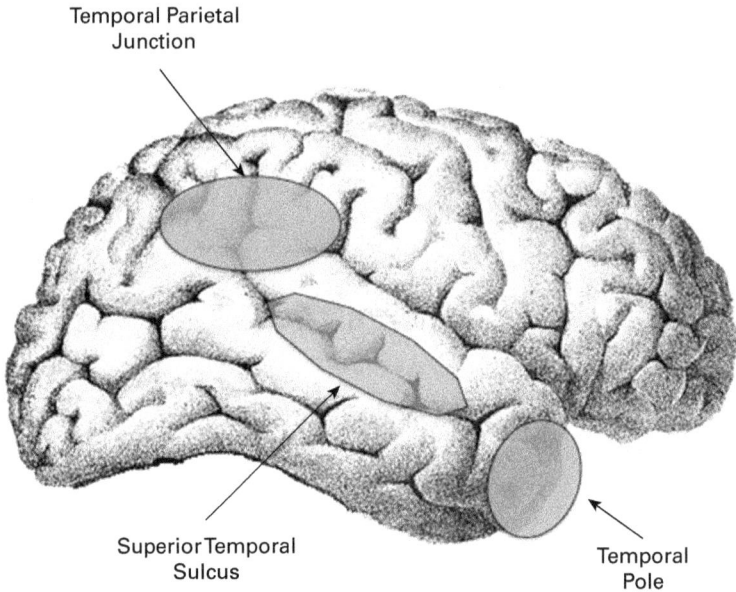

SOURCE Adapted from Brown (1894). Public domain, via Wikimedia Commons.

ple senses and the reorienting of attention in response to that information (Figure 6.4). In brief, the TPJ has been described as being activated by "people thinking about thinking people" (Saxe and Kanwisher, 2003).

To the degree to which tasks engage a TOM and require that the participant infer another's goals, perspectives, beliefs, and intentions, the TPJ is more strongly activated, whereas tasks that require assessments of how those things are relevant to one's self also co-engage the MPFC. Other regions implicated in the mentalizing system include additional areas of multimodal association cortex including the posterior portion of the superior temporal sulcus and the anterior polar region of the temporal lobes (Frith and Frith, 2003). The mentalizing system appears to not be involved in deliberative reasoning processes that lack a social component (Mitchell, 2009), but is instead engaged in proportion to the amount of reasoning about people and social situations demanded by different tasks (Saxe and Kanwisher, 2003; Van Overwalle, 2011).

Social Norm Violations and the Mentalizing System

As we have seen, beliefs and inferences about the prevailing social norms concerning green purchasing and other types of pro-environmental behaviors play an important role in predicting both purchase intent and real-world behaviors. Such thought processes fall very much inside the types of tasks that presumably engage the mentalizing system. Accordingly a great deal of recent research in the domain of social and affective neuroscience has focused on the issue of evaluating norms and responses to perceived norm violations.

One meta-analytic review of studies that used fMRI methods (Zinchenko and Arsalidou, 2018) looked for commonalities between tasks that required participants to judge scenarios that implicate moral norms. Or that tracked activity while participants played economic games with others (often hypothetical others in the form of computer programs). Some of these games may be familiar to readers who have studied microeconomic strategy, and include versions of the Prisoner's Dilemma, the Dictator Game, and the Ultimatum Game.

The latter game is easy to describe. It involves a single-round interaction between two players. One of them, the proposer, is given a pot of money and that player gets to propose a split of the money between the proposer and the other player, the responder. The responder has the choice of either accepting the proposal, or not. If the person tasked with responding then rejects the proposed split, the money is forfeited. Since the gain in monetary terms for the responder is maximized if anything offered is accepted, this task gets at trade-offs between economic gain and perceived violation of social norms for fairness and reciprocity. An even split tends to be accepted, as does a split slightly in favor of the proposer. But at some point the respondent tends to reject an inadequate proposed split, presumably out of spite.

In the meta-analysis, two patterns of activity were observed. In studies that merely represent social norms in terms of contrasting conditions where normative attitudes are presented or not, or that contrasted normative information with some other factual information, the vMPFC was consistently activated. In contrast, in studies where there was a norm violation in terms of fairness or honesty or some other issue in which the participants might take affront with the other player's behavior, the anterior insular cortex tended to be activated. For example, in an fMRI study of respondent players in the Ultimatum Game, the anterior insula was strongly activated when the respondent decided to reject an offer, and areas associated with cognitive control mechanisms (e.g., dorsolateral frontal cortex) were also strongly engaged (Sanfey et al, 2003). As you might remember the anterior insula is also activated when shoppers are confronted with high prices or in conditions in which high cognitive effort is demanded or where some anxiety-producing, emotionally negative choice must be made.

The mentalizing system is also activated in "trust games." In these scenarios a pair of players engage in multiple rounds of joint interaction. The games are structured such that monetary rewards for each player are maximized if they learn to effectively develop a shared norm of cooperation with the other player over time. There have been enough studies of brain activity during such games that patterns are starting to emerge (Alos-Ferrer and Farolfi, 2019). Generally, cortical areas involved with TOM activities like the TPJ tend to be activated throughout game play. And areas involved in self-reference and reward such as the MPFC and the NAcc tend to increase their activity over trials as a shared cooperation norm is developed.

But areas involved with risk assessment like the anterior insula and brain regions like the lateral prefrontal cortex involved in cognitive control tend to stay active even as trust builds, an effect that might reflect a continuous monitoring for any signs of betrayal. Tellingly, compared with healthy controls, patients with social anxiety disorders have reduced involvement in reward systems and increased involvement of the insula and frontal lobes in these situations. Such results are consistent with the notion that has been promulgated by some evolutionary psychologists that the social brain incorporates a "cheating detection mechanism" (Cosmides et al, 2010). This system appears to operate automatically, below the level of overt awareness (Van Lier et al, 2013), and it serves to maintain wariness in social encounters—facilitating the rapid detection of lies and cheating in social settings even in the presence of competing cognitive demands.

The Impact of Invoking Social Norms in Persuasive Communications

Another interesting line of research that implicates a role for the mentalizing system in social norm analysis has looked at the impact of persuasive messaging invoking norms on subjective beliefs and attitudes about a variety of topics. In one study a group of investigators in Japan (Yomogida et al, 2017) performed a study where participants were first asked to rate their agreement with a wide range of topics, including statements such as "Sugar is bad for your health." The participants' brains were then scanned while they listened to communications that provided normative information that either agreed or disagreed with a subset of the statements, as well as information directed towards some of the statements that did not implicate social norms. Afterwards the participants were required to again rate their degree of agreement with the longer list of statements.

Persuasion attempts directed at social norms both shifted rated agreement on the related topics and produced brain activation in the mentalizing system. In particular, persuasion attempts that invoked social norms activated the vMPFC and other mentalizing system regions such as the TPJ and temporal poles. In contrast, persuasion that didn't attempt to invoke social norms was both less effective at changing attitudes and failed to activate the mentalizing system.

Appealing to the Social Brain

Such findings from social neuroscience research have broad implications for how to best encourage green consumer choices and other pro-environmental decision-making. To start, the facts that appraisals of self-relevance and subjective valuation are tightly intertwined in the brain, and that activation of the vMPFC and associated areas is predictive of both product choice and the effectiveness of marketing communications, have clear yet somewhat counterintuitive implications about how to frame the benefits of green products. In particular, focusing attention primarily on environmental benefits is not likely to win you many converts.

The Social Brain and Pro-Environmental Behavior

Personal beliefs about behavioral efficacy and values such as environmental concern might explain some of the variance in green purchase intent and actual pro-environmental behaviors. But as we have seen, although a growing subset of people express some degree of environmental concern, not all people hold such concerns to the same degree. And most display a big gap between their environment-friendly intentions and related action. For the broad majority of individuals, sustainability issues are just one of many factors they weigh in purchase decisions, and for a small subset of individuals environmental claims might even be a reason to avoid a product.

Accordingly, framing product positioning and marketing communications to primarily focus on direct, personally relevant benefits to a consumer, benefits that engage the vMPFC, will generally lead to greater success in the marketplace (or alternatively, lead to more pro-environmental behavior in the private sphere) than will similar communications that instead focus on more abstract, impersonal, environmental benefits. Moreover, some empirical research has found that downplaying product greenness, and instead implying green benefits indirectly rather than leading with them, actually leads to better overall product evaluations than leading with a product's environmentally friendly attributes (Usrey et al, 2020).

Such framing doesn't have to be complicated, and creative teams tasked with creating messaging around pro-environmental behavior change or product benefit statements just have to keep one thing in mind. Communicate benefits that are about the things the target customer finds immediately most relevant rather than about abstract, possibly long-term, geographically and socially distant environmental issues. For food products, focus on a sustainable offering being delicious and healthy. And oh, yes, as an afterthought, that it also has less adverse environmental impacts than its traditional alternatives. For nonfood products, emphasize the problem the product will solve for the consumer, and communicate the green aspects of the product as an added benefit instead of talking about it as an attribute that might call into question the product's efficacy.

For those product benefits that reduce environmental impacts, channel those impacts into immediate personal benefits. If a product formulation reduces air or water pollution, focus on improving the "air that you breathe" or the "water that you drink" rather than on pollution as an abstract notion. If your product benefits include reductions in GHG emissions and those benefits can seem abstract and distant, don't focus on the impacts on polar bear ecosystems. Focus instead on reducing the current growth in the frequency and extent of wildfires and flooding and hurricanes.

Similarly, if your target market is of a certain age, focus your marketing tactics especially on the ways in which inaction can impact those most self-relevant to that population—their children and grandchildren. That is, "think about what recent changes in the frequency of wildfires or flooding or hurricanes might mean for your children and your grandchildren and their ability to live a good life and to get ahead in it." And, focus on the places they most care about. Like their homes, and the accessible wild-lands they cherish. Greenland or Antarctic glacier melt rates are of concern to scientists who work on those issues and activists that pay attention to them. But focusing on local environmental risks is much more likely to engage the brain's salience network.

The Social Brain and Greenwashing

An added return of not leading with environmental benefits in marketing communications, at least for those communications promoting green products, is that one is less likely to evoke concerns about greenwashing. As we saw earlier, advertising that makes specific green claims can be less effective at activating the reward system than advertising for equivalent products that don't make such claims. We have also seen that perceived greenwashing is a major barrier to consumer consideration and adoption of environmentally friendly products.

In this chapter we saw that the social brain's mentalizing system seems to include a "cheater detection mechanism" that serves to automatically detect potential violations of social or moral norms. This mechanism may well be invoked when considering brand communications, and strong environmental claims could result in consumers becoming mistrustful and wary in response to them. In contrast, vague claims do not seem to increase perceived greenwashing on the part of consumers, and the inclusion of nature imagery in communications can indirectly prime positive affective responses (Schmuck et al, 2018). Similarly, advertising that includes indirect sustainability claims such as those conveyed by third-party ecolabeling on packaging can increase a brand's association with sustainability with less risk of triggering mental counterarguing (Schmidt et al, 2017).

As a timely if mild example of greenwashing from my own life, in my home we now have a variety of bottles of hand sanitizer—as you likely do as well. The typical claim found on most bottles is that they are 99.9 percent effective at killing germs, and some might include subsidiary claims related to the inclusion of moisturizing or scent compounds. And most are mainly composed of ethyl alcohol, which is an organic compound derived from plants. Yet one bottle stands out. On the front panel there is also a green leaf, a prominent product claim that the alcohol it contains is "plant derived" and that, overall, it contains 98 percent plant-derived ingredients. The back panel also includes a litany of additional "reasons to believe" claims, including that it is vegan. Yet according to the UK-based website VeganFriendly, virtually all other hand sanitizer products are also technically "vegan" (VeganFriendly, 2021). So while this product is much like the majority of other hand sanitizer products on the shelf, it has highlighted "green" credentials, even though the credentials don't in fact significantly differentiate it from competitors. While in this case I am more amused than offended by the marketing tactic, other examples might be much more misleading in their claims, implying things that are not actually true. And it is hard to know which is which.

Invoking Social Norms to Encourage Pro-Environmental Behavior

Perceptions of prevailing social norms play an important role in the development of an individual's green purchase intent and the likelihood of someone engaging in pro-environmental behaviors, and information about prevailing norms can serve to regulate subjective valuation and reward anticipation components of the mentalizing system. It is not surprising, then, that invoking norms can be an effective tool for promoting pro-environmental behavior of one form or another (Manning, 2009).

Across cultures, the need to conform to the peer pressure of perceived social norms has been shown to be a powerful determinant of the adoption of pro-environmental behaviors (Culiberg and Elgaaied-Gambier, 2016), and a wide range of empirical research has demonstrated an impact of communicating social norms on pro-environmental behaviors. Such studies have ranged from increasing composting and recycling activity, reducing littering, increasing energy conservation and the adoption of solar panels, to increasing consumer selection of sustainable transportation options (reviewed in White et al, 2019). Interventions to successfully convey normative information can range from those that occur in the same context in which a targeted behavior will occur (for example, via a point-of-sale advertisement on a supermarket shelf) to those that occur remotely (for example, through television or out-of-home advertising). And the information content itself can range from just conveying summary information about group norms to activities that expose people to displays of the attitudes and behaviors of others (Yamin et al, 2019).

Social Norms and Green Status Signaling

That people seem to be motivated to conform to perceived social norms is consistent with the notion that they employ a sophisticated TOM to reflect on how their behavior might be evaluated by others. Another aspect of that type of social reasoning is that people also tend to change their behavior, including their purchase behavior, in ways to influence such evaluations. As we have seen, Adam Smith viewed people as very status conscious and concerned with how they were viewed by their peers, and thought that this fact could motivate their economic activity: "The wish to become proper objects of this respect, to deserve and obtain this credit and rank among our equals, may be the strongest of all our desires" (Smith, 1759).

And just as Veblen (1899) proposed that people engage in "conspicuous consumption" by using public evidence of their purchase decisions to flaunt their social status, the term "conspicuous conservation" has more recently been used to describe how one motivation for consumers to purchase environmentally friendly products might be to also signal the purchaser's social status (Sexton and Sexton, 2014). As one example of a class of behaviors that is sometimes pejoratively referred to as "virtue signaling" (Bartholomew, 2015), researchers have found that priming status-seeking motives in experimental settings can lead people to choose green products over attractive non-green products—at least when their behavior can be observed by others (Griskevicius et al, 2010). This aspect of the social brain suggests, then, additional routes toward driving green consumption—such as crafting advertising to activate perceptions of status benefits, and perhaps the development of marketing strategies that leverage social networks to spread the adoption of green consumption.

Social Contagion and Dynamic Norms

One of the virtues of virtue signaling is that it can be a spark for igniting the social contagion of green choices. The terms social or behavioral contagion refer to another type of social influence effect, one related to perceptions of emerging social norms. This phenomenon reflects the increased tendency of people to adopt behaviors that others whom they have been exposed to display—apparently whether or not such display behavior occurs in the real world or the virtual world. It builds on the notion that social modeling around the decision-making of early adopters can promote the diffusion of innovations (Schultz, 2014), as well as the finding that normative information can be most effective when it is communicated by an in-group influencer (Abrams et al, 1990).

Let's consider social contagion in the context of the anecdote I shared at the beginning of this chapter about the seeming propinquity effect in the diffusion of solar panels and electric vehicles (EVs) in my immediate neighborhood. Since only a minority of people at present actually drive EVs or install solar panels on their rooftops, a social modeling approach may at first seem to be problematic, as the existing norm is in fact to drive a gasoline-fueled vehicle and leave decisions about electrical power provision to their local utility—and hence an understanding of that existing descriptive norm could give the audience psychological license to maintain their current behavior. Despite this concern, geospatial evidence indicates that there are definite spatial clusters for both EV adoption (Liu et al, 2017) and solar panel adoption (Bollinger and Gillingham, 2012; Graziano and Gillingham, 2015), suggesting that people may be more influenced by the actions of their neighbors than by overall broader incident rates.

Consistent with this observation, Sparkman and Walton (2017) provide evidence that reference to "dynamic norms," that is, the notion that the current norm is changing, can create a "bandwagon" effect that can be effective at behavioral change. In particular, they report results from studies that attempted to persuade respondents to reduce their meat consumption. They found that when normative information is framed in terms that suggest that peers are actively changing their behavior (e.g., x number of people have recently started to do y), the intervention is more successful than when the same information is framed in more static terms (e.g., x number of people do y). This effect of communicating a dynamic norm is also consistent with *social diffusion* models of innovation and behavior change (Rogers, 2003), as it suggests that innovators and early adopters serve as a social model of the target behavior for the following majority to aspire to, which in turn then creates a status quo norm that eventually even laggards start to conform to.

Exploitation of the phenomenon of social contagion to promote green products really doesn't differ that much from other types of product promotion. For example, for big ticket items, leaning into conspicuous conservation and encouraging early adopters of prominent purchases such as electric vehicles and solar panels to be credible sources of product information for their neighbors is obviously important. But if advertisers also directly target those neighbors with marketing communications, they can exploit a potential opportunity in that those neighbors will be in a mind state more attuned to being receptive toward those messages than the general population might be.

These strategic efforts are not limited to physical proximity, though. For example, it appears that in terms of product adoption, social contagion effects extend into online social networks, with increased product adoption among close connections of friends who have publicized those products (Christakis and Fowler, 2009). For promoting pro-environmental products and behaviors, such influence appears to radiate outwards from immediate friends to at least the more credible social influencers that people follow (Fatima et al, 2019). There may also be value in green product placement in traditional media to impute the growing normalcy of such options (Fortuna, 2019). That is, while the brain science helps to illuminate it, exploiting the social imperative does not necessarily require a radically new approach from that of existing marketing science.

---

1 Behaviorally, perceptions about the existence of a relevant social norm can be a strong predictor of the likelihood that an individual will engage in a pro-environmental behavior.

2 The brain has specialized functional circuitry dedicated to assessing self-relevance and processing social information, including social norms. Engaging this system can help motivate behavior change.

3 The social information processing system is highly tuned for detecting social norm violations and "cheating" in general, and accordingly is primed to be triggered by marketing claims that incorporate "greenwashing."

4 In contrast, appealing to prevailing and emerging social norms in marketing communications can be an exceptionally effective tactic for encouraging pro-environmental behavior.

5 Social contagion or social proximity effects on "green" purchase behaviors suggest that even implicit conveyance of an emerging social norm communicated by the display by peers of their environmentally friendly purchasing can be a strong driver of new product adoption.

References

Abrams, D, Wetherell, M, Cochrane, S, Hogg, M A and Turner, J C (1990). Knowing what to think by knowing who you are: Self-categorization and the nature of norm formation, conformity and group polarization, *British Journal of Social Psychology*, 29, 97–119

Aharon, I, Etcoff, N, Ariely, D, Chabris, C F, et al (2001) Beautiful faces have variable reward value: fMRI and behavioral evidence, *Neuron*, 32, 537–551

Alos-Ferrer, C and Farolfi, F (2019) Trust games and beyond, *Frontiers in Neuroscience*, 13, 1–16

Amodio, D M and Frith, C D (2006) Meeting of minds: The medial frontal cortex and social cognition, *Nature Review Neuroscience*, 7, 268–277

Bartholomew, J (2015) I invented "virtue signalling". Now it's taking over the world, Spectator, 10 October, www.spectator.co.uk/article/i-invented-virtue-signalling-now-it-s-taking-over-the-world (archived at https://perma.cc/Q9DS-B4LF)

Baumeister, R F and Leary, M R (1995) The need to belong: Desire for interpersonal attachments as a fundamental human motivation, *Psychological Bulletin*, 117, 497–529

Bollinger, B and Gillingham, K (2012) Peer effects in the diffusion of solar photovoltaic panels, *Marketing Science*, 31(6), 900–912

Brown, S (1894) Outer surface of the human brain, commons.wikimedia.org/wiki/File:PSM_V46_D167_Outer_surface_of_the_human_brain.jpg (archived at https://perma.cc/CBA4-5PSW)

Byrne, R W and Whiten, A (1988) *Machiavellian Intelligence: Social expertise and the evolution of intellect in monkeys, apes, and humans*, Clarendon, Oxford

Christakis, N A and Fowler, J H (2009) *Connected: The surprising power of our social networks and how they shape our lives*, Little Brown and Co, New York

Cloutier, J, Heatherton, T F, Whalen, P J and Kelley, W M (2008) Are attractive people rewarding? Sex differences in the neural substrates of facial attractiveness, *Journal of Cognitive Neuroscience*, 20, 941–951

Cosmides, L, Barrett, H C and Tooby, J (2010) Adaptive specializations, social exchange, and the evolution of human intelligence, *Proceedings of the National Academy of Sciences*, 107, 9007–9014

Culiberg, B and Elgaaied-Gambier, L (2016) Going green to fit in: Understanding the impact of social norms on pro-environmental behaviour, a cross-cultural approach, *International Journal of Consumer Studies*, 40(2), 179–185

Dunbar, R I M (2009) The social brain hypothesis and its implications for social evolution, *Annals of Human Biology*, 36(5), 562–572

Fatima, S, et al (2019) The effect of social media influencer towards pro-environmental intention, *Business and Management Review*, 10(3), 63–68

Fornara, F, Molanario, E, et al (2020) The extended value-belief-norm theory predicts committed action for nature and biodiversity in Europe, *Environmental Impact Assessment Review*, 81, 1–9

Fortuna, C (2019) Green product placement is making sustainability cool and normal, cleantechnica.com/2019/09/18/green-product-placement-is-making-sustainability-cool-normal/ (archived at https://perma.cc/8BX7-4C4A)

Frith, C and Frith, U (2006) The neural basis of mentalizing, *Neuron*, 50, 531–534

Frith, U and Frith, C D (2003) Development and neurophysiology of mentalizing, *Philosophical Transactions of the Royal Society of London B. Biological Sciences*, 358(1431), 459–473

Ghazali, E M, Nguyen, B, Mutum, D S and Yap, S F (2019) Pro-environmental behaviours and value-belief-norm theory: Assessing unobserved heterogeneity of two ethnic groups, *Sustainability*, 11(12), 1–28

Graziano, M and Gillingham, K (2015) Spatial patterns of solar photovoltaic system adoption: The influence of neighbors and the built environment, *Journal of Economic Geography*, 15(4), 815–839

Griskevicius, V, Tybur, J M and Van den Bergh, B (2010) Going green to be seen: Status, reputation, and conspicuous conservation, *Journal of Personality and Social Psychology*, 98(3), 392–404

Krupenye, C, Kano, F, Hirata, S, Call, J and Tomasello, M (2016) Great apes anticipate that other individuals will act according to false beliefs, *Science*, 354(6308), 110–114

Leonard, C A and Williams, W J (2015) Characteristics of good poker players, *Journal of Gambling Issues*, 31, 44–67

Levy, D J, and Glimcher, P W (2012) The root of all value: A neural common currency for choice, *Current Opinion in Neurobiology*, 22(6), 1027–1038

Liu, X, Roberts, M C and Sioshansi, R (2017) Spatial effects on hybrid electric vehicle adoption, *Transportation Research Part D*, 52, 85–97

Manning, C (2009) The psychology of sustainable behavior: Tips for empowering people to take environmentally positive action, Minnesota Pollution Control Agency, September, www.pca.state.mn.us/sites/default/files/p-ee1-01.pdf (archived at https://perma.cc/9GV8-P9J8)

Martin, C and Czellar, S (2017) Where do biospheric values come from? A connectedness to nature perspective, *Journal of Environmental Psychology*, 52, 56–68

Mitchell, J P (2009) Social psychology as a natural kind, *Trends in Cognitive Sciences*, 13(6), 246–251

Northoff, G and Bermpohl, F (2004) Cortical midline structures and the self, *Trends in Cognitive Science*, 8(3), 102–107

Ochsner, K N, et al (2004) Reflecting upon feelings: An fMRI study of neural systems supporting the attribution of emotion to self and other, *Journal of Cognitive Neuroscience*, 16(10), 1746–1772

Premack, D and Woodruff, G (1978). Does the chimpanzee have a theory of mind?, *Behavioral and Brain Sciences*, 1(4), 515–526

Rogers, E (2003) *Diffusion of Innovations*, Free Press, New York

Sanfey, A G, Rilling, J K, Aronson, J A, Nystrom, L E and Cohen, J D (2003) The neural basis of economic decision-making in the Ultimatum Game, *Science*, 300, 1755–1758

Saxe, R and Kanwisher, N (2003) People thinking about thinking people: The role of the temporo-parietal junction in "theory of mind", *NeuroImage*, 19, 1835–1842

Schmidt, S, Langner, S, Hennigs, N, Wiedmann, K-P, Karampournioti, E and Lischka, G (2017) The green brand: Explicit and implicit framing effects of ecolabelling on brand knowledge, *Cogent Psychology*, 4(1), 1–23

Schmitz, T W and Johnson, S C (2006) Self-appraisal decisions evoke dissociated dorsal–ventral aMPFC networks, *NeuroImage*, 30(3), 1050–1058

Schmitz, T W and Johnson, S C (2007) Relevance to self: A brief review and framework of neural systems underlying appraisal, *Neuroscience and Biobehavioral Reviews*, 31(4), 585–596

Schmuck, D, Matthes, J and Naderer, B (2018) Misleading consumers with green advertising? An affect–reason–involvement account of greenwashing effects in environmental advertising, *Journal of Advertising*, 47(2), 127–145

Schultz, P W (2014) Strategies for promoting pro-environmental behavior: Lots of tools but few instructions, *European Psychologist*, 19(2), 107–117

Sexton, S E and Sexton, A L (2014) Conspicuous conservation: The Prius halo and willingness to pay for environmental bona fides, *Journal of Environmental Economics and Management*, 63(3), 303–317

Smith, A (1759) *The Theory of Moral Sentiments*, A. Millar, London and A. Kincaid and J. Bell, Edinburgh

Sparkman, G and Walton, G M (2017) Dynamic norms promote sustainable behavior, even if it is counter-normative, *Psychological Science*, 28(100), 1663–1674

Stern, P C (2000) Towards a coherent theory of environmentally significant behavior, *Journal of Social Issues*, 56, 407–424

Usrey, B, Palihawadana, D, Saridakis, C and Theotokis, A (2020) How downplaying product greenness affects performance evaluations: Examining the effects of implicit and explicit green signals in advertising, *Journal of Advertising*, 49(2), 1–16

Van Lier, J, Revlin, R and De Neys, W (2013) Detecting cheaters without thinking: Testing the automaticity of the cheater detection module, *PLoS ONE*, 8(1), 1–8

Van Overwalle, F (2011) A dissociation between social mentalizing and general reasoning, *NeuroImage*, 54(2), 1589–1599

Van Overwalle, F and Baetens, K (2009) Understanding others' actions and goals by mirror and mentalizing systems: A meta-analysis, *NeuroImage*, 48(3), 564–584

Veblen, T (1899) *The Theory of the Leisure Class: An economic study of institutions*, Macmillan, New York

VeganFriendly (2021) Is alcohol-based hand sanitiser vegan?, www.veganfriendly.org.uk/is-it-vegan/hand-sanitiser/ (archived at https://perma.cc/423B-MSQ5)

Vesalius, A (1543) *De Humani Corporis Fabrica Libri Septem* (On the Fabric of the Human Body in Seven Books), p 607, Johannes Oporinus, Basel

Wang, L, Zhang, G, Shi, P, Lu, X and Song, F (2019) Influence of awe on green consumption: The mediating effect of psychological ownership, *Frontiers in Psychology*, 10, 2484

White, K, Habib, R and Hardisty, D J (2019) How to SHIFT consumer behaviors to be more sustainable: A literature review and guiding framework, *Journal of Marketing*, 83(3), 22–49

Yamin, P, Fei, M, Lahlou, S and Levy, S (2019) Using social norms to change behavior and increase sustainability in the real world: A systematic review of the literature, *Sustainability*, 11(5847), 1–41

Yomogida, Y, Matsumoto, M, Aoki, R, et al (2017) The neural basis of changing social norms through persuasion, *Nature Scientific Reports*, 7(16295)

Zaki, J, Schirmer, J and Mitchell, J P (2011) Social influence modulates the neural computation of value, *Psychological Science*, 22(7), 894–900

Zinchenko, O and Arsalidou, M (2018) Brain responses to social norms: Meta-analyses of fMRI studies, *Human Brain Mapping*, 39, 955–970

07

Evading the Behavioral
Immune System

At the level of consumer behavior, the circular economy agenda of eliminating waste and keeping products and materials in use applies not just to the flow of physical materials through technical systems that provide us with all of the clothes and gadgets and other physical stuff that make our lives easier and more comfortable and stylish. It also critically applies to the biological systems that we depend on for the air we breathe, the water we drink, and the food we eat. To achieve a more sustainable way of living, consumers will need to adapt to being like astronauts living in Boulding's spaceman economy, one "in which the earth has become a single spaceship, without unlimited reservoirs of anything, either for extraction or for pollution, and in which, therefore, man must find his place in a cyclical ecological system" (Boulding, 1966).

What's it like to be a spaceman living in a closed system? In 2013 real-life Canadian astronaut Colonel Chris Hadfield became something of an internet star while he was serving as commander of the International Space Station (ISS). He shared the nature of life on an actual spaceship by posting pictures and videos on social media that documented the day-to-day activities of the ISS and conveyed its stunning views of Earth from space. Toward the end of his journey, he became a viral sensation by posting a well-crafted video, with over 47 million views to date, in which he was singing and playing an acoustic guitar while floating weightless on the ship and performing a cover version of David Bowie's *Space Oddity* (CSC ASC, 2013b).

It is a charming and poignant production that is well worth watching, but more important for our present purposes was another video he had posted a few weeks earlier that received much less attention. That video, entitled

"Astronauts drink urine and other wastewater," shared details of the water recycling system on the ISS. That entirely closed-loop system captures astronaut wastewater, including that used for personal hygiene purposes and that which is excreted: moisture from their breath, sweat, and urine. It then sterilizes the liquid and filters out contaminants. The end product is recycled water that is then reused to bathe, or drink, or rehydrate food. As Frank De Winne, a previous ISS astronaut from the European Space Agency, has colorfully noted: "On a given day, you drink a cup of coffee. The next day you drink the same cup of coffee again, and a few days later, you end up drinking your colleague's cup of coffee as well" (ESA, 2012).

Sounds a bit off-putting, but as Colonel Hadfield observed: "Before you cringe at the thought of drinking your leftover wash water and your leftover urine, keep in mind that the water that we end up with is purer than most of the water that you drink at home" (CSA ASC, 2013a). While that last bit is indeed a functional product benefit, it may not deliver quite the same emotional impact as describing something as pure, fresh water from a mountain spring. There may be some challenging emotional barriers that we will need to overcome in the transition to a more circular consumer economy.

The Disgusted Brain

Charles Darwin's third book *The Expression of the Emotions in Man and Animals* focused on the biology of emotion and its continuity across species. In it he identified six fundamental emotional states: happiness, sadness, surprise, fear, anger, and… disgust. The latter of these is one focus of this chapter. Darwin characterized the emotional experience of disgust as being elicited by a wide variety of stimuli, from direct sensations to abstract thoughts: "Disgust refers to something revolting, primarily in relation to the sense of taste, as actually perceived or vividly imagined; and secondarily to anything which causes a similar feeling, through the sense of smell, touch and even eyesight" (Darwin, 1872).

In some formulations basic emotional states can be differentiated by their various associations with specific expressive, behavioral, physiological, and subjective feeling dimensions (Ekman and Davidson, 1994). Accordingly, disgust elicits a distinctive and readily recognized facial expression—narrowed eyebrows, a wrinkling of the nose to narrow the nostrils, and a curled upper lip sometimes with protruding of the tongue (Figure 7.1). It is

FIGURE 7.1 Distinctive Facial Expression of Disgust

SOURCE DARWIN (1872). Public domain via Creative Commons.

strongly associated with an avoidance or withdrawal behavioral response that drives the individual away from the object that elicits it. It can be associated with nausea, a characteristic visceral physiological state. And it is reliably associated with a subjective feeling of revulsion.

The past few decades have seen a renaissance of research into the psychological and neural underpinnings of disgust, in large part due to the work of the psychologist Paul Rozin and his colleagues. Rozin is famed for conducting colorful laboratory research, such as examining the relative acceptance that experimental participants display for a piece of chocolate fudge shaped as a muffin versus the same fudge shaped to resemble dog feces. He has characterized the evolutionary roots of disgust as coming from the adaptive rejection of food that is potentially contaminated with infectious agents or toxins, but also claims that disgust has become a generalized response to many types of physical and even psychological contamination (Rozin and Fallon, 1987).

A wide range of potential physical contamination sources can elicit a disgust reaction. In addition to potentially spoiled or culturally inappropriate foods, these can include all manner of body effluence, depictions of poor hygiene, visible signs of infection, blood or body mutilations, dead bodies and decaying matter, and even some insects (e.g., cockroaches, maggots) and other forms of animal life. Since disgust appears to be a generalized emotional response associated with disease avoidance, it can also be elicited by other people or even inanimate non-biological objects when they possess features that suggest they have been contaminated in some way or otherwise connote a potential disease vector (Oaten et al, 2009).

Neuroimaging Disgust Reactions

A great deal of neuroimaging research has focused on trying to identify neural correlates of emotional reactions, including disgust. One area of the brain that is activated consistently by disgust-inducing stimuli is the anterior insula. When viewing emotionally neutral pictures relative to pictures designed to elicit feelings of either fear or disgust, brain activation was increased in the emotion-related amygdala for both the scary and disgusting pictures. But activation in the anterior region of the insula was only found to positively covary with subjective ratings of disgust (Stark et al, 2007).

That is, the same region of the brain that becomes highly active when a desired product has been paired with an excessive price and we choose to reject its purchase. That becomes active when the expected mental effort required to acquire a reward is high relative to the valuation of the potential payoff. And that is activated in the brain of the "responder" in the Ultimatum Game when that responder chooses to reject a monetary offer because it is perceived as unfair and in violation of an unwritten moral norm. The anterior insula tends to be activated when the person who owns it is experiencing something aversive that may signal a need for course correction.

This area has long been understood to be part of the primary "gustatory" or taste-processing cortex and to also be highly sensitive to olfactory inputs. It is also involved with the control of visceral sensations and the autonomic nervous system responses associated with them. Accordingly, the anterior insula is reliably activated by unpleasant smells and tastes and that activation tends to be correlated both with the autonomic responses and the nausea they can evoke. But its function appears to extend beyond the self-perception of disgust to having a role in the perception of the experience of disgust by others. Patients with brain damage affecting the anterior insula have been reported to display both reduced subjective sensations of disgust and a selectively impaired ability to recognize the expression of disgust in pictures of faces (Adolphs et al, 2003; Calder et al, 2000).

Convergent results have been provided by fMRI studies of the brains of intact healthy individuals. In one such study participants either inhaled odorants designed to elicit strong disgust reactions or watched video clips of scenes of others depicting the facial expression of disgust (Wicker et al, 2003). Both the personal experience of disgust and seeing disgust emoted by others were found to activate the same regions of the anterior insula. Similarly, in another study (Jabbi et al, 2008) participants had their brain scanned when they either tasted a disgusting-flavored liquid, watched film clips of actors tasting a beverage and looking disgusted in response, or simply read and imagined story scenarios involving disgusting things. All three types of stimuli elicited activation in the anterior insula of the participants relative to neutral control conditions.

SUBSPECIES OF DISGUST

Rozin and colleagues (Rozin et al, 2000) have proposed a differentiation between different types of disgust reactions:

- core disgust—that elicited by a real or perceived threat of eating something pathogenic in order to protect the body and avoid disease;
- interpersonal disgust—that elicited by potentially coming into contact with strangers who might be a source of pathogens;
- moral disgust—that elicited by violations of fairness, dishonesty, or some perceived social or cultural norm.

While physical or conceptual "core disgust" selectively activates the anterior insula, disgust involving assessments of the moral infractions of others appears to also disproportionally activate key nodes of the "mentalizing system," including the vMPFC and the TPJ (Schaich Borg et al, 2008). Similarly, patients with brain damage that impacts the vMPFC display reduced sensitivity to examples of interpersonal disgust while displaying relatively normal sensitivity to physical disgust (Ciaramelli et al, 2013). Such results suggest that our perceptions of disgust involve the "social brain," at least when those perceptions involve an interpersonal dimension. With respect to the relationship between social norm violation and attitudes toward greenwashing attempts we considered in the last chapter, suspicions about such marketing tactics may also reflect the elicitation of some degree of "moral disgust."

Disgust and the "Behavioral Immune System"

The notion that disgust is part of a generalized disease avoidance system that affects human psychology, interpersonal behavior, and many other aspects of everyday life has become almost doctrinaire in the behavioral research and evolutionary psychology communities (Apicella et al, 2018; Oaten et al, 2009; Tybur et al, 2013). Since actually getting infected in order to build up a physiological immune system response to a disease can be costly and sometimes deadly, it has been posited that we also possess a "behavioral immune system" (BIS) that helps us to pre-emptively avoid contact with potential pathogens (Schaller, 2006; Schaller and Park, 2011).

The BIS is assumed to include a variety of mental processes through which we implicitly gauge risks of being infected by evaluating threat-related environmental cues. Such cues are assumed to automatically elicit an aversive emotional reaction, prime associated mental representations, and rapidly activate avoidance behaviors. Since the consequences of missing an actual, proximal, threat-related stimulus can be particularly costly, the BIS can be easily triggered and accordingly tends to detect many false positive threats (Ackerman et al, 2018).

The Impact of the BIS on Interpersonal Interactions

Since other humans can be dangerous both in terms of potential disease transmission and on various other dimensions, the BIS is thought to be particularly tuned to infectious threats originating from unfamiliar people. Social psychologists have thus found the BIS notion to be a particularly rich area for research on interpersonal behavior. Such research has extended to studies of person perception, interpersonal attraction, prejudice, judgments of morality, and social conformity to cultural norms (Murray and Schaller, 2016). These aspects of the imputed BIS are closely related to Rozin's notions of interpersonal disgust and moral disgust.

For example, with respect to person perception, when research participants are implicitly primed with disease cues, they display more prejudice towards obese individuals, the elderly, people with disfigurements or disabilities, the homeless, and so on. Individual differences in disease risk and contextually specific cues can also heighten xenophobic attitudes and decrease sociability, as well as increase prejudice towards individuals not part of one's socially identified in-group (Ackerman et al, 2018; Faulkner et al, 2004). One can only imagine the role the BIS may play in heightening social anxiety and increasing political division during situations like the COVID-19 pandemic.

From Disgust to Magical Contagion

Rozin and his colleagues also introduced the topic of "magical contagion" to modern experimental psychology, although the roots of the notion extend back to the cultural anthropology literature of the 19th century (Frazer, 1890; Mauss, 1902). In the original formulation it refers to a primitive belief common to many cultures that intrinsic characteristics of one object can be transferred to a different object solely from some physical proximity or temporal continuity between them. In its more contemporary version, such contagion occurs when a source, which could be a person, place, or thing, passes some of its properties to a target, which could also be a person, place, or thing, through either physical or non-physical mechanisms of transference (Morales et al, 2018).

In Rozin's formulation, magical contagion was proposed to have two fundamental dimensions (Figure 7.2). With respect to the first:

> the "magic" can be positive or negative; that is, contact of an object with a loved or respected person can enhance the value of the object (positive contagion), whereas contact with a disliked or despised person (or an offensive substance such as feces) can devalue the object (negative contagion) (Rozin et al, 1986).

With respect to positive contagion, imagine that someone might pay a great deal more for a used piece of sports memorabilia that has been associated with a favorite player than they would pay for a brand-new piece of sporting

FIGURE 7.2 Dimension of Contagion: Valence and Direction of Causality

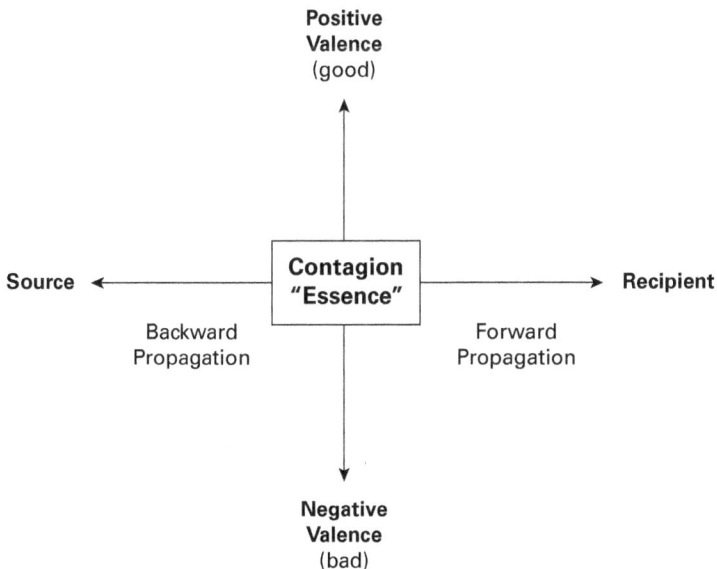

equipment straight out of the box. Conversely, with respect to negative contagion, imagine someone wanting to destroy some perfectly good or even valuable object because it had been a gift from an ex romantic partner that they had experienced a painful breakup with.

For the second proposed dimension of magical contagion, the "transmitted essence can mediate effects either in its source or in its recipient. In forward causation, the essence influences the entity it has contacted (the recipient)... in backward causation, action on the residue (essence) reflects back on its source" (Rozin et al, 1986). Forward causation in this respect might sometimes be somewhat rational in that it could lead to disease transmission, but often it is an overgeneralization of this possibility. In contrast, in the example of the estranged ex mentioned above, backward causation is more akin to incorporating some belonging of the former partner (and possibly a few stray hairs) into a voodoo doll, and then torturing the doll with the intent of harming the former partner.

Magical Contagion in the Laboratory

In both their initial report and much subsequent research, Rozin and colleagues (Rozin et al, 1986; Rozin and Nemeroff, 1990) have described a wide range of experimental evidence in support of an implicit tendency of study participants to act as if they reason under a spell of magical contagion. One example is provided by the dog feces-shaped fudge rejection result cited above. In another the researchers examined the preferences of participants for two types of juice. They then implicitly associated a dead sterilized cockroach with one of the two types of juice. That is, there was no direct contamination of the juice that the participants actually sampled. But nonetheless, on a retest trial with the same varieties of juice, the participants' own ratings for the type of juice that had been associated with the cockroach were dramatically lower than their original preference rating for that juice.

Magical Contamination Influences Consumer Behavior

Such laboratory results are curiosities that shed insight into human nature, but subsequent research has demonstrated that contagion beliefs also influence consumer behavior and preference both in the laboratory and in the marketplace.

A recent review of the literature on contagion effects in consumer contexts documented dozens of examples in which consumer research has provided convincing evidence of both negative and positive contagion effects (Huang et al, 2017).

For some examples on the negative side, people tend to rate new clothes as worse in quality and they are less willing to purchase them when it appears that other people have tried them on (Argo et al, 2006). And these preference differences appear to be associated with disgust reactions. Even the presence of disorganized store shelves (which might indirectly imply greater handling of items by other shoppers) can induce this effect (Castro et al, 2013).

Packaged products have also been shown to magically contaminate other packaged products. In another retail environment consumer marketing study (Morales and Fitzsimons, 2007), research participants were exposed to shopping carts that contained an attractive target product (e.g., a box of cookies) and a product that might implicitly activate some level of disgust reaction (e.g., a box of tampons). When the products were physically touching, respondents rated the cookie product quality as worse and were less willing to sample them than when the products were not touching. Of course, the potential for such contagion effects to occur is already well understood by many retail outlet managers at this point. At many retailers, stock personnel frequently can be seen busily straightening shelves. And when retailers consider product adjacencies on the shelf, no one stocks candy adjacent to bug spray.

Circularity, Biology, and the Behavioral Immune System

To achieve a sustainable economy, it is understood that we will need to rely upon a strategy of eliminating waste and pollution, of keeping materials in use in a circular flow, and of restoring the natural systems that both humanity and the rest of the biodiversity on the planet depend on. On the biological side of things, for consumers this means big changes in the way we use water and in the ways we produce and consume food. While implementing such changes it will be important to keep in mind that disgust is a powerful emotion, that there does seem to be something like a BIS, and its manifestations are not strictly rational.

Reflecting back to Colonel Hadfield's overview of the water recycling system on the ISS, let's consider the implications of closed-loop wastewater recycling at scale. And, specifically, ways in which to confront the "yuck" factor as it is technically referred to by researchers who study these things (Leong, 2010; Wester et al, 2016). The growing metropolitan area of San Diego, California where I live is semi-arid by nature. In an average year we only receive about 12 inches of rainfall. Since this area is hilly and covered by pavement in many places, much of that water just runs into the ocean. And as with the rest of the southwest region of the United States, a warming climate means we are more susceptible to droughts and our typical rainfall patterns are being disrupted. All of these factors mean that we currently import most of the water we use from elsewhere. And those supplies are becoming less reliable and, frankly, yuckier.

Our biggest source of imported water is piped from the Colorado River, and there are several large inland cities such as Las Vegas and Phoenix that are upstream from where we draw water. Those cities pull almost their entire water supplies from the river and clean it up and then use it. That is, it flows through their homes and industries and back into their wastewater management systems, where it is treated and then pumped back into the river such that we are on the receiving end of their treated sewage. Once it gets here it flows through our water systems into local homes and industries. And then it is treated at our local wastewater facilities and is pumped far out into the ocean.

The water isn't very good from an aesthetic viewpoint, but it is the default choice, the status quo, familiar and habitual and consequently not something most people think about very much—except for the fact that it is getting scarcer. Fortunately people are actually learning to reduce their freshwater use, so we are making progress on the resource reduction part of the sustainability equation. But there is growing awareness on the part of city planners and water management specialists that we need to start recovering and reusing as much of the water that is currently flowing out to sea as possible.

Accordingly, infrastructure plans are being made and feasibility projects are being conducted with just such a future development in mind. When those things start happening, the media starts covering it and op-ed writers and news program talking-heads start using terms like "toilet-to-tap," which in turn evokes emotional responses that undermine more rational perspectives on the part of community members concerning the advisability of moving in that direction.

This is by no means a unique local issue. It is familiar to many other regions facing these same problems. A review of media coverage on this topic in other areas with freshwater shortages (including Singapore and Australia) found that the way in which water-recycling developments were framed in the popular mind by the media in affected communities had a direct impact on the development of related social norms and popular beliefs (Leong, 2010). Yet there have also been successes in efforts aimed at helping communities overcome the "yuck factor" and accept recycled drinking water as the new norm. Let's consider how such successes can be achieved.

Reducing Disgust With Cognitive Reappraisal and Psychological Distancing

One approach to facilitating the self-regulation of emotions is to encourage participants to cognitively reappraise a situation by considering it from a more abstract and less immediate perspective. In one study in which participants were shown both emotionally neutral and disgust-inducing film clips (Goldin et al, 2008), the neutral film clips were rated as less disgust-inducing than the emotional clips, and more activation in the anterior insula and other disgust-associated regions was observed while participants watched the disgust-inducing clips relative to watching the neutral clips. In contrast, when participants were instead encouraged to review the films in a detached, objective manner from the perspective of a medical professional watching a training film, both disgust ratings and anterior insula activation were reduced for the emotionally loaded clips.

This sort of reappraisal or reframing approach appears to reduce disgust towards recycled wastewater. Quantitative survey research has confirmed that factors such as pro-environmental values, environmental knowledge, and risk tolerance are positive predictors of stated willingness to try recycled water (Wester et al, 2016). However, researchers have also observed that the degree to which one finds the idea disgusting is a much stronger negative predictor of such willingness. Even so, interventions where participants were provided with either a factual description of the recycling process or reframing descriptions that focused on positive rational or emotional benefits of using recycled water succeeded in reducing rated disgust towards recycled water and increasing willingness to try it.

Another way to encourage such reframing is to think like a strategic brand manager and/or a community-based marketer. For example, in promotional materials, the well-established, potable recycled wastewater product in Singapore is branded as *NEWater*, and in the pilot program at my local water utility the product is branded as *Pure Water*, in both cases focusing on the product benefit rather than source. And both in Singapore and in my local region, community outreach programs extend to allowing anyone interested to visit a facility, learn objectively about the process, and even sample the product as if you were in a wine-tasting room. I've done that, it's better than what I get out of my tap, I trust the process, and I am ready to sign up for home delivery.

But that's not the main plan. Another way to facilitate self-regulation of negative emotions is through the reappraisal mechanism of psychological "distancing" (Powers and LaBar, 2019). Distancing involves looking at something from a more remote perspective. That is, your BIS may be less alarmed if you think about some person with a communicable disease who lives in another town than if you imagine that the person next to you on the subway may be infected. Population-scale water recycling projects tend to exploit this effect as well. For the recycled water intended for human use, both in Singapore and in the project in my local community, the recycled water is pumped into reservoirs and aquifers and other storage facilities, where it is intermingled with the water originating from other sources, and then moved once again through the primary water purification plants that then produce the water that flows to the tap. The result of this, because of the intermingling of sources, is actually less "pure" than it would have been if taken directly from the recycling system. But at least it is more psychologically distant.

Disgust and the Problem of Food Waste

On another biological circularity front, given that the feeling of disgust most likely evolved as an adaptation to the possibility of consuming something that could cause disease or death, it is not surprising that it also plays a major role in food waste, especially in food waste at the consumer level. At least 40 percent of the agricultural products produced for food are never actually consumed by people and the associated waste is responsible for both a great deal of general environmental degradation and for a large fraction of the GHG emissions that humans are responsible for (Hawken, 2017).

At the household level over 60 percent of consumers explicitly state that their reasons for disposing of food they have purchased include concerns about food poisoning and a need to only eat "the freshest food" (Neff et al, 2015). Moreover, an individual consumer's general disgust sensitivity is a good predictor of how much food they typically waste (Egolf et al, 2018).

In recognition of the scope of the food waste problem and the challenges associated with addressing the issue, the US National Academies of Sciences, Engineering, and Medicine has recently published *A National Strategy to Reduce Food Waste at the Consumer Level* (NAS, 2020). In it they outline a variety of consumer-targeted interventions aimed at reducing food waste. One thing that doesn't appear to have much impact is an informational strategy of just increasing awareness of the problem. In fact, such a strategy may even backfire. Most people believe they waste less food than their peers (Neff et al, 2015), and so conveying a descriptive norm of wastage can appear irrelevant or even provide a moral license to waste more. In contrast, informational strategies aimed at educating consumers on how to reduce waste by modifying their shopping, food preparation, and food storage behaviors, and to help them better understand product expiration dates, appears to show promise, especially when combined with injunctive rather than descriptive normative information (Hebrok and Boks, 2017; Reynolds et al, 2019).

But to the extent which such consumer-level behavior change requires shifting well-ngrained habits, it is clear that the educational approach can only be part of the solution. Retailers can help by, for example, discouraging over-purchasing of perishable items in the first place by reducing reliance on pricing strategies (such as "buy one get one") that incentivize their custom-ers to buy more of such items than they are likely to use in a timely fashion.

And entrepreneurs are increasingly looking at technological solutions to make it easier to reduce food waste at the consumer level. For example, the OLIO smartphone app (olioex.com) connects neighbors and local businesses to make it easy to match people who have excess perishable foods and other items to share with other people nearby who may want them. Other techno-logical solutions include smart food storage containers and smart refrigerators that promise to track the expiration dates of perishable items and automati-cally alert users to any items at risk for spoilage (Kennedy, 2018).

Other innovators have focused on the rapidly growing market for "upcy-cling" pre-consumer food waste (cf. Peters, 2019). That is, taking either fruits and vegetables that might otherwise be wasted because they are too imperfect to sell to consumers in stores, or waste that is a byproduct of other food prep-arations (such as leftover grain mash from brewing operations, or the residual from the fruit that encases coffee beans that would otherwise be discarded), and turning what would otherwise be waste products into new consumer products. Such products can be healthy, tasty, and honestly marketed as sustainable in nature, turning what would otherwise be garbage into something that can be recycled through the food system.

One interesting approach to this issue turns food waste into high-quality nutritional protein. Sometimes referred to as "maggot farming" (Sguazzin, 2019), it involves using food waste of various forms to raise black fly larvae. The resulting mature larvae could in principal be converted directly into protein powder and incorporated into various food products intended for human use. But since maggots are exactly the type of thing that evokes a disgust reaction, it might be a hard sell. So instead, the larvae are fed to animals that provide more socially acceptable forms of protein such as those raised on fish and poultry farms. This form of upcycling can be viewed as... ahem... a chicken and egg solution to the problem of disgust and food waste.

Magical Contamination of the Technical Material Stream

While disgust sensitivity is especially acute for products that may be physically ingested, implicit concerns about contamination can have broader implications for circular economy efforts. At the level of consumer behavior, operations of the BIS might also impact efforts to reduce waste and keep materials in use in the "technical streams" (Ellen MacArthur Foundation, 2013) that provide us with physical goods and services.

To take a simple example, the "endowment effect" refers to a differential between how much people would be willing to pay for an item that they don't have, versus how much they would be willing to sell that same item for if they did have it. In general, they want more to part with something than they are willing to pay for it in the first place (Kahneman et al, 1991). Researchers at Carnegie Mellon University have found that if participants who have previously been endowed with a set of writing pens are then incidentally exposed to a disgusting film clip and afterwards are given an opportunity to sell their endowment, the typical differential was eliminated (Lerner et al, 2004). The disgust-eliciting film appeared to make them more eager to depart with their possession, an effect not observed in response to clips that were emotionally neutral or that evoked an emotion of sadness.

A follow-up study extended this "disgust-promotes-disposal" effect to relate it to the status quo bias that we have previously considered (Han et al, 2012). In that study participants were given a closed box that they were told contained office supplies. After viewing either a disgusting or neutral film clip, they were given the opportunity to either keep the box they were given or trade it for a new one. In the neutral condition participants displayed the typical status quo bias and chose to keep the box they already had. But participants who viewed the disgust-eliciting film were much more likely to want to trade their box away than were those in the neutral condition. Apparently magical contagion leads to the devaluation of material assets associated with a feeling of disgust, which may be one reason why (apart from instances of positive contagion such as sports memorabilia) people generally are willing to pay less for second-hand things than they are for new things of superficially the same quality (O'Reilly et al, 1984).

As we have seen, the BIS tends to make us wary in any situation in which products may have been in contact with unfamiliar people. Yet major efforts are under way to create product service models that may need to take the BIS under consideration. For example, in August 2020 the high-end UK-based department store chain Selfridges launched their "Project Earth" aimed at upending the traditional retail model in an effort to become more circular in nature and to minimize waste (Ecobahn, 2020). In addition to a commitment to source sustainable materials and design out waste, they have also adopted mechanisms to encourage keeping products in use longer—such as enabling shopping for pre-owned items and allowing customers to sell used items back into the system, options for renting fashion items rather than buying them outright, and in-store capabilities to facilitate repair of damaged items—all excellent and important innovations aimed at minimizing resource use and environmental contamination.

What is the risk of launching these types of new services in the midst of a global pandemic, when consumers are in a state of heightened concern about contagion? On the one hand, consumers have tended to display greater contamination concerns for products that come into contact with their body (especially when the other users are unknown), and used clothing definitely falls into that category (Hazee et al, 2019). On the other hand, Selfridges has the luxury of having high brand equity, and trusted brands can moderate any concerns about contamination from unknown strangers. Moreover, the moderating effect of a trusted, familiar brand seems to be particularly strong when contamination fears are heightened (Galoni et al, 2020).

Similarly, Selfridges' posh, well-organized stores can serve to minimize the potential for triggering implicit thoughts of contagion that might occur in less well-tended venues (Hazee and Van Vaerenberch, 2020). Advertising and in-store promotions can avoid images that depict strangers actually touching products on the shelf, which might inadvertently imply contagion. And, since it appears that activating the BIS can increase concerns about out-group members, advertising could serve to imply that other users of the services are all members of an elite in-group rather than some potentially threatening "other."

1 Disgust is a primitive and powerful reaction that evolved to protect us from pathogens. It is an emotional response, often irrational in nature, and one that can pose a challenge to the circular economy agenda.

2 The "behavioral immune system" is the notion that disgust underlies a psychological defense mechanism that results in avoidance reactions towards people or things that might convey pathogens, even if the potential for such contagion is so irrational as to require magical thinking.

3 The potential for eliciting disgust reactions is particularly high for products that might be ingested and especially those with ingredients recycled from the waste stream. Marketing tactics that reframe the issue with positive branding and that encourage cognitive reappraisal can mitigate this issue.

4 Automatic, implicit concerns about potential contamination can also affect non-ingestible products. Disorderly retail displays and poorly considered product adjacencies have been shown to elicit subtle disgust reactions.

5 Implicit disgust reactions can undermine circularity by encouraging early disposal, avoidance of the sharing economy, and activating suspicions about the history of used items. Green marketers need to be aware of such tendencies and employ tactics to minimize their influence.

References

Ackerman, J M, Hill, S E and Murray, D (2018) The behavioral immune system: Current concerns and future directions, *Social and Personality Psychology Compass*, 12(e12371), 1–14

Adolphs, R, Tranel, D and Damasio (2003) Dissociable neural systems for recognizing emotions, *Brain and Cognition*, 52(1), 61–69

Apicella, C L, Rozin, P, Busch, J T, Watson-Jones, R E and Legare, C H (2018) Evidence from hunter-gatherer and subsistence agricultural populations for the universality of contagion sensitivity, *Evolution and Human Behavior*, 39, 355–363.

Argo, J J, Dahl, D W and Morales, A C (2006) Consumer contamination: How consumers react to products touched by others, *Journal of Marketing*, 70, 81–94

Boulding, K E (1966) *The Economics of the Coming Spaceship Earth*, in H Jarrett (ed.) *Environmental Quality in a Growing Economy*, Resources for the Future/ Johns Hopkins University Press, Baltimore, MD

Calder, A J et al (2000) Impaired recognition and experience of disgust following brain injury, *Nature Neuroscience*, 3(11), 1077–1088

Castro, I A, Morales, A C and Nowlis, S M (2013) The influence of disorganized shelf displays and limited product quantity on consumer purchase, *Journal of Marketing*, 77(4), 118–133.

Ciaramelli, E, Sperotto, R G, Mattioli, F and di Pellegrino, G (2013) Damage to the ventromedial prefrontal cortex reduces interpersonal disgust, *Social Cognitive and Affective Neuroscience*, 8, 171–180

CSA ASC (2013a) Astronauts drink urine and other wastewater, 29 April, www. youtube.com/watch?v=ZQ2T9OJY1lg (archived at https://perma.cc/9U8D-NB78)

CSA ASC (2013b) "Space oddity, 12 May, www.youtube.com/ watch?v=KaOC9danxNo (archived at https://perma.cc/284D-DPN9)

Darwin, C (1872) *The Expression of the Emotions in Man and Animals*, John Murray, London

Ecobahn (2020) Selfridges sustainability: Project Earth, theecobahn.com/ideas/ selfridges-sustainability-project-earth/ (archived at https://perma.cc/ZJ8K-XJFA)

Egolf, A, Siegrist, M and Hartmann, C (2018) How people's food disgust sensitivity shapes their eating and food behaviour, *Appetite*, 127, 28–36

Ekman, P and Davidson, R J (1994) *The Nature of Emotion: Fundamental questions*, Oxford University Press, New York

Ellen MacArthur Foundation (2013) Towards the circular economy, www. ellenmacarthurfoundation.org/assets/downloads/publications/Ellen-MacArthur-Foundation-Towards-the-Circular-Economy-vol.1.pdf (archived at https:// perma.cc/U57B-6UJ9)

ESA (2012) Dutch Prime Minister 'phones' André Kuipers in space, www.esa.int/ Science_Exploration/Human_and_Robotic_Exploration/PromISSe/Dutch_ Prime_Minister_phones_Andre_Kuipers_in_space (archived at https://perma.cc/ X7FM-TKNM)

Faulkner, J, Schaller, M, Park, J H and Duncan, L A (2004) Evolved disease-avoidance mechanisms and contemporary xenophobic attitudes, *Group Processes and Intergroup Relations*, 7(4), 333–353

Frazer, J G (1890/1959) *The New Golden Bough: A study in magic and religion*, ed. T. H. Gaster, Macmillan, New York

Galoni, C, Carpenter, G S and Rao, H (2020) Disgusted and afraid: Consumer choices under the threat of contagious disease, *Journal of Consumer Research*, 47(3), 373–392

Goldin, P R, McRae, K, Ramel, W and Gross, J J (2008) The neural bases of emotion regulation: Reappraisal and suppression of negative emotion, *Biological Psychiatry*, 63(6), 577–586

Han, S, Lerner, J S and Zeckhauser, R (2012) The disgust-promotes-disposal effect, *Journal of Risk and Uncertainty*, 44, 101–113

Hawken, P (ed.) (2017) *Drawdown: The most comprehensive plan ever proposed to reverse global warming*, Penguin Books, London

Hazee, S, Van Vaerenberch, Y, Delcourt, C and Warlop, L (2019) Sharing goods? Yuck, no! An investigation of consumers' contamination concerns about access-based services, *Journal of Service Research*, 22(3), 256–271

Hazee, S and Van Vaerenberch, Y (2020) Customers' contamination concerns: An integrative framework and future prospects for service management, *Journal of Service Management*, 32(2), 161–175

Hebrok, M and Boks, C (2017) Household food waste: Drivers and potential intervention points for design: An extensive review, *Journal of Cleaner Production*, 151, 380–392

Huang, J Y, Ackerman, J M and Newman, G E (2017) Catching (up with) magical contagion: A review of contagion effects in consumer contexts, *Journal of the Association for Consumer Research*, 2(4), 430–443

Jabbi, M, Bastiaansen, J and Keysers C (2008) A common anterior insula representation of disgust observation, experience and imagination shows divergent functional connectivity pathways, *PLoS One*, 3(8), 1–8

Kahneman, D, Knetsch, J K and Thaler, R H (1991) Anomalies: The endowment effect, loss aversion, and status quo bias, *Journal of Economic Perspectives*, 5(1), 193–206

Kennedy, E (2018) Can kitchen tech reduce excessive food waste?, *CNN Business*, 11 July, money.cnn.com/2018/07/11/technology/startups/smarterware-fridgecam-food-waste/index.html (archived at https://perma.cc/XHQ6-6EXM)

Leong, C (2010) Eliminating "Yuck": A simple exposition of media and social change in water reuse policies, *International Journal of Water Resources Development*, 26(1), 111–124

Lerner, J S, Small, D A and Loewenstein, G F (2004) Heart strings and purse strings: Carryover effects of emotions on economic decisions, *Psychological Science*, 15(5), 337–341

Mauss, M (1902/1972) *A General Theory of Magic*, trans. Robert Brain, Norton, New York

Morales, A C, Dahl, D W and Argo, J J (2018) Amending the law of contagion: A general theory of property transference, *Journal of the Association for Consumer Research*, 3(4), 555–565

Morales, A C and Fitzsimons, G (2007) Product contagion: Changing consumer evaluations through physical contact with "disgusting" products, *Journal of Marketing Research*, 44, 272–283

Murray, D R and Schaller, M (2016) The behavioral immune system: Implications for social cognition, social interaction, and social influence, *Advances in Experimental Social Psychology*, 53, 75–129

NAS (2020) *A National Strategy to Reduce Food Waste at the Consumer Level*, National Academies of Sciences, Engineering, and Medicine, The National Academies Press, Washington, DC

Neff, R A, Spiker, M L, and Truant, P L (2015) Wasted food: U.S. consumers' reported awareness, attitudes, and behaviors, *PLoS ONE*, 10(6), 1–16

Oaten, M, Stevenson, R J and Case, T I (2009) Disgust as a disease-avoidance mechanism, *Psychological Bulletin*, 135(2), 303–321

O'Reilly, L, Rucker, M, Hughes, Marge Gorang, R and Hand, S (1984) The relationship of psychological and situational variables to usage of a second-order marketing system, *Journal of the Academy of Marketing Science*, 12(3), 53–76

Peters, A (2019) Everything you need to know about the booming business of fighting food waste, *Fast Company*, 19 June, www.fastcompany.com/90337075/inside-the-booming-business-of-fighting-food-waste (archived at https://perma.cc/MQN2-P3KZ)

Powers, J P and LaBar, K (2019) Regulating emotion through distancing: A taxonomy, neurocognitive model, and supporting meta-analysis, *Neuroscience and Biobehavioral Reviews*, 96, 155–173

Reynolds, C, Goucherc, L, Quested, T, Bromley, S et al (2019) Review: Consumption-stage food waste reduction interventions: What works and how to design better interventions, *Food Policy*, 83, 7–27

Rozin, P and Fallon, A (1987) A perspective on disgust, *Psychological Review*, 94(1), 23–44

Rozin, P, Haidt, J and McCauley, C R (2000) Disgust, in *Handbook of Emotions* (3rd edn, pp 757–776), Guilford Press, New York

Rozin, P, Millman, P R and Nemeroff, C J (1986) Operation of the laws of sympathetic magic in disgust and other domains, *Journal of Personality and Social Psychology*, 50(4), 703–712

Rozin, P and Nemeroff, C J (1990) The laws of sympathetic magic: A psychological analysis of similarity and contagion, in *Cultural Psychology: Essays on comparative human development* (pp 205–232), Cambridge University Press, Cambridge

Schaich Borg, J, Lieberman, D and Kiehl, K A (2008) Infection, incest, and iniquity: Investigating the neural correlates of disgust and morality, *Journal of Cognitive Neuroscience*, 20, 1529–46

Schaller, M (2006) Parasites, behavioral defenses, and the social psychological mechanisms through which cultures are evoked, *Psychological Inquiry*, 17(2), 96–101

Schaller, M and Park, J H (2011) The behavioral immune system (and why it matters), *Current Directions in Psychological Science*, 20(2), 99–103

Sguazzin, A (2019) Maggot farmer is expanding to California. Its mission: Turn trash into protein, *Los Angeles Times*, 31 October, www.latimes.com/business/story/2019-10-31/maggot-farmer-agriprotein-expanding-to-california# (archived at https://perma.cc/D9KP-EA2T)

Stark, R, Zimmermann, M, Kagerer, S, Schienle, A and Walter, B (2007) Hemodynamic brain correlates of disgust and fear ratings, *NeuroImage*, 37(2), 663–673

Tybur, J M, Lieberman, D, Kurzban, R and DeScioli, P (2013) Disgust: Evolved function and structure, *Psychological Review*, 120, 65–84

Wester, J, Timpano, K R, Cek, D and Broad, K (2016) The psychology of recycled water: Factors predicting disgust and willingness to use, *Water Resources Research*, 52, 3212–3226

Wicker, B, Keysers, C, Plailly, J, Royet, J P, Gallese, V and Rizzolatti, G (2003) Both of us disgusted in my insula: The common neural basis of seeing and feeling disgust, *Neuron*, 40(3), 655–664

08

Confronting the Need
for Cognitive Consistency

As we have seen, there is polarization in the general public when it comes to beliefs and attitudes about climate change. Across the general population there is a growing plurality of consumers who understand that climate change is happening, that it is due to human endeavor, and that it is a cause for serious concern. But there is also a small but fairly stable minority of people who say they are very sure that climate change is not happening, or that global warming is caused mostly by natural changes in the environment, not by human influences.

We have also seen that there is a subset of people who are almost militantly anti-green consumers. Members of that group lack any personal norms or sensitivity towards societal norms that might compel them in that direction, they display little in the way of environmental concern, and don't want to be hassled with thinking about it. According to researchers:

> this segment lacks expertise regarding green products, does not feel that green products are a good value or of high quality, lacks trust in green companies, and tends to believe that they alone cannot make a positive impact on the planet through green consumption (Gleim et al, 2013).

This chapter considers the implications that such deeply held beliefs and attitudes have for shifting market behavior towards a more sustainable direction. In it we will examine the psychological mechanisms that reinforce such hardened perspectives and the marketing considerations that they imply.

People Have a Strong Need to be Cognitively Consistent

In 1954 the social psychologist Leon Festinger and some of his colleagues (1956) infiltrated a UFO cult in Chicago. The widely publicized cult believed that an apocalyptic flood would occur before dawn on December 21 of that year, based on messages the cult's leader received from a superior race from another planet. And they were committed to a belief that the group members would be rescued from that event by a flying saucer at midnight the evening before the flood.

The degree of commitment on the part of many of the cult's members was so high that they quit their jobs or spouses or coursework, and sold their possessions or gave away their money in advance of the event. After midnight came and went, the cult members were troubled by their missed connection and struggled to find reasons for it. The leader informed them that a message had been received that the world had been spared the apocalypse because of the excellent proselytizing they had conducted, and hence no spaceship escape plan was needed. That settled, instead of modifying their beliefs, the relieved cult members continued to go about their work of sharing an updated doomsday message with more fervor and stronger commitment than before.

Many decades later, writing in the magazine *The Atlantic*, Elliot Aronson (a former student of Festinger's) and his coauthor Carol Tavris (2020) observed that once we make a decision about something, we seek to find reasons to justify it and to discount information inconsistent with it. They characterized the notion of "cognitive dissonance" (coined by Festinger) as a motivational drive that undermines our ability to rationally even-weight belief-inconsistent points of view or even to accept scientific facts as real. While their article was intended to consider the potential life-and-death consequences of such belief regulation mechanisms on polarized attitudes and ineffectual responses to the COVID-19 pandemic, they illustrated the issue with yet another spaceship-related anecdote.

This one was associated with the formerly San Diego, California-based "Heaven's Gate" religious cult. The premise of the cult held that when the Hale-Bopp comet was making a close pass by Earth in 1997, it was being followed in its tail by a spaceship, and that spaceship would transport true believers into some higher form of existence. According to Aronson and Tavris:

> Several members of the group bought an expensive, high-powered telescope so that they might get a clearer view of the comet. They quickly brought it back and asked for a refund. When the manager asked why, they complained that

the telescope was defective, it didn't show the spaceship following the comet. A short time later, believing that they would be rescued once they had shed their "earthly containers" (their bodies), all 39 members killed themselves (Aronson and Tavris, 2020).

Famously, all were wearing matching Nike athletic shoes for some reason, shoes in a currently discontinued style that because of some type of weird contagion now trade at a large premium for collectors of such things.

"Hobgoblin" or Cognitive Dissonance?

The fact that people strive to vigorously maintain and defend their mental models of the world, especially when those models are shared with social networks, has long been a focus of thoughtful consideration. The poet, philosopher, and armchair social psychologist Ralph Waldo Emerson, the major proponent of Transcendentalism in the first half of the 19th century, was very aware of the power of social norms and personal norms and the compelling conflict that occurs when people seek to deviate from them. He felt that the need to conform seemed to stifle individual development and creativity and therefore claimed: "Who so would be a man must be a nonconformist" (Emerson, 1841).

Likewise, he was notably not a fan of any intrinsic need to maintain consistent beliefs or attitudes. He felt people tended to determinedly hold on to past positions rather than being rational about changing their minds, mainly out of a need to not appear inconsistent and a little sketchy in the eyes of others. That is, he too would have also ascribed to the modern notion that people have a "Theory of Mind." In his essay *Self Reliance*, he disparaged the human need to strive to be internally consistent. In his words: "A foolish consistency is the hobgoblin of little minds, adored by little statesmen and philosophers and divines" (Emerson, 1841).

Leon Festinger also felt that the negative emotions experienced in response to a threat of being seen as inconsistent were a bit of a mental shackle. But in contrast to Emerson, he saw an opportunity to pursue an interesting research agenda instead of just cause to pontificate. Hot on the heels of his undercover cult-member adventure, he published his seminal work *A Theory of Cognitive Dissonance* (Festinger, 1957). In it he outlined the aversive feeling state of "cognitive dissonance": a feeling that arises in situations where one's sense of internal consistency is threatened by the existence of attitudes, beliefs, or behaviors that are in conflict with one another.

Two basic hypotheses about cognitive dissonance emerged from Festinger's early work on this topic:

- The uncomfortable feeling state of dissonance motivates the person to try to reduce the inconsistency at the source of it—by either changing their actions or changing their attitudes and beliefs to make them more consistent (Figure 8.1).

- Along with trying to actively reduce cognitive dissonance by making their actions and thoughts more consistent, people will also tend to avoid information and situations that might induce it in the future.

These general theoretical notions have inspired decades of experimental investigations exploring their implications. We'll consider the second hypothesis in the next section. With respect to the first, a variety of conditions have been shown to reliably produce the types of changes in actions or thought processes predicted by Festinger's theoretical view. Reviewing a few can be instructive.

Conditions Eliciting Cognitive Dissonance

One such condition involves belief disconfirmation like that involved in the Heaven's Gate example. Another dissonance-inducing condition involves getting someone to do something publicly that they wouldn't normally do when left to their own preferences, a method often referred to as "forced

FIGURE 8.1 Festinger's Theory of Cognitive Dissonance

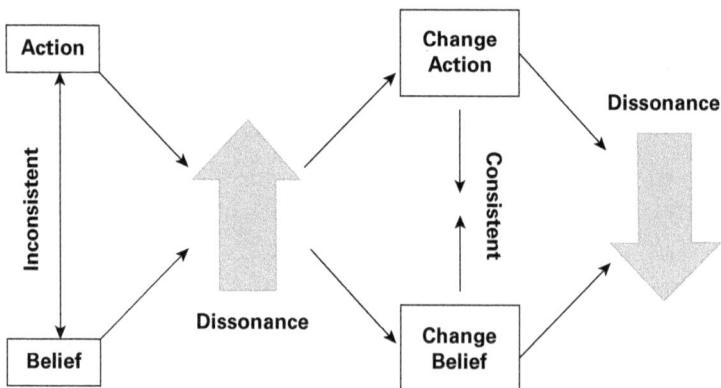

compliance" (Festinger and Carlsmith, 1959). In one such study researchers asked student participants to make a counter-attitudinal statement about a serious issue (Helmreich and Collins, 1968). Some students were asked to do so for an anonymous audio recording. Others were asked to do so for a non-anonymous video recording with no chance to change their minds and which might be shown to their classmates afterwards. Some of the students were paid a small amount for participating, while others were paid a larger amount.

The largest post-intervention changes in attitudes were found in the students in the most publicly committed group (non-anonymous video recordings) who received the lowest amount of payment (and hence could not easily rationalize that they were just doing it for the money). This latter result is interesting in that Festinger's original formulation focused primarily on resolution of inconsistencies internal to the individual, but the finding that the potential for public inconsistencies—differences between a new behavior and things an individual might have done or said in the past— greatly increased the amount of attitude change observed as a result of engaging in a counter-attitudinal behavior. This suggests that dissonance is especially acute when cognitive inconsistencies occur in a social context. Accordingly, for many decades researchers have incorporated this social dimension of cognitive dissonance into theories of "impression management," arguing that "the phenomenon will occur whenever an individual can be held intentionally responsible for his behaviors and is concerned with the attributions others make about him" (Tedeschi et al, 1971).

Subsequent research has come to suggest that dissonance is most pronounced when others might view an action as inconsistent with the view of oneself that one wants to portray to them (Bargh, 2018), which in turn helps us to better understand the power of social norms to influence behavior. It also suggests that Ralph Waldo Emerson was right to conclude that people are driven to appear consistent in the eyes of others.

Cognitive Dissonance and Consumer Behavior

A variety of evidence indicates that cognitive dissonance and efforts to reduce it can play an important role in consumer behavior (Cummings and Venkatesan, 1976). Some of that research has focused on leveraging laboratory research on the drive towards self-consistency as a tool to encourage pro-environmental behaviors in commercial settings. For example, in one large-scale study of real-world behavior, over 2,000 guests at a large business hotel were asked to make a commitment at check-in to save water and energy by reusing their bath towels, and were then given a small pin to wear to signal their commitment to being environmentally friendly (Baca-Motes et al, 2013).

Unknown to the participants, after check-out their towel use was scored as a primary measure, and a variety of other pro-environmental behaviors (such as turning off the lights on departure) were secondarily monitored. Compared with guests who were not asked to make such a commitment, the guests who had done so were 25 percent more likely to have reused at least one towel, and towel reuse among the committed guests increased 40 percent overall.

This type of behavior change is consistent with previous research on other forms of social nudges that have found positive impacts on this target behavior (Schultz et al, 2008). Baca-Motes and colleagues (2013) also found that although the commitment the guests had made was specific to towel reuse, those who made such a commitment were also more likely to have turned the lights off in their room on departure, suggesting the impact of having committed to a specific pro-environmental behavior generalized to other environmental concerns.

Other studies have focused on issues regarding how attitudes change once people choose between competing alternatives of similar value. In one of the earliest studies of this nature (Brehm, 1956), participants were asked to rate a variety of domestic appliances on their desirability, and then were provided a forced-choice situation in which they could choose one of two different appliances from the set as a reward for their participation. After making their choice they were again requested to rate the desirability of the list of appliances they had previously rated. On that second rating they tended to rate the option that they had selected to receive in the choice procedure higher than they had initially. And the rejected alternative was rated lower in desirability than they had rated it initially. Many subsequent studies have confirmed this basic effect.

Imaging the Brain During Cognitive Dissonance and Its Resolution

Let's look at the neural correlates of this tendency. While doing so, keep in mind that it is a concern for the green agenda, as it suggests that consumers' prior choices bias their future preferences.

What do studies that have examined choice show? One of the earliest studies of this nature was conducted using the forced-compliance type of experimental protocol (van Veen et al, 2009), and in general participants displayed the type of explicit attitude change that is expected in such circumstances. The brain imaging data during a conflict situation included increased activation in the anterior cingulate cortex and anterior insula, areas that we have seen are involved with processing response conflict and aversive affective reactions.

A very similar pattern of activation was observed in a study that induced dissonance by prompting participants to reflect on everyday personal experiences that were inconsistent with values they had expressed support for (de Vries et al, 2015). To the extent to which the anterior insula is involved with regulating autonomic nervous system reactivity, it is worthwhile to also note that a variety of evidence indicates that cognitive dissonance has frequently been associated with changes in metrics of autonomic arousal such as skin conductance, heart rate, and other metrics (Martinie et al, 2013).

Of key importance for current concerns are studies examining brain responses to dissonance induction in discriminative choice experiments, as well as the way in which those responses change after dissonance resolution. One hint of the changes in preferences that occur with dissonance resolution was observed in a study in which participants, while undergoing fMRI measurements, rated a series of possible future events in terms of how pleasurable they expected them to be (Sharot et al, 2009).

The participants were then required to choose between pairs of alternatives that they had previously rated as equivalent with respect to expected outcomes. After that choice they were again scanned while re-rating the same list of possible future events they had initially scored. Behaviorally they displayed the expected post-decision preference change in that the items they chose in the decision procedure were then rated as potentially more pleasurable than the items they rejected in the choice procedure. In terms of the brain imaging results, in the post-choice session the chosen items were associated with a relative increase in activation in brain reward centers relative to the pre-choice session, whereas rejected alternatives were associated with a decrease in activation in reward centers relative to the pre-choice period.

A broader picture of how attitudes and brain activation change after making a choice has been illustrated by a number of subsequent studies. First, as with the behavioral literature, increased attractiveness of selected options is consistently observed in post-choice ratings versus pre-choice ratings. Relatively difficult choices between similarly valued items are associated with greater activation in the anterior cingulate and anterior insula during the decision period than are easier choices of dissimilarly valued items, consistent with the notion that choosing between equally valued items results in greater cognitive dissonance (Kitayama et al, 2013; Izuma et al, 2010).

Post-choice activity appears to increase activity in the reward system including the NAcc region of the ventral striatum for chosen options but not for previously equally valued rejected options (Izuma et al, 2010). And a reappraisal process appears to be rapidly engaged in the decision-making period that incorporates a wide range of areas involved with cognitive control, self-reference, and valuation, with concomitant down-regulation of activation in the anterior insula and increased activation of the vMPFC and ventral striatum. This pattern of change was found to be predictive of a relatively increased subsequent preference for chosen items and decreased preference for rejected options (Jarcho et al, 2010; Qin et al, 2011).

What do such findings imply for our consideration of the green consumer? On the one hand, it is once again clear that people will be predisposed to continue with their previous choices rather than consider alternatives. It also suggests that when considering between new competing options, once one of those options is rejected it will become more likely to be rejected in future considerations. On the other hand, if a green option is selected in such a competition, it will enjoy the boosted preference that chosen options enjoy. Marketers would thus do well to make it easy for potential customers to choose their product on an initial encounter if they want to mold preferences and increase the likelihood of additional selection on future purchase occasions.

The Brain Builds Its Own Filter Bubbles

In his best-selling book *The Filter Bubble: What the internet is hiding from you*, the liberal activist and entrepreneur Eli Pariser described how personalization algorithms on the internet serve to create cozy cognitive cocoons (Pariser, 2012). Search engines, ecommerce companies, and social media feeds all are built on predictive preference models of what individual users might want to see based on data from their past click-through behavior, search history, location, any known demographics, and other data they might be able to access (including your financial history), and then use those models to customize what users are exposed to.

While being a very profitable business model that allows such companies to offer up addictive content, customized advertising, or particularly seductive product purchase opportunities, such "filter bubbles" hide information from users if that information might disagree with users' predilections or challenge their preconceived notions, which of course also insulates the users from any existential pain of cognitive dissonance. But as a consequence, it also essentially intellectually isolates them in ideological niches—constrained views of the world inhabited by like-minded affiliates.

The technology that enables such customization is very much a 21st-century development. But the brain has been evolving its own such dissonance reduction tools for thousands of generations. Let's consider the implications of Festinger's second hypothesis, that people will actively try to avoid information and situations that might induce cognitive dissonance, and the implication that people might instead seek out ideas and settings that are cognitively consistent with their existing attitudes and self-image. While cognitive dissonance appears to be an aversive affective state that we try to resolve by changing behaviors, beliefs, or attitudes, the cognitive processes that enable "confirmation bias" and "motivated reasoning" serve to help us to avoid that bad feeling in the first place. Those tendencies build an ideological filter bubble in the brain all on their own.

Confirmation Bias and Motivated Reasoning

Confirmation bias refers to an automatic tendency to notice, interpret positively, and remember information that reinforces an existing belief. Once a belief is formed there is a natural tendency to quickly detect and accept information that is consistent with it and ignore facts inconsistent with it.

Motivated reasoning on the other hand is a complementary bias to uncritically accept data and arguments consistent with a pre-existing belief, while also more critically scrutinizing data and arguments and their sources if they are inconsistent with such a belief. These effects are strongest for deeply held beliefs and in situations that can elicit strong emotional responses or threaten personal moral values—like issues related to politics, religion, health, family, etc. Confirmation bias and especially motivated reasoning have been characterized as tools that the brain uses to create solutions to problems it faces that minimize unpleasant feelings and maximize positive ones (Westen, 1994).

As noted in one early research project that examined these issues, people tend to:

> accept "confirming" evidence at face value while subjecting "disconfirming" evidence to critical evaluation, and, as a result, draw undue support for their initial positions from mixed or random empirical findings. Thus, the result of exposing contending factions in a social dispute to an identical body of relevant empirical evidence may be not a narrowing of disagreement but rather an increase in polarization (Lord et al, 1979).

To illustrate the effect, the authors exposed people who either supported or disapproved of capital punishment to two purported research articles about the topic—one that presented evidence for it and one that presented evidence against it. Both groups rated the article that confirmed their pre-existing attitude as having better methods and more convincing results. And the net effect of the articles was to increase polarization in attitudes between the groups after they had been exposed to them.

In the study by Lord and colleagues, the authors forced exposure of the relevant articles on the participants, but in the real world people tend to consider dis-confirmatory evidence even less. In a research literature that has grown to include hundreds of such investigations, confirmation bias appears to be ubiquitous in both informal reasoning situations and in the scientific process itself (Nickerson, 1998). It manifests itself most prominently when attitudes are strongly and confidently held (Pomerantz et al, 1995).

Amplifying Confirmatory Evidence and Discounting the Dis-confirmatory

A recent brain neurophysiology study suggests that under conditions of high confidence in a simple perceptual decision-making task, post-decision confirmatory information tends to be selectively amplified in the brain, whereas dis-confirmatory evidence tends to not even be processed (Rollwage et al, 2020). Analogous results were observed in a second study that employed fMRI scans during a more complicated task that included an interpersonal component (Kappes et al, 2020).

In that latter study pairs of participants were shown pictures of houses paired with a market price number, and they were asked to decide whether the true sales price was actually higher or lower than the price they were shown. They were also allowed to place a bet after making their decision, the magnitude of which was used as a measure of decision confidence. They were then shown the (purported) decision and the wager of the other member of the pair, which either agreed or disagreed with their own. And they were then given the opportunity to either stick with their initial decisions or alter them.

Behaviorally participants were more likely to take into consideration the choice and confidence level of their "partner" in cases where that partner agreed with them, and to discount any dis-confirmatory information in cases where the partner disagreed with their judgment. Similarly, the neuroimaging data displayed sensitivity to the partner's confidence level in agreement trials, but no such sensitivity in disagreement trials.

The tendency to discount dis-confirmatory information is especially strong when beliefs or attitudes have personal importance because they are attached to one's self-concept, personal values, or social group identification, and accordingly are resistant to change (Howe and Krosnick, 2017). These are also the conditions where people are most likely to engage in motivated reasoning. In a seminal review of the literature on this type of bias, Ziva Kunda referred to motivated reasoning as the "tendency to find arguments in favor of conclusions we want to believe to be stronger than arguments for conclusions we do not want to believe" (Kunda, 1990). That is, rather than just ignoring dis-confirmatory points of view, as appears to occur with confirmation bias, motivated reasoning can also involve mental counterarguing in an effort to find reasons to disbelieve evidence that runs counter to existing beliefs (Figure 8.2).

FIGURE 8.2 Motivated Reasoning and the Brain's Response to New Information

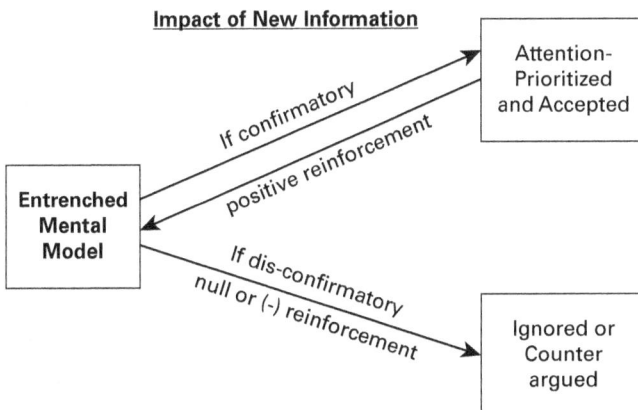

Motivated Skepticism

Some instances of motivated reasoning can be better characterized as "motivated skepticism" (Ditto and Lopez, 1992). This type of response appears to be an active cognitive process. In studies where participants are asked to rate statements as true or false, statements that are judged as true elicit greater activation in the vMPFC (Harris et al, 2009; Harris et al, 2008), an area we have seen is involved with judgments of self-relevance and personal value. When highly motivated political partisans have been asked to consider information that reinforced or threatened the image of a preferred candidate, activation was observed in a constellation of areas including the vMPFC, insula, and portions of the mentalizing network in ways that are not seen in cold, non-motivated reasoning tasks where people do not have a strong emotional predisposition towards information (Westen et al, 2006; Hyatt et al, 2015). In other political reasoning tasks, more activation has been found in the anterior insula and amygdala of participants who were most resistant to any change in their beliefs after being confronted with belief-challenging information than in participants who could be persuaded to modify their pre-existing perspective (Kaplan et al, 2016).

As we've seen, a high degree of belief polarization is associated with the topic of climate change and global warming. A somewhat hardened minority of the population, most commonly individuals that are relatively religious, politically conservative, and antagonistic towards government, persists in either disputing the existence of the phenomenon or doubting that it reflects human influences, despite massive evidence to the contrary. As a result, this is a growing area of interest for research on motivated reasoning and related issues.

In a recent review, Druckman and McGrath (2019) concluded that while the evidence for this resistance to update beliefs is consistent with the idea of motivated reasoning, it could also just reflect a more "cold" cognitive analysis, where people try to form accurate beliefs but differ in terms of what the true believers trust to be credible evidence. But of course, that is pretty much mincing words, when the scientific consensus and day-to-day reality points both to the existence and human source of the change in climate.

Motivated Skepticism and Failures of Self-Insight

Of key relevance here is research that has shown that individuals who cling to extreme beliefs in the face of dis-confirmatory evidence also tend to display a type of metacognitive failure in their performance of even low-level perceptual discrimination judgment tasks (Rollwage et al, 2018). Participants in that study displayed reduced insight into how correct their responses were and a reduced tendency to update their confidence when presented with dis-confirmatory evidence after making a perceptual decision.

Such evidence suggests that there may be a tendency among people who hold extreme beliefs to also fail to update their self-assessments in general, even in a domain wholly different from any emotional context or extreme sociocultural belief that they hold. Strong believers also tend to suffer from a "false consensus" bias in that they are disproportionately prone to also believe that other people share their viewpoint, beyond any facts to the contrary (Ross et al, 1977). As an example, with respect to climate change beliefs, research from Australia indicates:

> that opinions about climate change are subject to strong false consensus effects, that people grossly overestimate the numbers of people who reject the existence of climate change in the broader community, and that people with high false consensus bias are less likely to change their opinions (Leviston et al, 2012).

This view of a cognitive deficit or limitation in perceptual processing in extremists is consistent with emerging data that suggests there exists "motivated attention" for detecting or failing to detect relevant climate-change-related data. In one eye-tracking and behavioral study, liberal or conservative participants were exposed to graphs of longitudinal data that either were labeled as reflecting global temperature change data from 1880–2013 or as reflecting some neutral dimension over the same timeframe. That study found that political orientation was associated with how visual attention was deployed and how accurate estimates of change over a specific interval were when the graphs were labeled as climate data as opposed to neutral labeling (Luo and Zhao, 2019).

In the face of presumably strongly held beliefs, automatic biases to overlook dis-confirmatory information when possible, and dissonance-reducing tendencies to be hyper-skeptical about such information when it can't just be ignored, is there any hope of shifting the attitudes of people with such polarized views in order to reduce their denial of things like climate change? There are reasons to think that some skeptical attitudes towards climate change can in fact be reduced both by personal experiences and by informational interventions, at least among a persuadable middle.

In one study researchers measured the implicit attitudes of residents on the US East Coast towards hypothetical political figures either committed or opposed to policies for combatting climate change (Rudman et al, 2013). At an initial measurement period, participants displayed an implicit negative attitude towards a "green" politician. In a twist of fate, over a period of 14 months, two devastating hurricanes then impacted the region after the initial measurement period. Following the storms, the researchers re-examined implicit attitudes towards green politicians and found a complete reversal of the original bias, instead finding an implicit positive attitude in favor of the green politician—especially among participants who had personally experienced the effects of the hurricanes. They also found an overall shift toward increased explicit belief in anthropogenic sources of climate change between the two test periods.

Another study (Beattie and McGuire, 2020) found that exposing research participants with low levels of environmental concern to emotionally loaded informational videos about climate change positively modified implicit attitudes towards low-carbon-footprint products as well as expressed product preference. Such results suggest that interventions intended to increase environmental knowledge and concern can be effective, at least among people who are not overtly skeptical and defensive about the issue at hand.

Motivated Skepticism and Green Marketing

Writing about denial and skepticism in his ground-breaking book *Don't Even Think About It: Why our brains are wired to ignore climate change*, George Marshall, founder of the Climate Outreach and Information Network based in Oxford, England, notes that with respect to climate change, "More than any other issue it exposes the deepest workings of our mind, and shows our extraordinary and innate talent for seeing only what we want to see and disregarding what we would prefer not to know" (2014).

So how does one address the skeptics in denial? The best tactics to take with environmental skeptics and climate change deniers may be to not cause them associated dissonance in the first place. While people with liberal political leanings and high levels of environmental concern might respond to marketing appeals that highlight environmental benefits of products and services, others with more conservative political leanings can still find other benefits attractive if those benefits are framed in a way that doesn't conflict with their personal identity and values.

Consider that someone with high environmental concerns might buy an energy-efficient light bulb that is priced higher than an incandescent light bulb based on the notion that it is better for the environment, whereas someone without those concerns might nonetheless find them attractive because of overall energy and cost savings. Similarly, research on adoption of rooftop solar has suggested that people of more conservative leanings will respond to benefits of the technology that are framed not in terms of environmental impacts but rather in terms of cost savings, and in terms of a libertarian-leaning ideology of increasing energy independence and economic liberty (Mooney, 2015a, 2015b). From another perspective, Tesla's success in the electric car market has depended as much or more on high performance, attractive styling, and a general "cool" factor rather than any overt appeal to environmental benefits.

One doesn't have to be a committed environmentalist to be persuaded to buy green, but to reach those who aren't so sustainably predisposed, it is critical to make sure a product offering has functional or emotional benefits that extend beyond just the environmental ones.

Green Skepticism and Greenwashing

An example of motivated reasoning that is undoubtedly underpinned in part by the same psychological proclivities as those responsible for climate change skepticism is the somewhat broader emerging concept of "green skepticism." This concept refers to the tendency of consumers to doubt the environmental benefits or the environmental performance of a green product. As noted above, a small subset of the population has strongly held anti-green attitudes and is highly skeptical of green marketing claims. While this extreme group is a minority of the population, their attitudes are shared to at least some degree by a much broader range of consumers.

A number of empirical studies have now demonstrated that while factors such as environmental concern and perceived behavioral efficacy are positive predictors of green purchase intent (GPI), green skepticism negatively moderates GPI (Albayrak et al, 2011; Kwong and Balajii, 2016; Leonidou and Skarmeas, 2017). Others have found that a major factor promoting green skepticism is, once again, consumer concerns about greenwashing or unsubstantiated pro-environmental claims in product or corporate advertising (Chang, 2011; Kwong and Balajii, 2016; Nguyen et al, 2019; Silva et al, 2019).

That is, while some green skeptics might be unconvinced about the extent of human impacts on the environment in general, others might well possess some level of environmental knowledge and concern. But both subgroups might also—rightly in some instances—be skeptical about the claims made by marketers concerning the actual greenness of their product and service offerings.

Building on our earlier observations, people tend to be wary of others in general, and they are particularly sensitive to any perceived violation of norms around fairness and trust. The greenwashing effect tends to be greater when environmental claims are made more strongly and explicitly, and can in some instances lead to reduced ratings of product attractiveness (Chang, 2011) and even negative "word of mouth" (Leonidou and Skarmeas, 2017).

Fortunately marketers have several tools at their disposal to counter green skepticism. First and foremost, don't engage in greenwashing tactics. People are quick to detect it. If they do, it's likely to shift their attitudes against both the product and the manufacturer. If maintaining the trust of your customers and keeping them loyal for the long run is important for your business model, deceiving them is not an effective way to do so. Plus, they will tell their friends. It could even be illegal in some instances, if often only laxly enforced.

Second, even if your product has real and verifiable sustainability bene-fits, you might want to soft-sell them. Strongly worded claims are more likely to elicit skepticism and can lead to your product being implicitly asso-ciated with negative emotional reactions. In contrast, implying green benefits indirectly rather than leading with them can improve overall product evalu-ations (Usrey et al, 2020).

Third, to build trust, use widely recognized third-party certifications on your packages and advertising where appropriate. And support educational efforts to promote the certifying bodies and explain the certifications to consumers. A preponderance of evidence suggests that—when understood by consumers—such certifications can provide a quick method to convey the greenness of products without necessarily eliciting a green skepticism response. Finally, make it easy for potential consumers to choose your product in the first place, as cognitive dissonance will only lead to it becom-ing less attractive as a future option if a competing product is first chosen instead of it.

1   When an individual's beliefs and actions are inconsistent, especially in the eyes of others, they are often driven by an uncomfortable feeling of cognitive dissonance to bring those beliefs and feelings into better alignment. While this fact can pose challenges for efforts to expand the market for green products and services, it can also be leveraged to the advantage of green marketers.

2   If one can influence an initial green product choice by a consumer, that consumer will likely display an increased preference for that product and enjoy it more on future choice occasions. Similarly, if one can elicit a small public commitment by someone to engage in a pro-environmental behavior, they are more likely to engage in that behavior in the future.

3   People try to actively avoid experiencing cognitive dissonance by prioritizing information that confirms their predilections and avoiding or discounting information that might challenge their beliefs or actions; that is, they engage in confirmation bias and motivated reasoning.

4   Many people possess some degree of "green skepticism" with respect to marketing claims about product characteristics, especially those consumers who are relatively low in environmental concern; accordingly, clumsy greenwashing tactics may well backfire with much of one's potential audience.

5   For green skeptics, rational appeals for a change in beliefs or choice behavior are unlikely to be effective if the rationale focuses on environmental benefits over other concerns. To target that audience, instead focus on other types of product benefits (cost-effectiveness, health, performance) or emotional benefits (style, status) instead of sustainability-oriented issues.

References

Albayrak, T, Caber, M, Moutinho, L and Herstein, R (2011) The influence of skepticism on green purchase behavior, *International Journal of Business and Social Science*, 2(13), 189–197

Aronson, E and Tavris, C (2020) The role of cognitive dissonance in the pandemic, *The Atlantic*, 12 July, www.theatlantic.com/ideas/archive/2020/07/role-cognitive-dissonance-pandemic/614074/ (archived at https://perma.cc/AHK9-6M2G)

Baca-Motes, K, Brown, A, Keenan, E A and Nelson L D (2013) Commitment and behavior change: Evidence from the field, *Journal of Consumer Research*, 39, 1070–1084

Bargh, J A (2018) It was social consistency that mattered all along, *Psychological Inquiry*, 29(2), 60–62

Beattie, G and McGuire, L (2020) The modifiability of implicit attitudes to carbon footprint and its implications for carbon choice, *Environment and Behavior*, 52(5), 467–494

Brehm, J (1956) Post-decision changes in desirability of alternatives, *Journal of Abnormal and Social Psychology*, 52(3), 384–389

Chang, C (2011) Feeling ambivalent about going green, *Journal of Advertising*, 40(4), 19–32

Cummings, W H and Venkatesan, M (1976) Cognitive dissonance and consumer behavior: A review of the evidence, *Journal of Marketing Research*, 13(3), 303–308

de Vries, J, Byrne, M and Kehoe, E (2015) Cognitive dissonance induction in everyday life: An fMRI study, *Social Neuroscience*, 10(3), 268–281

Ditto, P H and Lopez, D F (1992) Motivated skepticism: Use of differential decision criteria for preferred and nonpreferred conclusions, *Journal of Personality and Social Psychology*, 63(4), 568–584

Druckman, J N and McGrath, M C (2019) The evidence for motivated reasoning in climate change preference formation, *Nature Climate Change*, 9, 111–119

Emerson, R W (1841) Self-Reliance, in C E Eliot (ed.), *Essays and English Traits*, Harvard Classics, Volume 5, 1965 edition, P.F. Collier & Son Corporation, New York

Festinger, L (1957) *A Theory of Cognitive Dissonance*, Stanford University Press, Palo Alto, CA

Festinger, L and Carlsmith, J M (1959) Cognitive consequences of forced compliance, *Journal of Abnormal and Social Psychology*, 58(2), 203–210

Festinger, L, Riecken, H W and Schachter, S (1956) *When Prophecy Fails: A social and psychological study of a modern group that predicted the destruction of the world*, Harper Collins, New York

Gleim, M R, Smith, J S, Andrews, D, and Cronin, J (2013) Against the green: A multi-method examination of the barriers to green consumption, *Journal of Retailing*, 89(1), 44–61

Harris, S, Kaplan, J T, Curiel, A, Bookheimer, S Y, Iacoboni, M and Cohen, M S (2009) The neural correlates of religious and nonreligious belief, *PLoS ONE*, 4(10), e7272

Harris, S, Sheth, S A and Cohen, M S (2008) Functional neuroimaging of belief, disbelief, and uncertainty, *Annals of Neurology*, 63, 141–147

Helmreich, R and Collins, B E (1968) Studies in forced compliance: Commitment and magnitude of inducement to comply as determinants of opinion change, *Journal of Personality and Social Psychology*, 10(1), 75–81

Howe, L C and Krosnick, J A (2017) Attitude strength, *Annual Review of Psychology*, 68, 327–351

Hyatt, C J, Calhoun, V D, Pearlson, G D and Assaf, M (2015) Specific default mode subnetworks support mentalizing as revealed through opposing network recruitment by social and semantic FMRI tasks, *Human Brain Mapping*, 36(8), 3047–3063

Izuma, K, Matsumoto, M, Murayama, K, Samejima, K, Sadato, N and Matsumoto, K (2010) Neural correlates of cognitive dissonance and choice-induced preference change, *Proceedings of the National Academy of Sciences*, 107(51), 22014–22019

Jarcho, J M, Berkman, E T and Lieberman, M D (2010) The neural basis of rationalization: Cognitive dissonance reduction during decision-making, *Social Cognitive and Affective Neuroscience*, 6(4), 460–467

Kaplan, J, Gimbel, S and Harris, S (2016) Neural correlates of maintaining one's political beliefs in the face of counterevidence, *Scientific Reports*, 6, 39589

Kappes, A, Harvey, A H, Lohrenz, T, Montague, P R and Sharot, T (2020) Confirmation bias in the utilization of others' opinion strength, *Nature Neuroscience*, 23, 130–137

Kitayama, S, Chua, H F, Tompson, S and Han, S (2013) Neural mechanisms of dissonance: An fMRI investigation of choice justification, *NeuroImage*, 69, 206–212

Kunda, Z (1990) The case for motivated reasoning, *Psychological Bulletin*, 108(3), 480–498

Kwong, G S and Balajii, M S (2016) Linking green skepticism to green purchase intent, *Journal of Cleaner Production*, 131, 629–638

Leonidou, C N and Skarmeas, D (2017) Gray shades of green: Causes and consequences of green skepticism, *Journal of Business Ethics*, 144(2), 401–415

Leviston, Z, Walker, I and Morwinski, S (2012) Your opinion on climate change might not be as common as you think, *Nature Climate Change*, 3(4), 334–337

Lord, C, Ross, L and Lepper, M (1979) Biased assimilation and attitude polarization: The effects of prior theories on subsequently considered evidence, *Journal of Personality and Social Psychology*, 37(11), 2098–2109

Luo, Y and Zhao, J (2019) Motivated attention in climate change perception and action, *Frontiers in Psychology*, 10, 1541

Marshall, G (2014) *Don't Even Think About it: Why our brains are wired to ignore climate change*, Bloomsbury, New York

Martinie, M A, Milland, L and Olive, T (2013) Some theoretical considerations on attitude, arousal and affect during cognitive dissonance, *Social and Personality Psychology Compass*, 7(9), 680–688

Mooney, C (2015a) The best way to get conservatives to save energy is to stop the environmentalist preaching, *Washington Post*, 12 February, www.washingtonpost.com/news/energy-environment/wp/2015/02/12/the-best-way-to-get-conservatives-to-save-energy-is-to-stop-the-environmentalist-preaching/ (archived at https://perma.cc/KM3D-HJZB)

Mooney, C (2015b) Solar energy is playing surprisingly well in conservative parts of the U.S., *Washington Post*, 13 February, www.washingtonpost.com/news/energy-environment/wp/2015/02/13/why-solar-energy-is-playing-well-in-conservative-parts-of-the-u-s/ (archived at https://perma.cc/4LS5-F6SS)

Nickerson, R S (1998) Confirmation bias: A ubiquitous phenomenon in many guises, *Review of General Psychology*, 2(2), 175–220

Nguyen, T T H, Yang, Z, Nguyen, Z, Johnson, L W and Kao, T K (2019) Greenwash and green purchase intention: The mediating role of green skepticism, *Sustainability*, 11, 2653

Pariser, E (2012) *The Filter Bubble: What the internet is hiding from you*, Penguin Press, London

Pomerantz, E M, Chaiken, S and Tordesillas, R S (1995) Attitude strength and resistance processes, *Journal of Personality and Social Psychology*, 69(3), 408–419

Qin, J, Kimel, S, Kitayama, S, Wang, X, Yang, X and Han, S (2011) How choice modifies preference: Neural correlates of choice justification, *NeuroImage*, 55(1), 240–246

Rollwage, M, Dolan, R J and Fleming, S M (2018) Metacognitive failure as a feature of those holding radical beliefs, *Current Biology*, 28, 4014–4021

Rollwage, M, Loosen, A, Hauser, T U, Moran, R, Dolan, R J and Fleming, S M (2020) Confidence drives a neural confirmation bias, *Nature Communications*, 11(1), 2634

Ross, L, Greene, D and House, P (1977) The "false consensus effect": An egocentric bias in social perception and attribution processes, *Journal of Experimental Social Psychology*, 13(3), 279–301

Rudman, L A, McLean, M C and Bunzl, M (2013) When truth is personally inconvenient, attitudes change: The impact of extreme weather on implicit support for green politicians and explicit climate-change beliefs, *Psychological Science*, 24(11), 2290–2296

Schultz, P W, Khazian, A M and Zaleski, A C (2008) Using normative social influence to promote conservation among hotel guests, *Social Influence*, 3(1), 4–23

Sharot, T, De Martino, B and Dolan, R J (2009) How choice reveals and shapes expected hedonic outcome, *Journal of Neuroscience*, 29(12), 3760–3765

Silva, M E, Sousa-Filho, J M, Yamim, A P and Diógenes, A P (2019) Exploring nuances of green skepticism in different economies, *Marketing Intelligence & Planning*, 38(4), 449–463

Tedeschi, J T, Schlenker, B R and Bonoma, T V (1971) Cognitive dissonance: Private ratiocination or public spectacle?, *American Psychologist*, 26(8), 685–695

Usrey, B, Palihawadana, D, Saridakis, C and Theotokis, A (2020) How downplaying product greenness affects performance evaluations: Examining the effects of implicit and explicit green signals in advertising, *Journal of Advertising*, 49(2), 1–16

van Veen, V, Krug, M, Schooler, J W and Cameron, C (2009) Neural activity predicts attitude change in cognitive dissonance, *Nature Neuroscience*, 12(11), 1469–1474

Westen, D (1994) Toward an integrative model of affect regulation: Applications to social–psychological research, *Journal of Personality*, 62, 641–667

Westen, D, Blagov, P S, Harenski, K, Kilts, C and Hamann, S (2006) Neural bases of motivated reasoning: An fMRI study of emotional constraints on partisan political judgment in the 2004 U.S. presidential election, *Journal of Cognitive Neuroscience*, 18(1), 1947–1958

09

Public Policy and Internalizing Externalities

A key barrier to the broader adoption of green products and services is that sustainable production processes are often more expensive than traditional manufacturing, resulting in products that have a harder time being price competitive. But much of the reason for that gap is the fact that some true costs of production (and post-consumption disposal) are not actually priced into producer–consumer transactions. Rather they are externalized and passed on to people not part of those transactions. Let's consider how public policy can help correct that market failure, and additional ways in which governments and other actors could accelerate the behavior changes needed to enable sustainable consumption.

Natural Capital

"Capital," as everyone who has taken introductory economics understands, includes owned resources that appear on a balance sheet—the physical, financial, or abstract things like brand equity and goodwill that allow an entity to create more resources. "Natural capital" refers to the world stock of both renewable and nonrenewable stuff, including the minerals and dirt and water and air, and all the living things on the planet. That part of our world and its depletion is typically not regularly accounted for on balance sheets, or priced into products—a neglect that leads to market failures.

The notion of natural capital was first introduced into the modern vernacular in the book *Small Is Beautiful: A study of economics as if people mattered*, written by the German-born British economist Ernst Friedrich

Schumacher. That book was one of the earliest popular texts to consider emerging environmental problems in the light of economic considerations. In it, Schumacher argued for adoption of decentralized and human-scale production methods that could enable more sustainable forms of societal development. He observed that by failing to treat natural resources as capital rather than income to be expended, those resources would eventually be depleted and accordingly not available for the future production needs of subsequent generations.

His point was that under the current economic trajectory, society was gradually bankrupting itself by destroying much of the natural capital it needed to progress. As a founding member of the environmental economics movement of his time, he stated:

> Ever bigger machines, entailing ever bigger concentrations of economic power and exerting ever greater violence against the environment, do not represent progress: they are a denial of wisdom. Wisdom demands a new orientation of science and technology towards the organic, the gentle, the non-violent, the elegant and beautiful (Schumacher, 1973).

Schumacher's sentiments remain very relevant these many decades later.

But... Clean Is Beautiful Too

One of the things that Schumacher pointedly considered as nonrenewable natural capital resources that were worthy of conserving and stewardship were fossil fuels. In retrospect this was not surprising, because for 20 years before retiring and starting to write *Small is Beautiful*, he served as chief economic advisor to the British National Coal Board. In that position he promoted the idea that coal should be the primary resource for fulfilling the world's energy needs, as it was more plentiful than oil, which then was primarily sourced from relatively unstable countries, and which was destined to have escalating prices and to run out sooner than coal. So burn coal instead.

This reflects the priorities of economic thinking at that time, which largely ignored the degrading effects of carbon pollution on economic progress. It also reveals obliviousness concerning the fact that the GHG emissions associated with burning fossil fuels in general, and especially coal in particular, has great potential for destroying "natural capital." The term "carbon dioxide" doesn't even appear in Schumacher's book.

One can't blame Schumacher for this lapse in judgment, as general awareness of the growing threat of global warming did not really emerge as a pressing issue until long after his death. It is only in recent decades that the potential impacts of GHG emissions have started to be considered in policy discussions and seriously examined as to how to best account for the costs of those impacts (Bastien-Olvera and Moore, 2020). The emerging notion that much of our existing fossil fuel reserves would also become "stranded assets" as the world moves towards increased reliance on renewable resources might also have seemed foreign to Schumacher (Livsey, 2020). And as coal-fired power plants are shuttered, coal's prominence as an energy resource will likely never again approach its pre-pandemic peak. Indeed, the notion that coal is on its way out has been cited as the number one clean energy development of 2020 (Stone, 2020).

Externalities Distort the Market Equilibrium for Pricing and Production

There is an old joke that conjures up Adam Smith's metaphor of an "invisible hand" that guides market matters: An ecologist and an economist have fallen off the roof of a skyscraper. As they plummet towards disaster, the ecologist is very frightened and warns of their impending doom. The economist in contrast is calm and serene and reassuringly says, "Don't worry… demand will create a parachute." Rather than engage in such magical thinking, let's explore the active role that policymakers can take in shaping green consumption.

In neoclassical economics, the notion of Pareto efficiency, named after the early 20th-century Italian economist Vilfredo Pareto, refers to a theoretical condition in which an individual or societal condition can't be better off without making some other individual or societal condition worse off. This is supposed to be an optimal condition for all participants in an economy, but it is very much a theoretical idealized notion and seldom represents any true state of affairs. That is in part because some things that should be priced into production processes are just "externalized" as an unaccounted-for drawdown of natural capital, which in turn distorts the market by making the apparent equilibrium price of some things cheaper than they would otherwise be. There might be a point where supply meets demand, but it's not a societally optimal point.

This situation hides costs that might shift preferences if they were revealed. That is, we might consume less of a thing if all of its externalized costs were accounted for in its price. An "externality" can be conceived of as a cost or benefit that accrues to someone who did not choose to suffer or enjoy that cost or benefit. For reference, the word externality is also missing from Schumacher's book. While in principle the term refers to both cost and benefits, in reality many key externalities are all about a short-term illusion of benefits. For consumers, those benefits are related to cheaper products when environmental impacts have been externalized. And for producers, those benefits are for higher profits for production processes that ignore environmental impacts. In reality, such short-term benefits reflect acts of borrowing from the future, and in the longer term the externalities that permitted them will need to be re-accounted for in terms of the collective costs of biosphere degradation.

In policy circles there is a growing effort to "internalize" such externalities so that they are more properly accounted for up-front, such that consumers and producers can be properly informed about the costs and benefits of their transactions and thus can make choices that better reflect them. For example, one could in principle correct for such market failures by adding a tax to the price of some product for which its creation or disposal imposes some externalized societal cost, which would in turn increase the costs to the consumers of that good while reducing the quantity of the injurious product demanded in the first place (Figure 9.1). What the best use is for such tax revenues though is of course something of a quandary in and of itself. We'll come back to this.

FIGURE 9.1 Expected Impact of Taxing a Negative Externality

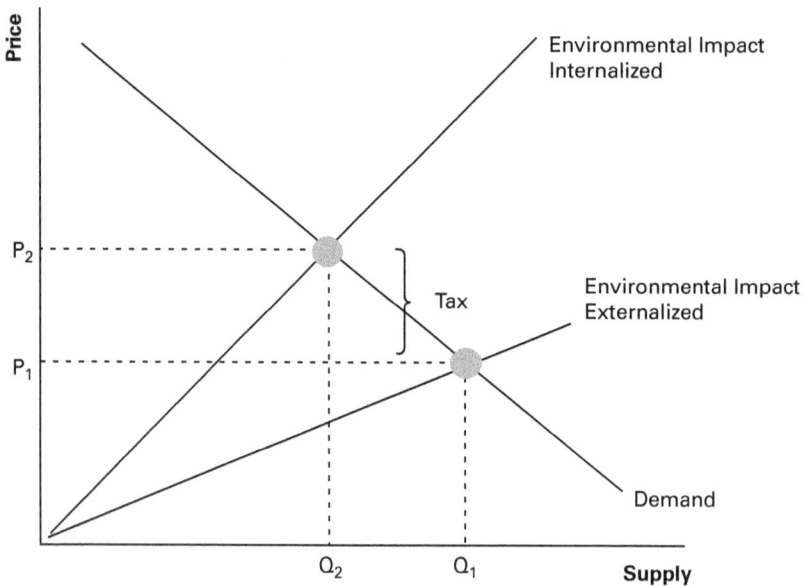

Barriers and Benefits and Behavior Change

As we have seen, a fairly well-developed body of literature describes how people develop intentions to engage in pro-environmental behaviors. Some conceptual frameworks incorporate an individual's beliefs about whether a target is a good thing, whether other people also think so, and their beliefs about whether engaging in a behavior can lead to an effective outcome. The stronger each of these beliefs is, the more likely the individual will be motivated to engage in the behavior.

But motivation alone is often not enough. A well-meaning individual might have a green intention but lack knowledge or skills to act on it, or may be sidetracked by automatically engaging in some other, more habitual behavior. Or structural barriers may exist that can impede the behavior from taking place.

Motivation, Opportunity, and Ability All Contribute to Green Behaviors

Other theories of motivated behavior have more directly incorporated such factors into predictive frameworks. For example, the Swedish economic psychologists Folke Ölander and John Thøgersen (1995) argued that improved understanding of consumer behaviors that have an environmental impact will be key to any efforts to shape those behaviors. They synthesized the literature to develop a model of consumer behavior that relied on three general categories of variables: motivation, opportunity, and ability (MOA).

The general outline of this MOA framework is depicted in Figure 9.2. To the left of the diagram appears the motivational component, which much like TPB Azjen's TBP incorporates beliefs about, and attitudes toward, the target behavior, as well as perceptions of prevailing social norms about the behavior that serve to drive behavioral intent. Whether that intent is actualized depends in large part on other constraints, such as whether the potential actor has the opportunity to engage in the behavior, whether the context the behavior would take place in is conducive to it, and whether the actor has the knowledge, skills, and habits required to perform the behavior.

This framework was intended to help categorize alternative directions that public policy might take to influence a desired behavior, and it is extensible to the problem of shaping green purchase decisions. For example, one might decide to try to increase the motivation for engaging in the behavior by increasing the incentives for it or by communicating relevant social norms. One might instead find in some situations that it is more

FIGURE 9.2 Motivation, Opportunity, and Ability Framework

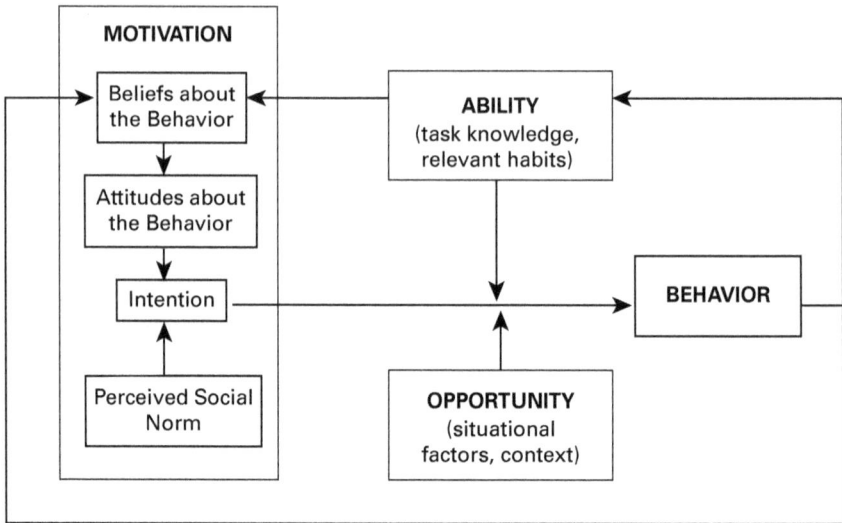

SOURCE Adapted From Ölander and Thøgersen (1995).

critical to enhance opportunities for engaging in the behavior by removing perceived barriers to it or by improving infrastructure to support it. And in some circumstances, one might need to address the individual's abilities by either making the target behavior easier, engaging in educational efforts to help the individual to develop the knowledge and skills needed to successfully perform the behavior, or by providing informational prompts to remind them to do the behavior. The feedback arrows in the diagram depict a virtuous circle in that when the behavior is successfully conducted, the individual can refine their beliefs about the behavior as well as their knowledge and skills in order to develop habits that make the behavior easier in the future.

This conceptual framework has guided a variety of interventions intended to promote pro-environmental behaviors or to discourage competing behaviors. Ölander and Thøgersen (1995) and several other groups (reviewed in Geiger et al, 2019) have used this framework to identify drivers of recycling behavior. It has also been used to evaluate the factors that contribute to household water use and conservation behavior (Addo et al, 2018), as well as for interventions helping to identify motivations and barriers to reducing household food waste (Graham-Rowe et al, 2014; NAS, 2020).

Increasing Motivation While Removing Barriers to Sustainable Behaviors

The MOA framework is also compatible with behavior change interventions often undertaken in the applied psychology field of community-based social marketing (CBSM) (McKenzie-Mohr et al, 2012). In the context of promoting pro-environmental behaviors, practitioners of CBSM seek to first identify a specific target behavior to attempt to change, and then try to systematically identify the key barriers and benefits associated with the behavior:

> Barriers refer to anything that reduces the probability of engaging in the target behavior. Typically barriers are structural… but they can also be personal costs that an individual associates with the behavior. Benefits refer to a person's beliefs about the positive outcomes associated with the behavior. This could include saving money, protecting the environment, or receiving social recognition (Schultz, 2014).

Once the barriers and benefits associated with a behavior are identified, CBSM practitioners then develop behavior change programs to either reduce the barriers to the behavior and/or increase the perceived benefits that motivate the behavior (cf. Figure 9.3). For example, if perceived benefits are low, a policymaker might want to use incentives of some sort to increase motivation toward the behavior. If instead perceived benefits are high and barriers are not prohibitive, educational efforts or the use of prompts to activate the behavior might be adequate. In contrast, if instead perceived barriers are

FIGURE 9.3   Changing Benefits and Barriers to Encourage Green Behavior

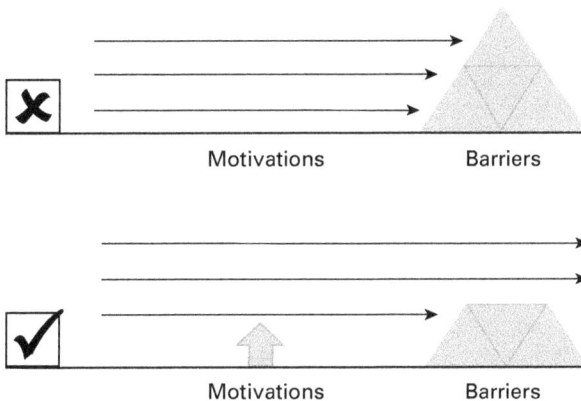

SOURCE Adapted from Schultz (2014).

high, a decision-maker might instead seek ways to make the behavior easier by reducing structural barriers to performing it, at least to the extent that the benefits of the target behavior outweigh any costs associated with doing so.

In general, the design of such an intervention will seek to modify the situation such that the benefits of performing the behavior overcome any barriers to doing so. Of course, if one wants to discourage a behavior, one could increase barriers to the behavior while also reducing any perceived benefits of engaging in it. For example, in many regions of the world, cigarette smoking has been effectively reduced by creating areas where smoking is prohibited, eliminating advertising promoting it, educating people about its ill effects, and imposing a disincentive in the form of higher taxes (and in some cases social ostracism) for engaging in it. In some countries and social groups, combinations of these factors have served to reduce smoking by 50 percent or more from earlier historical peaks. We'll consider incentives and disincentives more in the next section. For now, I'll focus on issues related to barriers.

Reducing Barriers to Making Green Consumption Decisions

When reviewing perceived barriers to engaging in more sustainable purchase decisions, we have seen that consumers feel they lack awareness of green options, lack knowledge needed to evaluate costs and benefits, and lack availability of green options where they shop. All of these barriers are things that can be addressed by manufacturers and retailers.

In an effort to reduce barriers to sustainable shopping, the ecommerce giant Amazon has announced a "Climate Pledge Friendly" program that labels products with one of 19 certifications for sustainability that can help green consumers to identify products from brands that have worked to reduce their carbon footprint and make other progress toward sustainable operations. At launch, the program included over 25,000 products from the grocery, household, fashion, beauty, and personal electronics categories—all searchable and available for online ordering and home delivery. "Climate Pledge Friendly is a simple way for customers to discover more sustainable products that help preserve the natural world," said Jeff Bezos, Amazon founder and CEO (Amazon, 2020).

At the other end of product life, the disposal of packaging and other material waste is a prototypical externality that is not priced into purchase transactions. We'll consider this issue later, but here it is important to note that while most people indicate an intention to recycle materials, one has to know what's recyclable and what is not, and there is a long history of consumer confusion on the issue. That type of barrier is in part an educational issue, and in response to the problem the Sustainable Packaging Coalition (a consortium of leading CPG manufacturers) has introduced a smarter labeling system called How2Recycle. Such labeling is incorporated on packages to provide consumers convenient instructions as to whether the package is recyclable, the specific component of the package that the label refers to, the type of material the package is made from, any specific instructions (such as cleaning) that should be followed in recycling the package, and a website link for more information should it be needed. While this is all helpful information in an easy-to-digest format, recent survey research suggests that less than a quarter of consumers claim to consistently look at such recycling labels before discarding packaging, suggesting that brands will need to invest more in creating awareness of this type of information on the part of consumers (Shelton, 2020).

Other barriers to recycling have historically related to more structural issues. That is, if one has to sort household recyclable materials into material categories, store those materials at home, and then eventually physically take them to a recycling center if one is accessible, the difficulty of doing such tasks can dissuade many consumers from even trying. Yet the amount of household waste that consumers attempt to recycle has increased dramatically over recent decades (EPA, 2017). Much of the increase is due to the greatly added convenience in many areas of single-stream recycling and curbside municipal pickup, where all the materials can be added to a single bin and the contents of which can then be periodically whisked away to a sorting center.

A more circular option to the issue of recycling is to simply make packaging refillable rather than recyclable. At the annual meeting of the World Economic Forum in 2019, 25 major global brands became part of the Loop Alliance, a pilot project to eliminate waste by switching from single-use packaging to refillable packaging. In this model consumers order products from Loop or a retail partner's website. The products are delivered in waste-free durable containers for which a deposit is paid, but those containers can be conveniently returned to the manufacturer by door-side pickup, where they are cleaned and refilled and put back into service:

> Loop brings back the old "milkman model," where products are delivered to customers at the same time empties are picked up, washed, refilled and restocked for delivery to another customer. The customer gets the product but the company owns the package (Makower, 2019).

And the retailers benefit from the advantage of "locking in" customers as repeat purchasers by increasing barriers to switching out of the system.

Reducing Barriers to Choosing Sustainable Transportation Options

Another big environmental problem includes the externalities associated with the ways we get around. Transportation is associated with almost 25 percent of GHG emissions globally, and in areas with a mild climate like where I live (which requires less heating and cooling), that number rises to over 40 percent. Accordingly, a major priority for many legislatures and other civic organizations is to reduce those numbers, which in turn will require that consumers change the ways in which they use transport. One type of human-scale technology that Ernst Schumacher might have approved of is the bicycle, in that it doesn't emit anything or use any fossil fuels or any other natural resources for that matter beyond those involved in its manufacture. On top of that it is health-promoting, can be a faster way to get about in some urban environments than gas-guzzling vehicles, and doesn't require one to share space on public transit with other people in the midst of a global pandemic.

Given such benefits, bicycle ridership is having a bit of a moment. For example, in the United Kingdom, the National Health Service has recently prescribed bike riding both as a way to reduce obesity and avoid exposure on public transit, going so far as to offer "Fix your bike" monetary vouchers to potential riders to encourage them to get any needed repairs completed and to help them get back on the road (BBC, 2020).

But barriers exist, especially in busy cities. First, many city dwellers don't own them. And second, in accidents with automobiles on busy city streets, bicycle riders don't usually fare well. In response, policymakers concerned both with carbon emissions and general quality of life issues in cities are addressing these physical barriers by instituting bike share programs, by creating bike storage facilities, by building dedicated bike lanes on roads while reducing those allocated to other types of vehicles, and even by rethinking city spaces to eliminate private vehicle traffic altogether.

Analogously, GHG emissions reductions in coming years will depend in significant part on replacement of the gasoline-powered vehicle fleet with electric vehicles. But many people live in situations where they don't have easy access to means for charging such vehicles. And at least in the early stage of EV adoption, potential drivers of EVs have suffered from "range anxiety," that is, a fear of adoption based on the notion that their batteries will run out of juice before they can get to where they want to go (Bonges and Lusk, 2016). In response to such issues, legislatures and civic leaders throughout the world have begun to address the need for a build-out of charging infrastructure and research on improved battery-storage technology to support a transition to an electrified automobile fleet. Of course, such a transition must also address the relatively high up-front expense of electrical vehicles and the pricing of fossil fuels in a way that ignores their environmental externalities, so let's turn to that topic.

Incentives, Disincentives, and Motivation

Another way to overcome barriers to engaging in pro-environmental behaviors is to increase the individual's motivation for surmounting those barriers by one means or another. "Intrinsic motivation" is that driven by one's existing attitudes, beliefs, and values. With sufficient intrinsic motivation, some tasks can be rewarding in and of themselves. Accordingly, one way to increase a pro-environmental behavior might be to work toward raising the individual's environmental concern and hence intrinsic motivation through information campaigns, persuasive appeals, and communication of related emerging social norms. By doing so one might achieve lasting behavior change that generalizes to other aspects of the individual's consumer behavior. But as we've seen, historically that hasn't worked very well, and for some individuals such an approach can serve to just strengthen pre-existing resistant attitudes and beliefs.

An alternative approach, as any pricing strategist or tax policy wonk could tell you, is to instead provide some "extrinsic motivation" by increasing the financial incentives for doing the desired behavior and/or increasing the financial penalty for not engaging in it. And generally, the larger the incentive or disincentive, the more likely a behavior change will occur. For example, across OECD countries, those with the highest gasoline taxes tend to also have the most fuel-efficient vehicle fleets and broader use of public transportation, while those with the lowest gasoline taxes trend in the opposite direction. As common sense would suggest and as empirical data confirms, the brain tends to like a bargain and finds things that are overly costly to be unrewarding and aversive.

> Changing the financial incentive landscape for pro-environmental behaviors also has risks associated with it, as such changes can yield unintended consequences. One such consequence is that requiring people to rationalize their behavior with respect to incentives can also change existing attitudes toward those behaviors. With respect to the use of financial incentives for encouraging energy conservation, researchers have warned that "strong and obvious incentives have the potential of converting people who value energy conservation into people who conserve only because it pays" (Stern and Kirkpatrick, 1977).

Challenges With Incentivizing Pro-Environmental Behavior

The opposite can also happen—weak incentives can also change attitudes. This can be illustrated by a foundational study in the field of cognitive dissonance research (Festinger and Carlsmith, 1959), one that employed the "forced compliance" method for inducing attitude change. In that study participants were required to engage in boring tasks—such as spending an hour just turning pegs in a pegboard. Afterwards they were paid either just $1 or $20 to tell a waiting "participant" (actually a confederate of the researchers) that the tasks they will be performing were really interesting to do. After engaging in this bit of persuasion, the participants were asked to complete a post-experiment evaluation. Those participants who were paid only $1 to persuade the confederate actually rated the boring tasks as more fun and interesting than did the participants who received $20 for their deception. The researchers concluded from this that requiring participants to deceive a stranger in public in return for only $1 caused more cognitive dissonance in the participants than doing it for $20. And since the behavior had already been committed and hence couldn't be changed, the only route for the nominally paid participants to resolve any dissonance they suffered was to change their attitudes about the objectively tedious experience to align those attitudes with the behavior itself.

The important thing to note is that this sort of result suggests a need to modify any incentive-based economic theories that might assert that the bigger the reward the more likely an individual's attitudes will change— instead, attitude change is only likely to occur if the incentive-induced behavior is inconsistent with the individual's values, beliefs, or attitudes. Similarly, Thøgersen (1994), in considering the impacts of policies that include economic incentives and disincentives on promoting pro-environmental behaviors, has argued that when implementing a proposed extrinsic reward structure, a stronger focus should be placed on considering how it could influence the attitudes and perceptions toward the pro-environmental behavior it is meant to influence.

In research examining the effects of garbage fees and recycling incentives on attitudes toward waste processing, Thøgersen noted that "reframing" the activities as something that invokes personal economic cost–benefit analysis based on extrinsic motivators might sometimes undermine or shift the intrinsic motivation of environmental concern that might otherwise promote the behavior. Beyond just pro-environmental behaviors, subsequent research has found that extrinsic incentives can undermine intrinsic motivation for prosocial behaviors in general (Kamenica, 2012).

Incentives also work differently for infrequent behaviors than for behaviors that are repeated. Using tax breaks or rebates to encourage purchases made only rarely, like home solar arrays, energy-efficiency upgrades, or electric vehicles, can encourage individuals who might not otherwise make those purchases when up-front costs are steep, the payoff period is long, and the technologies have not yet reached the stage where they are the social norm.

But using incentives to encourage behaviors that occur more frequently can have some drawbacks. Instrumental learning refers to the type of associative learning where the strength of a behavior is modified by a reward (or a punishment). When financial incentives serve as a reward for a behavior, removing that reward can lead to the behavior being extinguished. Furthermore, rewards in the form of financial incentives might influence a very specific behavior, but that change typically will not generalize to other pro-environmental behaviors in the way that changing an individual's level of environmental concern might. As Schultz (2014) notes, there are even "instances of moral licensing effects, wherein a person who adopts a pro-environmental behavior because of a contingency is subsequently less likely to choose other pro-environmental actions."

Despite Such Challenges, Incentives Can Be Effective

Although such concerns are good to keep in mind, there are some cases where incentives have been shown to work well in the context of repetitive consumer behaviors. A prime example is the implementation of beverage container deposit laws. Common in some countries, and a little spotty or non-existent in others, the general notion is that you pay a deposit on a beverage bottle or can at the point of purchase, and that deposit is refunded when you return the container to a retailer or recycling center. Simple enough, and in comparison with a tax it is in principal cost-neutral for the consumer, at least in terms of financial costs if the returns are performed.

Despite the on-again off-again nature of such laws (Jorgensen, 2013), and the fact that the big beverage brands and retailers have often tried to undermine them (Nash-Hoff, 2015), they nonetheless clearly work. In places where they exist, beverage containers end up being recycled at much higher rates than in places without container deposit laws, and they make up a much smaller percentage of litter. Yet the consumption of the affected beverages themselves mainly doesn't differ among people who live in areas with container deposits versus people living in other locations.

Internalizing the Externality of Carbon Pollution

Similarly, an increasingly popular notion for internalizing the externalities of carbon pollution is to rely on carbon taxes for a solution to the problem of global warming and climate change. When a fossil fuel is burned, its carbon content is converted into carbon dioxide and other compounds and the carbon dioxide produced is one of the main GHGs that result in global warming. A carbon tax is a tax levied on the carbon content of fossil fuels (ideally set at a level to compensate for the perceived "social cost of carbon," that is, its negative externality). While it could be levied at many points in the value chain, one simple notion is to levy it at the point of production as a licensing fee that fossil-fuel companies would initially pay in order to extract the fuel from a mine or wellhead.

In principle this added production cost would then be passed on to consumers in the form of higher prices for fossil fuels and things made from them, which in turn would reduce demand for them while increasing demand for alternatives. Most economists concur that such taxes would be the most effective and efficient way to curb GHG emissions, with the lowest impact to the economy overall. According to the World Bank, through 2019 over 50 national or subnational governments have either already enacted such a tax or announced plans to do so. And research to date on cases where such taxes have been implemented has demonstrated that, in practice, they are effective at curtailing GHG emissions (Metcalf, 2019). An added potential side benefit is that, since plastics are created from oil-derived petrochemicals, carbon taxes could also increase the costs of virgin plastics and thereby provide a price signal to increase plastic waste recovery and recycling (Mosko, 2016).

Why haven't such taxes become even more widespread? Primarily because of industry resistance, political resistance, and consumer resistance. Entrenched fossil-fuel companies want to sell as much of their product as possible. Political bodies are sensitive to their industry supporters and many have a rigid anti-tax perspective. And consumers, especially lower-income consumers, are concerned that increased prices for products they need would be hard to bear. At least part of those latter concerns are semantic in nature. For example, if a levy is described as an "upstream" fee that producers pay to offset their carbon emissions, consumers are more likely to support the notion than they are if it is instead framed as a "downstream" direct consumer tax (Hardisty et al, 2019). But beyond such framing effects, carbon taxes could be implemented in a regressive way that disproportionally impacts those that are least able to afford them. And it is generally agreed that addressing public opposition to carbon taxes will be key to promoting their further adoption (Carattini et al, 2018).

What to do With Carbon Tax Revenue?

There is a good deal of political debate about the best use of such tax revenue. Should it be used to reduce taxes on the least fortunate? Or used to support R&D on the development of renewable energy sources? Or used to build out new public power infrastructure? And what sort of command-and-control entity would make such decisions?

An increasingly popular idea is that the revenue derived from carbon fees should simply be rebated directly back to consumers on a flat per capita basis. In doing so, individuals could decide to reduce their purchases associated with high GHG emissions, and instead to shift those expenditures to products that are less impacted by the fees—and as a result enjoy a net positive benefit from the scheme at the expense of those who continued with a high-emission lifestyle. This market-based method for achieving emissions reductions without increasing overall taxes, often referred to as a "carbon fee and dividend" (CFD) system, was the topic of an open letter published in the *Wall Street Journal* in 2019 and endorsed by dozens of leading economists, including 28 Nobel Prize winners (Climate Leadership Council, 2019), with over 3,000 more subsequently joining as co-signees.

The CFD approach has also garnished widespread support by some environmental activist groups and has a growing consensus of support among business leaders, so it is likely that some version of a CFD scheme could emerge as a common standard. And it has not gone unnoticed that the impact of a carbon dividend on the purchase decisions of early adopters of low-carbon technologies could yield an additional benefit through social contagion effects. Much like the observation I made in a previous chapter concerning neighborhood effects in the spread of home solar arrays and electric cars, the economist Robert Frank observes that:

> By making solar power cheaper in comparison with fossil fuels, for example, the tax would initially encourage a small number of families to install solar panels on their rooftops. But as with cigarette taxes, it's the indirect effects that really matter (Frank, 2020).

Frank further explains that: "According to a 2012 study by the economists Bryan Bollinger and Kenneth Gillingham, a carbon tax that induced a family to install solar panels could be expected to stimulate a neighbor's copycat installation within four months, on average." And that through such indirect effects:

> [in] just two years' time, these figures suggest, the initial new installation will lead to 32 new installations. Contagion doesn't stop there, either, since each of these families will have shared news about their projects with friends and family in other locations (Frank, 2020).

Regulatory Policies to Enable Circular Consumption

As outlined in the first chapter of this book, a true circular economy is a self-contained system that designs out waste and pollution, keeps products and materials in use, and serves to restore natural systems. However, to realize this transforming ambition will require big and more or less concurrent changes in business models and product design, in regulatory regimes and government policy protocols, and as we have been discussing here, changes in consumer and civic culture and behavior (Piscicelli and Simon, 2016). A majority of consumers are at least subjectively on board with this agenda and express a willingness, if not eagerness, to buy more durable products and second-hand used or refurbished products when appropriate. Provided it's reasonably cost-effective, they are willing to get a product repaired if needed rather than discarding and replacing it. And some are already experimenting with "shared' product use through renting/leasing arrangements. But the same consumers often lack critical information about product durability and reparability to inform their purchase decisions, and if sharing arrangements are too complicated, they tend not to bother (European Commission, 2018).

As we have seen, there remains a large gap between the stated willingness of consumers to participate in the circular economy and their actual engagement with it. Consumers are aware of this gap; while most aspire to more sustainable lifestyles, many of those aspirants will admit to not often achieving it. When asked why, respondents assume some of the blame and admit motivational deficits—they find it inconvenient and time-consuming, they don't really trust brands and the companies that manage them, they lack belief in their ability as an individual to make a difference, and they don't perceive a shared normative imperative to change their purchase behavior.

But beyond such deficits in intrinsic motivation, consumers also perceive a systemic lack of extrinsic motivators for behavior change in that many barriers to green consumption are systemic in nature. Such barriers include unaffordability and a lack of adequate structural support from private sector entities like companies and NGOs, and especially from governments (GlobeScan, 2019). There is growing pressure on organizations to address these barriers, and ways in which to do so are becoming more obvious.

Eliminating Planned Obsolescence and Enabling Easy Repair

To take the example of extending product life, there is a growing reaction against the product design practice of "planned obsolescence," that is, deliberately designing products to be fragile and expensive or difficult to repair and relatively easy to just replace with a new one—a manufacturing practice widely recognized to waste material resources and increase greenhouse gas emissions, while also resulting in more landfill waste.

One reaction to this practice is a growing "Right to Repair" movement that has adherents working towards making it easier for individuals to fix rather than replace things and to reduce manufacturer-imposed barriers to doing so. Writing in the *New York Times*, Paolo Rosa-Aquino notes that, as a deliberate business strategy, manufacturers:

> have made it increasingly difficult over the years to repair things, for instance by limiting availability of parts or by putting prohibitions on who gets to tinker with them. It affects not only game consoles or farm equipment, but cellphones, military gear, refrigerators, automobiles and even hospital ventilators, the lifesaving devices that have proven crucial this year in fighting the Covid-19 pandemic (Rosa-Aquino, 2020).

Advocates in the movement have been pushing lawmakers at many levels of government to adopt legislation promoting the after-market repair industry and to discourage anti-competitive practices that create barriers to engaging in it.

Product Design for Emotional Durability

On the brand marketer side of the equation, there is growing recognition that manufacturers can both advance the circular agenda while gaining brand equity and opening up better options for premium pricing by designing products that are both physically and "emotionally" durable. "Simply put, emotional durability is the idea of designing products that people want to keep. Where physical durability resists wear and damage, emotional durability resists our natural tendency to want the next new thing" (Phipps, 2019).

Don Norman, one of the godfathers of the field of cognitive science and an expert on user experience design, has made the point that we don't just use products; sometimes we become emotionally involved with them (Norman, 2004). For products that are low in emotional durability, their perceived value starts shrinking as soon as you walk out of the store with them and drops dramatically with the first signs of wear and tear. In contrast, products with high emotional durability—imagine a favorite pair of faded jeans that incorporate the emotional halo of all the good times you had wearing them while becoming more comfortable and better-fitting as they age—tend to increase in perceived value over time and become harder to part with. Others like product design guru Jonathan Chapman from Carnegie Mellon University's School of Design argue that "the onset of ageing can concentrate, rather than weaken, the experience of an object" and that "if we are to create sustainable fashion we must design products that celebrate the process of ageing, and the accumulation of grime and wear and tear" (Chapman, 2015).

Incorporating Lifecycle Costs Into Product Pricing

Another way in which governments and other actors can support the circular agenda is by requiring that a product's lifecycle costs be incorporated into the consumer's purchase price. As we have seen, targeted financial incentives and disincentives can be important tools for shaping consumer behavior to better align with policy objectives, increasing the costs of throwing out a recyclable bottle and polluting the atmosphere with carbon, while rewarding the return of that bottle and the purchase of low-carbon options. But more can be done. From the consumer's perspective, purchase costs would be higher for things that must be recycled and can't just be reused, and discounted for products that come in refillable containers. And costs should rise even more for products that can be neither used nor recycled and instead become part of the waste stream.

Often referred to as "extended producer responsibility" (EPR), this notion can be fundamental to the achievement of waste reduction. In the sustainable design world, manufacturers would share in the responsibility for end-of-life disposal costs in a way that encourages the design of products in ways that minimize negative health and environmental externalities, and in a way that influences consumers to choose those products over unsustainable alternatives. EPR has been frequently employed as a strategic policy approach for almost three decades in Europe and is becoming increasingly common in other modern economies. While in practice it has most commonly been adopted to account for costs for products that are toxic or otherwise costly to manage, in principle the notion extends to all waste, and could serve to mitigate the moral dilemmas and environmental impacts of producers and consumers failing to pay the full social costs of their actions (Moreno *et al*, 2016; OECD, 2014).

1   Facilitating green consumption and encouraging other pro-environmental behaviors requires that effective marketing strategies be complemented by effective regulatory and public policy strategies. To make sustainable products and services price-competitive will in part require that the negative externalities associated with traditional consumption be instead priced into market transactions.

2 Behavior change strategies to inspire green consumption will involve reducing barriers to making pro-environmental choices while increasing the motivational benefits for doing so. Governments, corporations, and NGOs all have a role to play in the effort to craft market structures and regulatory processes that support a viable sustainable economy.

3 Tax strategies such as reducing greenhouse gas emissions through the imposition of a carbon fee would allow market forces to work towards mitigating global warming without the imposition of restrictive command and control measures. Consumers would be incentivized to choose low-carbon products and manufacturers would have additional motivation to reduce the carbon footprint of their production processes.

4 Consumer rights organizations are increasingly demanding a "right to repair" and the shift to a circular economy is driving a consensus that products need to be amenable to an extended lifecycle. To best anticipate this inevitability, product designers will need to shift from a mindset of planned obsolescence toward instead one of creating products that have both physical and emotional durability.

References

Addo, I B, Thoms, M C and Parsons, M (2018) Household water use and conservation behavior: A meta-analysis, *Water Resources Research*, 54(10), 8381–8400

Amazon (2020) Amazon launches "Climate Pledge Friendly" to make it easier for customers to discover and shop for sustainable products, www.businesswire.com/news/home/20200923005297/en/ (archived at https://perma.cc/LA5U-S6FJ) [last accessed November 17, 2020]

Bastien-Olvera, B A and Moore, F C (2020) Use and non-use value of nature and the social cost of carbon, *Nature Sustainability*, doi.org/10.1038/s41893-020-00615-0

BBC (2020) "Fix your bike" vouchers launch, as cycling to be prescribed on NHS, *BBC News*, 28 July, www.bbc.com/news/business-53558629 (archived at https://perma.cc/T7WU-U77F)

Bonges, H A and Lusk, A C (2016) Addressing electric vehicle (EV) sales and range anxiety through parking layout, policy and regulation, *Transportation Research Part A*, 83, 63–73

Carattini, S, Carvalho, M and Fankhauser, S (2018) Overcoming public resistance to carbon taxes, *Wiley Interdisciplinary Reviews: Climate Change*, 9(2), e531

Chapman, J (2015) *Emotionally Durable Design: Objects, experiences and empathy*, 2nd edn, Routledge, Oxford

Climate Leadership Council (2019) Economist's statement on carbon dividends, *Wall Street Journal*, 16 January, www.econstatement.org/ (archived at https://perma.cc/895S-6APK)

EPA (2017) National Overview: Facts and figures on materials, wastes, and recycling, www.epa.gov/facts-and-figures-about-materials-waste-and-recycling/national-overview-facts-and-figures-materials#NationalPicture (archived at https://perma.cc/3EZK-QXTT)

European Commission (2018) Behavioural study on consumers' engagement in the circular economy, ec.europa.eu/info/sites/info/files/ec_circular_economy_final_report_0.pdf (archived at https://perma.cc/U9GB-PCYF)

Festinger, L and Carlsmith, J M (1959) Cognitive consequences of forced compliance, *Journal of Abnormal and Social Psychology*, 58(2), 203–210

Frank, R H (2020) Behavioral contagion could spread the benefits of a carbon tax, *New York Times*, 19 August, www.nytimes.com/2020/08/19/business/behavioral-contagion-carbon-tax.html (archived at https://perma.cc/CL7V-5AR2)

Geiger, J L, Steg, L, van der Werff, E and Ünal, A B (2019) A meta-analysis of factors related to recycling, *Journal of Environmental Psychology*, 64, 78–97

GlobeScan (2019) Healthy and sustainable living: A global consumer insights study, globescan.com/wpcontent/uploads/2019/09/Healthy_Sustainable_Living_2019_GlobeScan_Highlights.pdf (archived at https://perma.cc/Z5GJ-EBPX)

Graham-Rowe, E, Jessop, D C and Paul, S (2014) Identifying motivations and barriers to minimizing household food waste, *Resources, Conservation and Recycling*, 84(84), 15–23

Hardisty, D J, Beall, A, Lobowski, R, Petsonk, A and Romero, R (2019) A carbon price by another name may seem sweeter: Consumers prefer upstream offsets to downstream taxes, *Journal of Environmental Psychology*, 66, 101342

Jorgensen, F A (2013) A pocket history of bottle recycling, *The Atlantic*, www.theatlantic.com/technology/archive/2013/02/a-pocket-history-of-bottle-recycling/273575/ (archived at https://perma.cc/F55K-SJDF)

Kamenica, E (2012) Behavioral economics and the psychology of incentives, *Annual Review of Economics*, 4, 13.1–13.26

Livsey, A (2020) Lex in depth: The $900B costs of "stranded energy assets", *Financial Times*, 3 February,www.ft.com/content/95efca74-4299-11ea-a43a-c4b328d9061c (archived at https://perma.cc/3KM9-JE9S)

Makower, J (2019) Loop's launch brings reusable packaging to the world's biggest brands, *GreenBiz*, www.greenbiz.com/article/loops-launch-brings-reusable-packaging-worlds-biggest-brands#: (archived at https://perma.cc/U6CT-ZUPN)

McKenzie-Mohr, D, Lee, N, Schultz, P W and Kotler, P (2012) *Social Marketing to Protect the Environment: What works*, Sage, Thousand Oaks, CA

Metcalf, G (2019) Carbon taxes: What can we learn from international experience?, *Econofact*, econofact.org/carbon-taxes-what-can-we-learn-from-international-experience (archived at https://perma.cc/4M9M-A66S)

Moreno, M, De los Rios, C, Rowe, Z and Charnley, F (2016) A conceptual framework for circular design, *Sustainability*, 8, 937

Mosko, S (2016) Carbon tax reduced warming, plastic pollution, *Earthtalk*, earthtalk.org/carbon-tax/ (archived at https://perma.cc/VFB6-YML8)

NAS (2020) *A National Strategy to Reduce Food Waste at the Consumer Level*, National Academies of Sciences, Engineering, and Medicine, National Academies Press, Washington, DC

Nash-Hoff, M (2015) Why are there so few states with "Bottle Bill" laws?, *Industry Week*, www.industryweek.com/the-economy/regulations/article/22008100/why-are-there-so-few-states-with-bottle-bill-laws (archived at https://perma.cc/NHE3-VBAZ)

Norman, D (2004) *Emotional Design: Why we love (or hate) everyday things*, Basic books, New York

OECD (2014) Creating incentives for greener products: Policy manual for eastern partnership countries, www.oecd.org/env/creating-incentives-for-greener-products-9789264244542-en.htm (archived at https://perma.cc/4JW8-PPFP)

Ölander, F and Thøgersen, J (1995) Understanding consumer behavior as prerequisite for environmental protection, *Journal of Consumer Policy*, 18, 345–385

Phipps, L (2019) Playing for keeps: Is designing emotional durability the key to a circular economy?, *GreenBiz*, www.greenbiz.com/article/playing-keeps-designing-emotional-durability-key-circular-economy (archived at https://perma.cc/N4ZN-F4US)

Piscicelli, L and Simon, G D (2016) The potential of design for behaviour change to foster the transition to a circular economy, Presented at the 50th Anniversary Conference of the Design Research Society, 27–30 June, Brighton, UK

Rosa-Aquino, P (2020) Fix? Or toss? The "Right to Repair" movement gains ground, *New York Times*, 23 October, www.nytimes.com/2020/10/23/climate/right-to-repair.html (archived at https://perma.cc/AQF3-C3VA)

Schultz, P W (2014) Strategies for promoting proenvironmental behavior: Lots of tools but few instructions, *European Psychologist*, 19(2), 107–117

Schumacher, E F (1973) *Small is Beautiful: A study of economics as if people mattered*, Blond and Briggs, London

Shelton, S (2020) The How2Recycle label needs a massive campaign and brands should make it happen, sheltongrp.com/the-how2recycle-label-needs-a-massive-campaign-and-brands-should-make-it-happen/ (archived at https://perma.cc/2T7M-LGZT)

Stern, P C and Kirkpatrick, E M (1977) Energy behavior: Conservation without coercion, *Environment: Science and Policy for Sustainable Development*, 19(9), 10–15

Stone, L (2020) The top eleven clean energy developments of 2020, rmi.org/the-top-11-clean-energy-developments-of-2020/ (archived at https://perma.cc/4W8W-C4A9)

Thøgersen, J (1994) Monetary incentives and environmental concern: Effects of a differentiated garbage fee, *Journal of Consumer Policy*, 17, 407–442

Conclusion

Greening Consumption and the Post-Consumerism Mindset

In this book we have explored aspects of the consumer's brain and modes of thinking about the world that may pose barriers to the smooth transition to a more sustainable economy. We have also reviewed the types of beliefs and attitudes that have been found to be predictive of green purchasing and other forms of pro-environmental behaviors that people might engage in. We saw that Veblen (1899) viewed the traditional consumer way of thinking as one that creates a vicious cycle, where inter-individual social comparison processes regarding one's personal relative share of material things is a source of dissatisfaction—dissatisfaction that then manifests itself as an endless need to mount a hedonic treadmill and work to catch up. And despite such plodding efforts, we have also seen that beyond some state of material wealth adequate to meet one's basic needs, having adequate financial resources to acquire more stuff does little or nothing to increase satisfaction or any general sense of wellbeing (Helliwell et al, 2020).

But a question arises as to the degree to which this mindset of unhappy competitive materialism is the existing organic state of human nature versus one induced or learned by the cultural context one exists in. If it's the latter, it might be more amenable to changing. With respect to this question, it is interesting to note that some research suggests that such a materialistic mindset is normally latent but that it can be activated by situational factors. In a series of experiments, Bauer and colleagues found that simple environmental cues can significantly change the degree to which participants displayed a materialistic mindset, as well the affective and social impacts of adopting such a mindset (Bauer et al, 2012).

In one study they had separate groups of individuals first view a series of images of either luxury goods (such as jewelry, clothing, expensive cars) or natural scenes without products in them, and simply rate the pleasantness of each image on a scale. Following that exercise, in an ostensibly different study, the participants from both groups were then asked to rate questionnaire items from an inventory used to assess concerns related to materialistic issues. The researchers found that participants who had viewed images of luxury goods indicated that they had greater materialistic aspirations, heightened negative affect, and reduced interest in social involvement, relative to the group that had rated the natural images. In other studies, the group also found that a variety of incidental cues that "primed" a consumerism mindset in one way or another could, relative to a control condition, increase competitiveness and selfishness by participants, while also reducing interpersonal trust and their sense of personal responsibility over resource use. It appears, then, that the degree to which one displays a materialistic mindset depends on situational factors and presumably the activation of cognitive structures associated with those factors.

As we have seen, people with more environmental knowledge, those who understand that they are a part of a larger interdependent ecology, tend to be more likely to make green purchases and engage in other pro-environmental behaviors. They are also less likely to confront the world with an egoist, materialist mindset and more likely to display a "biospheric" value orientation in which they "judge phenomena on the basis of costs or benefits to ecosystems or the biosphere" (Stern and Dietz, 1994). Critics of the traditional, consumerist society, such as the environmentally oriented economist and sociologist Juliet Schor (1999) and the environmental philosopher Kate Soper (2017), have forcefully made the case for the obvious need for, and some hopeful nascent signs of, an emergence of a new post-consumerist mindset that values sustainable consumption and fair trade, that recognizes the need for taxing externalities, and that values subjective wellbeing over material wealth and GDP growth.

There is also growing acknowledgement that hastening the transition to a more sustainable economy will require targeted educational efforts by governments, corporations, and other organizations—efforts to promote environmental literacy and systems thinking in order to inculcate in the minds of citizens a more biospheric-oriented mental model for consumer behavior. Before considering this issue further, let's review the ground we have covered.

The Emerging Portrait of the Consumer in a Green Economy

What have we learned so far? One, we've seen that an increasing majority of people already realize that their way of life is having adverse environmental impacts, and that those impacts are starting to become more concrete and personal. We also know that a vanguard of such people understands the implications of their impacts and are trying to change their ways; that a broad center of such people understands those impacts but are less motivated or don't know how to change; and that there exists a group of laggards who remain oblivious to the consequences of their actions, who may be actively hostile to the notion that they need to change, and who are motivated to find reasons not to.

The first group needs to be supported, the second group needs to be both supported and incentivized and educated, and the third group needs to be dragged along, reluctant or not, in part through disincentives that make their behavior less adaptive and their exploitation of social norms less successful. We have also learned that all of these people will require reduced barriers to realizing lives that are more sustainable, and that they will need help from brands, retailers, NGOs, and policymakers to reduce those barriers, to make green choices easier such that they become the new status quo, the default, habitual choice, the social norm, the moral imperative.

While the gap between green intentions and green actions may be wide, it is not a chasm that is unbridgeable. Getting across that gap requires abandoning the quaint notion that real human decision-makers are part of the same species as *homo economicus*, or even the notion that such a creature actually exists anywhere at all in the real world, as well as abandoning the notion that the marketplace as currently constructed finds optimal demand–supply balance points that best represent everyone's interests.

Bridging that gap similarly requires accepting the fact that the decisions of people are not simply rational—and even if their decisions were rational, those decisions-makers would not have adequate information given that the marketplace deck is stacked against them in that pricing decisions don't include the long-term costs of environmental externalities. These are the simple facts on the ground. What other insights can we extract given what we know about the way in which the brains and minds of consumers work?

Don't Expect "Conscious Consumers" to Just Rise Up and Do the Right Thing

People have a limited ability to think hard about most things, and they find that being forced to think hard about routine things to be both aversive and not worth the trouble unless the stakes are high. To make their ways of life efficient and relatively painless, they develop expectations and routines and don't like to deviate from them. That is, they mainly operate on autopilot. This simple fact has several key implications.

First, marketing specifically to the "conscious consumer" is a good way to limit market share. While a majority of the population realizes in the abstract that current consumption trends are unsustainable, the segment of consumers who claim that they are highly motivated to act on that understanding is very much smaller. And actual engagement with the sustainable economy seems to have hit a bit of a barrier of late. The Conscious Consumer Spending Index is an annual survey started in 2013 to gauge commitment to green spending, and the 2019 and 2020 editions tied for the lowest level of engagement since the survey began (CCSI, 2020).

Second, while many people profess a willingness to pay more for more sustainable products and services, higher prices for "green" offerings is frequently cited as a major barrier to more widespread adoption of such products and services. This is especially true for the larger audience who is less committed to change, not least because such a pricing strategy limits the audience to those who are in a position to be able to afford it while effectively marginalizing the price-sensitive but otherwise well-intentioned consumer. And as pricing strategists know well, even brand loyalists can be convinced to shift their habitual purchase behavior when confronted with a compelling point-of-purchase discount by a competitor.

Third, getting consumers to modify their normal, often habitual, purchase behavior can require that marketers increase the motivation that consumers have for making a switch as well as making it easy for them to consider the new alternative during what has been referred to as a "first moment of truth" (Lafley and Charan, 2008). While this presents a challenge for brands seeking to introduce novel green products into the marketplace, it represents an opportunity for brand category leaders to further lock in their customers by increasing the sustainability profile of their products and packaging and thereby decreasing the likelihood that their customers might be tempted to defect in the first place.

Remember That Valuation and Personal Relevance Are Closely Related

The regions of the brain involved with assessing the relative valuation of product propositions overlap with those for assessing whether something is personally relevant, and assessments of personal relevance are a very important part of assigning value to things in the environment. Such valuation calculations are discounted both by the amount of mental effort required to consider a product proposition, as well as the remoteness in time and personal distance of any proposed benefits a potential purchase might provide.

These facts suggest that while an ecologically well-informed consumer who possesses strong biospheric values might respond to product propositions that include temporally and spatially distant and somewhat abstract environmental benefits, not many others will. Even otherwise well-meaning middle-of-the-road aspiring green consumers probably won't bother. And they certainly won't if they have to weigh those uncertain benefits against excessive mental effort or price concerns.

Such facts also have implications for communication strategies in general and especially for the effectiveness of advertising that is intended to be persuasive. People value things that are immediately and personally relevant. While Maslow's hierarchy of need states (Maslow, 1943) has been widely disparaged, for good reasons, his lower-level needs clearly predominate human concerns. People need to eat and be sheltered. They need to feel secure in that shelter and not fear for their wellbeing. And they need to be part of a social group that can help protect them when they need it to.

None of these issues are particularly controversial. But they have important implications for marketing practice. In particular, it makes no sense at all to focus on impersonal abstract or future benefits to the environment when communicating green product benefits. Instead, whenever possible, focus on immediate product benefits (efficacy, nutrition and health, fun, safety, taste, price, etc.). Sustainability-related benefits are a plus, a reason not to reject a product, but not a headline or reason in themselves to make a product choice. Ben and Jerry's ice cream is widely associated with the social equity and environmental values of its founders, but they are mainly successful in the marketplace by integrating those values with the fact that their products not only have green ingredients, but also are delicious and positioned as fun and quirky. At the same time, they keep their pricing in line with other premium brands.

And while it's tempting to talk about distant melting ice sheets and starving polar bears, don't. In marketing communications, it is much more effective to focus on the here and now. Don't focus so much on the future. Remind people of the growing amount of plastic products they now see on their sidewalks and beaches and the litter they see on their streets. And of the hurricanes and wildfires that are ravaging their communities. And focus on the air and water pollution that is contaminating their neighborhoods and impairing the health and lifespans of the people who live in them.

Instead of talking about personally and geographically distant product benefits, do this: focus the marketing conversations on the here and now, or on the target audience's immediate family members. That is, talk about green product benefits in terms of improving the health of consumers, improving the air they breathe, the water they drink, and the food they eat. To the extent that a product or service choice will also lead to future environmental benefits, communicate those instead in terms of how the target audience's most emotionally important concerns will be affected. Communicate to them in terms of the implications for their offspring. For example, indicate that while the climate crisis might be generally important, it is an existential threat to their children and grandchildren.

Consumption Happens in a Social Context

When considering consumer preferences, it is sometimes tempting to think of them in terms of the individual choice-taker and their independent rational cost–benefit analyses concerning any opportunity they are confronted with, that people are self-contained in their considerations. If my neighbor decides to buy an electric vehicle, it is because they have a personal preference for doing so, not because I have one. Yet we know that is not entirely true. The deep-seated need to be accepted by a social group has been characterized as a "fundamental human motivation" (Baumeister and Leary, 1995), and it would be highly unlikely for this motivation to not influence shopping behavior. Implicitly or explicitly, purchase decisions have a social dimension, and considerations that include social concerns end up recruiting different functional networks in the brain than considerations that lack them.

Understanding the social dimensions of consumer choice is important for marketers because it can both inform strategies for encouraging behavior change and help them to avoid threats and missteps. Communications that highlight existing or emerging social norms as a "reason to believe" can be powerfully persuasive. Strategies that leverage social contagion effects can help innovative ideas and novel products spread in the marketplace, and social comparison intuitions can lead to diffusion of green shopping preferences. Encouraging public commitments to take pro-environmental actions can increase the likelihood that those actions will be taken in the future, even in private. And helping virtue-signalers to signal their virtue to others amounts to freely earned media impressions.

On the side of avoiding potential threats and missteps, it is useful to remember that the social brain seems to incorporate a "cheating detection mechanism" that makes us wary of others and alert to possible norm violations. Activation of this system results in the same type of withdrawal reactions that are produced by price gouging and disgusting things. One consequence of this is that people are very attuned to any attempted greenwashing efforts that they might detect. They may be quick to devalue products and develop a mistrust of brands that deploy such tactics, independent of any true benefits that an offering may provide. Similarly, the social brain incorporates something of a "behavioral immune system" that makes us wary of any potential contamination imparted by others, and that system is not strictly rational. Being conscious of the possibility of triggering this system can be key to the successful design and marketing of the types of sharing, reuse, and repurposing product systems emerging in the nascent circular economy.

Consumer Knowledge Is an Asset and Consumer Ignorance Is a Barrier

The Sustainable Development Goals (SDGs) are 17 interwoven global developmental targets that were set by the United Nations General Assembly for achievement by the international community by 2030. Launched with much fanfare and an extensive marketing campaign in 2015, they incorporate a variety of social and environmental aspirations including targets for clean air and water, renewable energy and climate action, and more sustainable production and consumption. They were intended to impart common knowledge and to focus a universal collective effort towards their achievement.

A 2019 global survey commissioned by the World Economic Forum found that, overall, around three out of four adults worldwide had heard of the SDGs (World Economic Forum, 2019). But that headline number is a bit misleading in that awareness varied greatly across the globe. In some countries, like China and Turkey, 90 percent or more of respondents indicated that they had heard of them, and over half of the respondents felt they were very or somewhat familiar with them. However, general awareness in some richer countries—including the UK, Japan, Canada, and the United States—extended to only around half of all adults, and only 20 percent or less in each of these cases considered themselves very or somewhat familiar with the SDGs.

This relative obliviousness to what are global concerns of pressing consequence highlights a knowledge gap in key parts of the consumer-based economy that can undermine the sustainability agenda. It suggests a growing need for broadly educating consumers about the importance of becoming good environmental citizens. The likelihood that someone will be motivated to develop "green purchase intentions" or to engage in other pro-environmental behaviors is closely related to the amount of environmental knowledge and concern they possess, as well as the degree to which they understand that they exist as part of nature and live in a broader interconnected ecology.

We have also seen a variety of types of evidence indicating that a lack of knowledge about the environment and the importance of sustainable consumption can pose a major barrier to green consumer choice. On the somewhat benign end of that spectrum lie the facts that consumers may lack information needed to evaluate product characteristics and marketing claims, may fail to understand the relationship between their individual choices and the environmental impacts of those choices, and may not have the resources necessary to accurately weigh environmental impacts relative to other product characteristics in their decision-making. On the more malignant end of the ignorance spectrum, consumers can become suspicious or actively hostile toward efforts to shift their behavior in a more sustainable direction. To better understand these issues, let's consider the type of curricula that is emerging that might help people to learn how to more adaptively go about their lives in the 21st-century marketplace.

Rethinking Consumer Literacy in the Anthropocene

One common definition of "sustainable development" is development that "meets the needs of the present without compromising the ability of future generations to meet their own needs" (WCED, 1987). Yet the mental models that people typically operate under focus on obtaining short-term rewards while minimizing mental and physical effort and without regard to longer-term or more distant impacts. These two things are in need of better alignment. As Albert Einstein noted, "a new type of thinking is essential if mankind is to survive and move toward higher levels" (Einstein, 1946).

There is a growing recognition in the sustainability community that our mental models of the world and our place in it, especially the aspects of those models relating to resource limits, the interconnectivity of Earth systems, and the externalized and deferred impacts of economic transactions, are in sore need of some updating (Garrity, 2018)—updating that inculcates more systems thinking, more environmental knowledge, improved understanding of the broader impacts of consumerism, and an increased empathy for future generations, updating that shifts our perspective on the world such that we move from an "egocentric to ecocentric" (Vijayakumar and Seetal, 2020) point of view. That is, others are catching up with the thinking of Kenneth Boulding (Boulding, 1966).

Environment-Oriented Consumer Literacy for the New Millennium

When I was growing up, certainly when I was but a primary or secondary school student, there was nothing in the formal curriculum that explicitly taught me to think about my relationship to the environment and the implications of my impacts on it. Meaningful knowledge about how ecosystems work and how people understand their relationship to the environment was only covered when I was at the university level, and then only because I chose to seek out such coursework—there was no formal requirement to become literate in sustainability or in the environmental dimensions of how one is to comport oneself as a responsible citizen in a bounded world. If anything, such considerations were studiously avoided.

Fortunately, that has been changing. For over 20 years it has been recognized that formal, systematic environmental education and the fostering of environmental concern is a key element in the development of a pro-environmental worldview, one that increases the likelihood that citizens will engage in pro-environmental behaviors (Hawthorne and Alabaster, 1999). Such a stance is gradually becoming part of the normal way that children are taught to think about the world. And those children are starting to really harangue us, with increasing urgency, to think more responsibly about the world that they will inherit.

While some of this rising awareness is organic, much of it has also been deliberate and strategic on the part of educators. For example, the development of the idea of "environmental citizenship" has been central to the growth strategy of the European Union in that the engagement with, and participation of, EU citizens in a greening of the economy has been at least superficially viewed as essential to both preserving the biosphere and creating a more socially just economic system, in order to enable a more livable and harmonious world. Formal environmental education has been seen as a key part of that development effort (Hadjichambis and Reis, 2011).

Similarly, on the other side of the Atlantic, over the last decade the North American Association for Environmental Education, with support from the US National Science Foundation, has been developing an "Environmental Literacy Framework" that aims to initiate study in primary school and endorses a lifelong approach to the understanding of how human endeavor is embedded in the natural world (Hollweg et al, 2011). That framework defines an environmentally literate individual as one who possesses knowledge and understanding of environmental concepts and issues, who has the thinking skills and biospheric empathy to constructively engage with such issues, and who has the motivation to modify one's behavior in accordance with such engagement. That framework has led to the development of a strategy and target curriculum to "green" the US educational system in order to grow a new generation of environmental citizens (NEEF, 2015).

In addition to embedding environmental issues into the everyday STEAM curriculum, the strategy includes a thesis of "no child left inside," that is, it emphasizes the importance of direct contact with nature as critical for developing a better understanding of it and for developing a biospheric mindset. In my younger child's primary school experiences, this has included things from trips to nature preserves, to having butterfly and nature gardens in the schoolyard, and a "green team" working on environmental projects. Of course, through most of the Holocene this would have been unnecessary as any child would have grown up in the natural world and accepted a direct relationship with nature as the social norm. But that natural learning arc has long been broken.

Given that we have seen that much consumer behavior is more or less "mindless," it's also worth noting that there is a growing movement to incorporate "mindfulness" training into environmental education practice. Mindfulness is generally defined as being conscious or aware of something, and mindfulness training involves exercises to improve one's awareness of what's happening in their mind at the moment and recognizing and accepting their thoughts and feelings. Proponents of this perspective note that increased mindfulness may help people to get off the consumerist "hedonic treadmill." Research indicates it can also improve subjective happiness and decrease materialistic values, while increasing empathy and compassion with conspecifics and the biosphere as a whole. Advocates suggest that "promoting mindfulness practice in schools, workplaces and elsewhere could be construed as a policy that pays a 'double dividend' in that it could contribute both to more sustainable ways of life and to greater well-being" (Ericson et al, 2014).

New Economic Thinking as a Component of Consumer Literacy

It seems clear that part of the way to build environmental literacy would be to also revise the way economics is taught so as to increase emphasis on the implications of planetary limits on GDP growth, as well as on measures of maximizing the "collective good" that don't depend on exponential GDP growth—especially since countries from Bhutan to Costa Rica and from the Netherlands to New Zealand are emphasizing happiness and a sense of personal wellbeing as more important markers of development (Bahree, 2020).

As we have seen, for the last 70 years rapid GDP growth has been associated with rapid resource depletion and increases in pollution, changes that in large part are due to overconsumption by people in affluent countries. A review of these issues noted that the:

> affluent citizens of the world are responsible for most environmental impacts
> and are central to any future prospect of retreating to safer environmental
> conditions [and] long-term and concurrent human and planetary wellbeing
> will not be achieved in the Anthropocene if affluent overconsumption
> continues, spurred by economic systems that exploit nature and humans
> (Wiedmann et al, 2020).

The authors rightly observed that better understanding of the drivers of overconsumption, and overcoming the barriers to reducing consumption and shifting it to more sustainable products and services, will be critical to changing the trajectory. Hopefully the sort of issues that we have covered herein can help form a basis for such a research agenda.

Wiedmann and colleagues (2020) subscribe to a path forward that is aligned with the ideas of the English economist Kate Raworth. Raworth is often cited with respect to her phenomenal 2017 book *Doughnut Economics: Seven ways to think like a 21st-century economist*. In it she addresses issues related to social justice and the need to raise the living standards of the most distressed people in the world, in contradistinction to the fact that current consumption patterns currently exceed the carrying capacity of the planet.

Her term "doughnut economics" pertains to a visualization of how to achieve a solution of those two inter-related problems that fit between both extremes. It is manifested as a set of two concentric circles. The interior, innermost circle represents the space that much of the world finds itself in, without the resources to maintain a decent quality of life. The outermost circle represents the boundaries beyond which the biosphere is being corroded and degraded in ways that may come irreversible. And in between is the donut in which we may find a "safe and just space for humanity" (Raworth, 2012). Such a conceptualization might be a new mental model well worth inculcating in 21st-century citizens.

Thinking for the Long Term

The high internal discount rate that people ascribe to the value of distant returns also appears to be a target to address in terms of improving environmental literacy and for updating the mental models underlying the existing consumerist mindset. That is, just as people tend to discount future monetary gains and prefer financial rewards up front, they also tend to discount future environmental or health benefits, especially if those benefits are in competition with cheaper alternatives in the here and now. While increasing understanding of how exactly people discount the future with respect to environmental outcomes is an interesting topic of psychological research (Green and Richards, 2018; Hardisty and Weber, 2009), in a society with long time horizons one might question whether temporal discounting with respect to the environment makes sense on the surface. At the immediate, individual level it might, but if one's concerns extend beyond one's immediate self-interest, even a low discount rate will eventually shift the costs of environmental degradation onto future generations. And such issues are in fact of concern to many people. Accordingly, inculcating notions of having a time horizon that extends beyond one's self, as well as respect for "intergenerational equity" (Padilla, 2002), also seem to be requisite understanding for the modern environmentally literate consumer.

The American science fiction author Kim Stanley Robinson explores these issues in his 2020 novel *The Ministry for the Future*. That story, set in the near term, follows the actions of an organization established specifically to represent the interests of the citizens of the world's future generations, through an advocacy approach that represents the rights of those yet-to-be as equal to those of the current generation. Though reflective of the current zeitgeist, these notions are not new. The sociologist and peace activist Elise Boulding (and spouse of Kenneth Boulding) has often been quoted as observing that: "Modern society is suffering from 'temporal exhaustion.' If one is mentally out of breath all the time from dealing with the present, there is no energy left for imagining the future" (Boulding, 1978). In the middle of a global pandemic and a ceaseless news cycle, in an era in which the term "doomscrolling" was added to our collective vocabulary, the notion of temporal exhaustion is eminently relatable. But identifying ways to overcome that exhaustion and develop a longer-term perspective seems key to a successful transition to a more sustainable consumer economy.

One way to inculcate longer-term thinking is to change how we think about our orientation in history. The Italian-American scientist Cesare Emiliani was a founder of the field of paleoceanography, the study of the history of the ocean's geological past. He proposed that we should share a planet-wide calendar system that dates things in a way that is unbiased by country, culture, recent history, or political or religious orientation. His idea was at once simple and profound (Emiliani, 1994). He suggested that at the turn of the millennium we should have simply added 10,000 years to the Gregorian calendar year, to approximately represent the time that has passed from the start of the Holocene, that stable climatic period in which all of modern society emerged from our hunter-gather past. Under this "Holocene Era" calendar, the first publication of this book would be in the palindromic year 12021 HE.

Acknowledgement of the need for longer-term thinking and intergenerational justice now appears to be spreading. Richard Fisher, writing for the BBC on "The perils of short-termism: Civilisation's greatest threat," notes that:

> researchers, artists, technologists and philosophers are converging on the idea that short-termism may be the greatest threat our species is facing this century. They include philosophers arguing the moral case for prioritizing our distant descendants; researchers mapping out the long-term path of Homo sapiens; artists creating cultural works that wrestle with time, legacy and the sublime; and Silicon Valley engineers building a giant clock that will tick for 10,000 years (Fisher, 2019).

They also include a growing contingent of activists of all ages imagining the future impacts of present practices, and who are intent on ensuring that corporations and governments do too. Where I live on the west coast of the United States, the nonprofit organization Our Children's Trust has been filing lawsuits on behalf of young people demanding that the government take climate action as they are otherwise infringing on the right of their generation to have a stable climate system. And on the other end of the age spectrum, an organization called Stay Cool for Grandkids encourages more mature adults toward engaging in actions to mitigate the impact of environmental degradation on future generations. The Extinction Rebellion movement that emerged in 2018 in the UK has explicitly aimed to use civil disobedience to compel action against climate change and the threat of ecological collapse. And the Fridays For Future climate strike movement inspired by Greta Thunberg, the Swedish teenager and global phenom, has motivated millions of her peers to extend their temporal horizons and to loudly object to what they see coming.

Social philosopher Roman Krznacic, in his book *The Good Ancestor: A radical prescription for long-term thinking*, brands such members of this growing new environmental movement, those dedicated to intergenerational justice and long term-thinking, as "time rebels" (Krznaric, 2020). And as the environmental impacts of consumer behavior grow more immediate and acute, the ranks of time rebels appear destined to only grow. Marketers and policymakers who have more than a very short-term time horizon would be wise to understand and share their concerns, and to help develop practices and product offerings that better address them.

La Jolla, California, January, 12021 HE

References

Bahree, M (2020) Why these countries value happiness over endless economic growth, *Huffington Post*, www.huffpost.com/entry/economy-growth-gdp-happiness_n_5fad6f57c5b6d647a39cf60c (archived at https://perma.cc/98FC-CMNG)

Bauer, M A, Wilkie, J E B, Kim, J K and Bodenhausen, G V (2012) Cuing consumerism: Situational materialism undermines personal and social well-being, *Psychological Science*, 23(5), 517–523

Baumeister, R F and Leary, M R (1995) The need to belong: Desire for interpersonal attachments as a fundamental human motivation, *Psychological Bulletin*, 117(3), 497–529

Boulding, E (1978) The dynamics of imaging futures, *World Future Society Bulletin*, XII, 1–8

Boulding, K E (1966) The economics of the coming Spaceship Earth, in *Environmental Quality in a Growing Economy*, ed H Jarrett, Resources for the Future/Johns Hopkins University Press, Baltimore, MD

CCSI (2020) Is good still growing? Highlights from the eighth annual Conscious Consumer Spending Index, *Good Must Grow*, goodmustgrow.com/ccsi (archived at https://perma.cc/3GBX-T2PX)

Einstein, A (1946) Interview, *New York Times*, 23 June, www.nytimes.com/1946/06/23/archives/the-real-problem-is-in-the-hearts-of-men-professor-einstein-says-a.html (archived at https://perma.cc/5PLY-68G3)

Emiliani, C (1994) Calendar reform for the year 2000, *Eos*, 75(19), 217–219

Ericson, T, Kjønstad, B G and Barstad, A (2014) Mindfulness and sustainability, *Ecological Economics*, 104, 73–77

Fisher, R (2019) The perils of short-termism: Civilisation's greatest threat, *BBC News*, 1 September, www.bbc.com/future/article/20190109-the-perils-of-short-termism-civilisations-greatest-threat (archived at https://perma.cc/LR9N-ZPNL)

Garrity, E J (2018) Using systems thinking to understand and enlarge mental models: Helping the transition to a sustainable world, *Systems*, 6, 15

Green, G P and Richards, T J (2018) Discounting environmental goods, *Journal of Agricultural and Resource Economics*, 43(2), 215–232

Hadjichambis, A C and Reis, P (2011) Introduction to the conceptualisation of environmental citizenship for twenty-first-century education, in *Conceptualizing Environmental Citizenship for 21st Century Education*, eds A C Hadjichambis, P Reis, D Paraskeva-Hadjichambi, et al, pp 1–14, Springer Open

Hardisty, D J and Weber, E U (2009) Discounting future green: Money versus the environment, *Journal of Experimental Psychology: General*, 138(3), 329–340

Hawthorne, M and Alabaster, T (1999) Citizen 2000: Development of a model of environmental citizenship, *Global Environmental Change*, 9, 25–43

Helliwell, J F, Layard, R, Sachs, J D, and De Neve, J-E (2020) World Happiness Report, worldhappiness.report/ (archived at https://perma.cc/RS55-LLN9)

Hollweg, K S, Taylor, J, Bybee, R W, Marcinkowski, T J and McBeth, W C (2011) Developing a framework for assessing environmental literacy, *North American Association for Environmental Education*, cdn.naaee.org/sites/default/files/envliteracyexesummary.pdf (archived at https://perma.cc/P9PL-DLUL)

Krznaric, R (2020) *The Good Ancestor: A radical prescription for long-term thinking*, The Experiment, New York

Lafley, A G and Charan, R (2008) *The Game-Changer: How you can drive revenue and profit growth with innovation*, Crown Business, New York

Maslow, A H (1943) A theory of human motivation, *Psychological Review*, 50(4), 370–396

NEEF (2015) Environmental literacy in the United States: An agenda for leadership in the 21st century, *North American Association for Environmental Education*, naaee.org/eepro/resources/environmental-literacy-united-states (archived at https://perma.cc/G747-JGXV)

Padilla, E (2002) Intergenerational equity and sustainability, *Ecological Economics*, 41(1), 69–83

Raworth, K (2012) A safe and just space for humanity, *Oxfam*, www.oxfam.org/en/research/safe-and-just-space-humanity (archived at https://perma.cc/HWM9-7E95)

Raworth, K (2017) *Doughnut Economics: Seven ways to think like a 21st-century economist*, Chelsea Green Publishing, Hartford, VT

Robinson, K R (2020) *The Ministry for the Future*, Orbit, Hachette Book Group, New York

Schor, J (1999) The new politics of consumption, *Boston Review*, bostonreview.net/archives/BR24.3/schor.html (archived at https://perma.cc/CF5R-MWZH)

Soper, K (2017) A new hedonism: A post-consumerism vision, thenextsystem.org/learn/stories/new-hedonism-post-consumerism-vision (archived at https://perma.cc/WY2S-95AT)

Stern, P C and Dietz, T (1994) The value basis of environmental concern, *Journal of Social Issues*, 50(3) 65–84

Veblen, T (1899) *The Theory of the Leisure Class: An economic study of institutions*, Macmillan, New York

Vijayakumar, S and Seetal, R (2020) We must move from egocentric to ecocentric leadership to safeguard our planet, *World Economic Forum*, www.weforum.org/agenda/2020/01/egocentric-to-ecocentric-leadership/ (archived at https://perma.cc/WCH2-4WL2)

WCED (1987) *Our Common Future*, Oxford University Press, New York

Wiedmann, T, Lenzen, M, Keyßer, L T and Steinberger, L K (2020) Scientists' warning on affluence, *Nature Communications*, 11, 3107

World Economic Forum (2019) Global survey shows 74% are aware of the Sustainable Development Goals, www.weforum.org/press/2019/09/global-survey-shows-74-are-aware-of-the-sustainable-development-goals/ (archived at https://perma.cc/Y8Z2-Q8PD)

INDEX

NB: page numbers in *italic* indicate figures or tables.

From 4 December 2025 the EU Responsible Person (GPSR) is:
eucomply oÜ, Pärnu mnt. 139b – 14, 11317 Tallinn, Estonia
www.eucompliancepartner.com

www.ingramcontent.com/pod-product-compliance
Lightning Source LLC
Chambersburg PA
CBHW041208220326
41597CB00030BA/5123

* 9 7 8 1 3 9 8 6 0 1 0 0 0 *